LEARNING TO WRITE WITH PURPOSE

SOLVING PROBLEMS IN THE TEACHING OF LITERACY
Cathy Collins Block, Series Editor

Recent Volumes

Learning to Write with Purpose

Effective Instruction in Grades 4–8

Karen Kuelthau Allan
Mary C. McMackin
Erika Thulin Dawes
Stephanie A. Spadorcia

THE GUILFORD PRESS
New York   London

© 2009 The Guilford Press
A Division of Guilford Publications, Inc.
72 Spring Street, New York, NY 10012
www.guilford.com

Printed in the United States of America

This book is printed on acid-free paper.

Last digit is print number: 9   8   7   6   5   4   3   2   1

Library of Congress Cataloging-in-Publication Data

Learning to write with purpose : effective instruction in grades 4–8 /
by Karen Kuelthau Allan … [et al.].
       p. cm.—(Solving problems in the teaching of literacy)
    Includes bibliographical references and index.
    ISBN 978-1-60623-125-8 (pbk.)—ISBN 978-1-60623-126-5 (hardcover)
    1. English language—Composition and exercises—Study and teaching
(Middle school)—United States.   I. Allan, Karen Kuelthau, 1942–
    LB1576.L3739 2009
    808.′0420712—dc22
                                                          2008040914

About the Authors

Karen Kuelthau Allan, PhD, is Professor in the Language and Literacy Division of the School of Education at Lesley University, where she teaches graduate courses in writing, reading, and research and also mentors adjunct professors. She has published several articles and books, most recently the second edition of *Literacy and Learning in the Content Areas: Strategies for Middle and Secondary School Teachers*. Dr. Allan is an active presenter at professional conferences, as well as a past president and board member of professional organizations. Her research interests are persuasive writing, poetry writing, and strategic reading. Revisiting her elementary teaching years, she often collaborates with teachers and students to pursue her research interests.

Mary C. McMackin, EdD, is Professor in the Language and Literacy Division of the School of Education at Lesley University, where she teaches and serves as faculty mentor for a graduate course, "The Teaching of Writing K–12." She has coauthored four books and has published several articles, most recently an article on differentiated instruction in *The Reading Teacher*. Dr. McMackin presents at local, regional, and national conferences and is on the board of the Massachusetts Reading Association and the Massachusetts Association of College and University Reading Educators. Her research interests include differentiated instruction, elementary and middle school poetry instruction, and nonfiction writing. Dr. McMackin began her career as an elementary school teacher and continues to work closely with children and teachers.

Erika Thulin Dawes, EdD, is Assistant Professor in the Language and Literacy Division of the School of Education at Lesley University, where she teaches courses in children's literature, literacy methods, and writing instruction. She is the author of a *Language Arts* article titled "Constructing Reading: Building Conceptions of Literacy in a Volunteer Read-Aloud Program" and worked with Dr. Barbara Kiefer of Ohio State University to create the ancillary materials to *Charlotte Huck's Children's Literature*, including classroom response guides to children's literature award winners. Dr. Dawes's research interests include practices of reading aloud, early childhood literacy, and social contexts for literacy learning. She has been an elementary-grades teacher, curriculum coordinator, and supervisor of literacy in public schools.

Stephanie A. Spadorcia, PhD, is Associate Professor in the Language and Literacy Division of the School of Education at Lesley University. Her research and teaching focus on literacy instruction for struggling readers and writers as well as students across the disability continuum, assessment of reading and writing difficulties, and using technology to support literacy instruction. Dr. Spadorcia has published articles and book chapters and presented nationally on these topics. She is a member of the Center for Literacy and Disability Studies at the University of North Carolina at Chapel Hill, conducting research and development work on literacy instruction for students with disabilities. Dr. Spadorcia works closely with schools on providing comprehensive literacy instruction to support all students. She has been a special education teacher and reading specialist in the public schools.

Preface

Over the past several years, the federal government has showered a great deal of attention and funding on reading and mathematics instruction. Far less visible, yet equally compelling, is our nation's concern over the quality of our students' writing. Indicators such as the *Nation's Report Card: Writing 2002* suggest that approximately 70% of students in grades 4, 8, and 12 are at or below the basic level of writing. Many upper elementary and middle school students write in a vacuum without consideration of their purposes or the needs of their readers; trust one inflexible and often ineffective writing process; fail to evaluate their writing to see where their messages are incomplete or unclear; and rely on a limited number of revision and editing strategies.

The intent of this book is to re-vision teachers' writing instruction to connect students' writing to particular readers with whom they have a purpose to communicate. To show the writer–reader connection, we created our communication model that describes how teachers and students can think about their intended audiences. In addition, we discuss the writer's cognitive processes in order to show how writers convey their messages. Throughout the book, our communication model and the writer's cognitive processes form our presentation of effective teaching practices and students' writing growth.

Although this book was written for preservice and inservice teachers who work with students in grades 4–8, many of the concepts, instructional practices, and strategies apply to writers of all ages. For example, our communication model of the writer–reader relationship is universal in that it addresses fundamental dimensions of writing that influence writing quality and that should be evident in the writing of primary, elementary, middle school, high school, and college students. The same can be said of the writer's cognitive processes we discuss.

Throughout the text, we present classroom scenarios and examples of student writing. Many examples come directly from classrooms we've visited or in which we've worked. In some cases, we have created hypothetical examples to illustrate a key point. In doing so, we offer a range of classroom possibilities that showcase good instructional practices.

CONTENT AND ORGANIZATION

We've organized the book into 11 chapters. The first two chapters introduce the theoretical foundation for the remainder of the book—our communication model and a writer's cognitive processes. Chapters 3 and 4 take us inside diverse classrooms where we witness how teachers and students function as communities of writers. The next three chapters (Chapters 5–7) are genre chapters, in which we present instructional practices that teachers and students use when writing to explore ideas, to entertain, and to inform. In Chapters 8 and 9, we consider *what* to revise (evaluation) and *how* to revise (revision), respectively. Then, since high-stakes standardized tests affect all educational stakeholders, we devote Chapter 10 to this genre. Finally, we focus our attention on teachers in Chapter 11, celebrating and encouraging teachers as writers and teachers of writers.

Specifically, in Chapter 1, we introduce a research-based communication model that focuses on purpose and audience. We propose that in order to be effective, writers must attempt to judge how much they have in common with their intended readers along the four dimensions of our communication model: world knowledge (content information), discourse knowledge (understanding of genres and how they function), recognition of time and space (contextual knowledge), and sociocultural memberships (social languages, ways of thinking, and beliefs). In this chapter, we introduce the components of our communication model and illustrate how we apply it by describing the distances between particular student writers and their audiences of proximate and distant readers.

In Chapter 2, we investigate how students write—the processes they use to communicate through written language. Processes, as well as environments in which writers write, influence how and what gets written; therefore, we present a model of the writer's cognitive processes, which we've adapted from existing research-based models. Our model consists of three processes: planning, producing text (generating and transcribing), and reviewing (evaluating, revising, and editing)—plus monitoring (metacognitive thinking about what writers know and their processes). Although these processes aren't linear, we separate and define each one, and then move from theory to practice as we explore the processes and monitoring of two students, an experienced writer and a struggling writer. Because determining what goes on inside a writer's head can be challenging, we include an Inquiry Guide to a Writer's Cognitive Processes. The guide pinpoints writing behaviors that teachers can observe and discuss with students. It also includes possible issues writers may be facing and suggests actions teachers can use to help students engage in processes that will assist them in meeting their purposes and audiences' needs. At the end of the chapter, we include an annotated list of technology resources that support writers' processes.

Chapter 3 begins with a peek into a fourth-grade classroom in which the teacher and students work together as a community of writers. In addition, we give an overview of the teacher's instruction as it moves from direct teaching to guided practice to independent application. We explore characteristics of effective writing classrooms, which are framed by both the components of the writer's cognitive processes and the four dimensions of our communication model. Taken together, the characteristics help teachers and students create safe classroom communities where everyone investigates and practices being effective writers.

Students in today's classrooms come from a variety of family structures, economic backgrounds, home languages, unique interests, cultural experiences, and academic strengths. In Chapter 4, we focus on classroom diversity and explore how teachers can gather information about each student's understanding of writing. A research-based developmental continuum, which we created, allows teachers to document students' current understanding of the writing processes and the dimensions of our communication model. The continuum enables teachers to mark growth of one student, several students, or an entire class over time.

The next three chapters—Chapters 5, 6, and 7 (and 10, which we'll address below)—are genre chapters. Our focus for these chapters is on instructional practices for a variety of purposes, audiences, and genres. In Chapter 5, we concentrate on writing to explore ideas and look closely at journal writing. Journals can serve as safe places where students and teachers investigate the dimensions of our communication model across disciplines, practice generating and transcribing texts, and reread existing entries to use in planning and producing extended pieces of writing. Although teachers don't generally grade journals because, for the most part, students are writing for themselves, they do want to know how students can grow in their ability to use journals effectively. Building on the developmental continuum we introduced in Chapter 4, we present a continuum for producing journal entries. We limit the continuum to producing text because journal writers seldom plan or review entries.

In Chapter 6 and its companion, Chapter 7, we focus on instructional practices for writing to entertain and writing to inform, respectively. In Chapter 6, we investigate personal narrative and memoirs, fictional and imagined events, and poetry. In Chapter 7, we discuss the genres of persuasion, explanation, and how-to. Consistently, we explain how a teacher prepares to teach each genre; use an inquiry process to introduce specific characteristics of each genre; and present a classroom scenario with examples of student writing to illustrate how a teacher supports students through the planning, producing, and reviewing of their pieces. In addition, we include a developmental continuum for each genre with which teachers can track students' writing growth in each genre or across genres. At the conclusion of each chapter, we provide an annotated list of mentor texts.

Writers need to be able to determine *what* they need to revise and edit (Chapter 8) before they think about *how* to engage in these processes (Chapter 9). In Chapter 8, we look at evaluating writing, the first component in the reviewing process. When we evaluate writing, we look at the product, the writer, and the processes the writer used to create the text. To evaluate *product*, we align common traits of good writing (idea development, organization, sentence fluency, voice, word choice, and conventions) to our communication model and then separate each one into smaller elements, which we display on an easy-to-use Evaluation Guide. To evaluate the *writer*, we try to determine why the writer composed the text the way he or she did. We ask how the writer's world knowledge, discourse knowledge, understanding of time and space, and awareness of sociocultural memberships influenced the writing. Finally, when evaluating *processes*, we summarize our discussions on the writer's cognitive processes that we explored in Chapter 2.

Building on our discussion of what to revise in Chapter 8, we turn our attention to *how* to revise in Chapter 9. In this chapter, we explore why many upper elementary and middle school students struggle with revision and editing. Arranged according to the four dimensions of our communication model, we describe two-dozen actions that students can use to communicate effectively across genres, purposes, and audiences. As in Chapters 6 and 7, we provide an annotated list of mentor books to use as exemplars for the actions introduced in this chapter.

Since mandatory standardized testing plays such a pivotal role in writing curriculum, instruction, and assessment, we dedicate Chapter 10 to a discussion of high-stakes testing. We provide a rationale for treating standardized test writing as a genre and for teaching the genre just prior to the administration of the test. Then, as with the other genre chapters in this text, we define the characteristics of this genre and supply a classroom scenario that illustrates how a teacher provides instruction in planning, producing, and reviewing responses. Emphasizing the need to analyze prompts using the four dimensions of our communication model, we provide sample analyses for an open-ended response prompt, a science prompt, and a response to literature prompt. Finally, we summarize the impact of high-stakes testing on writing instruction across the country.

In the final chapter of this book, Chapter 11, we shift our attention away from students to applaud teachers. We celebrate the writing teachers do and encourage their writing for themselves, familiar readers, and unknown audiences by including concrete suggestions for professional writing. The more we as teachers experience writing across genres and for a variety of purposes and audiences, the better prepared we are to provide our students with a repertoire of skills and strategies they can use to communicate their ideas purposefully and effectively to audiences both in and outside of the classroom.

SPECIAL FEATURES

- *Communication model*—a research-based model that reflects the writer–reader relationship along four dimensions: world knowledge, discourse knowledge, time and space, and sociocultural membership.
- *Writer's cognitive processes*—a research-based model that recognizes the recursive processes writers use to convey meaning in written texts: planning, producing (generating and transcribing texts), and reviewing (evaluating, revising, and editing texts), and an inquiry guide to a writer's processes.
- *General developmental continuum*—grounded in theory and research, the developmental continuum defines the characteristics of novice, developing, and experienced writers within the framework of our communication model and the writer's cognitive processes.
- *Genre-specific developmental continua*—built on the general developmental continuum, a continuum defines the characteristics of novice, developing, and experienced writers for each of the genres we discuss in Chapter 5 (journal entries), Chapter 6 (personal narratives, fiction, poetry), and Chapter 7 (persuasion, explanation, how-to).
- *Evaluation guide*—based on the common traits of effective writing but organized by the dimensions of our communication model, the evaluation guide presents questions for teachers to use when assessing written products.
- *Classroom scenarios and student writing samples*—particularly throughout Chapters 6 and 7, where we show how teachers support students' learning to write in different genres.
- *Annotated lists of mentor texts*—to accompany Chapters 6, 7, and 9.
- *Technology resources*—particularly at the conclusion of Chapter 2, where we include an annotated list of technology tools that can help students plan, produce, and review texts.
- *Application boxes*—suggested actions designed to help teachers connect the content of each chapter with their instructional practices.

ACKNOWLEDGMENTS

Writing this book has been a collaborative effort not only among the four authors but also among classroom teachers and their students, Lesley University colleagues, and Guilford Press staff. We have many people to thank.

First, we thank the many classroom teachers and their students with whom we've collaborated in their classrooms and in our graduate courses. Our work with them enabled us to refine and revise ideas that resulted in this book. In particular, we thank Tricia Stodden, Karen Clements, and Stephanie McLaughlin, whose teaching enabled students to write effectively. Over the years countless teachers and their students have taught us more than they realize.

Second, we thank our colleagues at Lesley University. We thank our literacy division colleagues for the many discussions about teaching and literacy. We thank our Division Director, Dr. Margery Staman Miller, for her watchful encouragement and support in arranging our teaching loads so that we had opportunities to write. We thank Dr. Mario Burunda, Dean of the School of Education, for his encouragement. Finally, we thank the grantees of the Russell Professional Grants and the President's Opportunity Grants for the grants that allowed a reduction in our teaching units, giving us time to write.

Third, we thank Diane Lowe of Framingham State University and the other reviewers of the book proposal and mauscript. They thoughtfully and thoroughly challenged our thinking and so strengthened this book. We thank them for the time they willingly gave, their comprehensive comments, and their knowledge of writing and teaching.

Fourth, we thank the people at The Guilford Press, especially Publisher of Education Chris Jennison and Editor Craig Thomas, who shepherded the book from proposal to production. We also thank Joi Rowe, Marketing Assistant; Lauren Foust, Administrative Assistant; Nina Hnatov, Copy Editor; and Laura Specht Patchkofsky, Senior Production Editor.

Finally, we thank our extended families and close friends, who have experienced this book with us. Through life's experiences, they granted us the time and support to be once again at the computer revising yet another draft.

KAREN KUELTHAU ALLAN
MARY C. MCMACKIN
ERIKA THULIN DAWES
STEPHANIE A. SPADORCIA

Contents

Chapter 1

Communicating Ideas
Writers to Readers

"Something is wrong," said Ms. Arnold on the first day of science class. "A report issued by the town indicates that there is too much salt in the drinking water." Ms. Arnold asked her eighth graders to take out their new science notebooks and record the following two facts:

- There is too much salt in our drinking water.
- One hundred percent of the water from the Franklin Brook watershed goes into our drinking water.

Next, in small groups, students recorded questions they generated from these two facts: How did the salt get there? What could be done to reduce it? Why can't you taste the salt?

For the entire year, teams of eighth-grade students, four content-area teachers (science, English language arts, social studies, and mathematics), a special educator, and an aide generated research questions, hypothesized possibilities, made field visits to a local watershed, collected data, analyzed the data, and drew conclusions about the excess salt in the water supply. Concurrently, they collected the same data at BOSS— Back of the School Site—a control site. Over the course of the year, they used writing to express their learning; they took notes, answered essay test questions, wrote letters to newspaper editors, prepared reports for oral presentations to multiple audiences, and even drafted blues songs. In Chapter 7, "Writing to Inform," you'll learn more about this expeditionary project and its impact on the Franklin Brook neighborhood. We introduce the project here to call attention to the fact that the students involved in this project communicated what they learned by writing to different audiences.

Teaching writing is one of the most interesting and at the same time one of the most difficult instructional activities teachers face. We all know that writing is much more than composing a draft and fixing it up. Throughout this book, we address the challenges associated with teaching writing. We begin this chapter by sharing a theoretical communication model we created. We connect back to this model as we introduce sound teaching practices in the remainder of the book. Our two goals are (1) to help students increase their capacity to compose texts successfully for a variety of purposes, audiences, and situations; and (2) to support teachers in their inquiries about their students' writing.

In this chapter, we:

- Establish communication as the construction of shared meaning.
- Introduce our communication model that emphasizes relationships between writers and readers.
- Consider the writer–reader relationship across purposes and audiences.

We begin by defining communication.

COMMUNICATION AS THE CONSTRUCTION OF SHARED MEANING

Students (or teachers) commonly set purposes for reading. Effective readers tend to set purposes before and sometimes while reading (Duke & Pearson, 2002). A reader, for example, might try to find out if a boy in a story will win the prize money and save his grandfather's farm in *Stone Fox* (Gardiner, 1980); or perhaps if wolves should be reinstated into regions of the United States in *Once a Wolf* (Swinburne, 1999). But do writers set purposes for their writing? Do they think about why they write, who will read the writing, and the impact the purpose has on what and how they communicate? Of course they do. Before and while drafting, writers ask themselves if they are writing to inform, to entertain, to persuade, to remember information, to present a position, to give advice, to provide evidence, or to maintain friendships. They consider what to communicate to their audience. As they compose, they continually evaluate whether they are achieving their purpose for writing and meeting the needs of their readers (Applebee, 2000; Hayes, 2000).

Common everyday experiences, curricula connections, and issues that interest students can provide genuine purposes for writing. They can ask and answer their own questions, record their wonderings and discoveries, and document their thinking and learning. Yet, sadly, many school writing assignments are designed for the purpose of building skills (Roe & Ross, 2006) and for an audience of the classroom teacher (Johns, 2002; Kaufer & Carley, 1994).

We sometimes associate purposes and audiences with writing, when in fact they impact all aspects of our lives—not just our writing. Something as routine as dinner, for example, can change dramatically depending on the occasion and the people with whom we are dining. Think about preparing a typical Saturday evening meal for those with whom you interact regularly. You probably are not too concerned about how the table is arranged or whether you remembered to put out the condiments, since everyone already knows where they are and can help themselves. Now think about preparing a special, formal holiday dinner for people you do not come in contact with on a daily basis. You might break out the china, arrange the table with flowers, and tailor your entrée to meet the specific dietary needs of your guests.

Similarly, when writing for those close to them, students do not need to be too concerned with how their ideas are organized or whether they include relevant details because the reader can easily fill in the gaps. If students always write for themselves, their peers, and their teacher—those with whom they interact regularly—they never practice constructing meaning for readers who come to the text without a great deal of shared understandings. In later chapters, we explore writing opportunities that can expand students' repertoire of strategies and processes used to construct meaning for multiple purposes and audiences. Students who write for a variety of purposes learn how purpose changes their writing process and the final product (National Council of Teachers of English/International Reading Association, 1996). Similarly, when students write for different audiences, they learn how to change their processes and products to meet audiences' needs. Keeping in mind purpose and audience, as well as the writer–reader relationship, we developed our communication model, which we describe in the next section.

OUR COMMUNICATION MODEL

In face-to-face conversations, speakers can usually assess whether their listeners understand what is being said. Facial expressions, gestures, and interjections help speakers adjust their thinking and speaking to meet the needs of their listeners (Martlew, 1983). When friends get together, one word can often trigger memories of an entire event. Friends talk in telegraphic speech and can be easily understood. The conversation may be completely incomprehensible, however, for someone who is not from this same circle of friends, unless the entire event is explained in detail.

Similarly, writers share unique relationships with their readers. Sometimes writers draft pieces they alone will read (e.g., a reminder to pick up dry cleaning, or a list of holiday gifts to buy). Sometimes they draft pieces for close friends (informal thank you notes or e-mails). In these cases, writing can be similar to the telegraphic speech of face-to-face conversations. Shared experiences and mutual knowledge enable readers to infer the missing information in the writer's intended message.

Sometimes, writers do not know who will read their pieces or when the pieces will be read. For example, on essays students write for state standardized tests the reader is not known to the students. Writers need to adjust what they write and how they write to meet the needs of diverse distant readers. As you will see in our communication model described below, writers' perceptions of purposes and audiences inform all decisions they make throughout their writing.

We have created a communication model that reflects our interpretation of research (Britton, Burgess, Martin, McLeod, & Rosen, 1975; Gee, 1996; Graham & Perin, 2007; Kaufer & Carley, 1994; McCutchen, 2006; Moffett, 1981; Nystrand, 1986) and our years of classroom experiences. We hold that writers and readers are members of sociocultural groups that share some degree of world knowledge, discourse knowledge, and time and space. We refer to these elements as the dimensions of our communication model. Each dimension is defined in the following section of this chapter.

First, we take a look at a visual representation of our communication model (see Figure 1.1). Notice that the writer is at the center of the model. Also notice four stars. The stars symbolize "distance" between writer and reader on each dimension. Although distance is somewhat arbitrary, the stars help us visually represent writer–reader relationships. Since the stars in Figure 1.1 are close together, we can assume that the writer and reader share many commonalities. If the stars were to appear farther away from the writer, they would indicate that the writer and reader do not share the same amount or types of knowledge or that the writer does not know what knowledge he or she shares with his or her reader.

In addition to the stars on our model, there are three concentric ovals, labeled *considerable, partial,* and *limited/uncertain.* The inner oval, *considerable,* signals a close relationship between writer and reader. They know each other and share ample common understandings. You might think of this oval as being similar to the relationship that exists between close friends in face-to-face conversations.

When a star falls within the *partial* oval on a dimension, the writer and reader share few commonalities. Writers must attend to the differences that result from this distance. Careful attention must be paid to

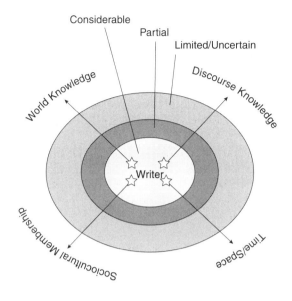

FIGURE 1.1. Our communication model.

what is being said and how it is being said. This oval might represent relationships that exist between younger and older students in a school.

When a star falls within the *limited/uncertain* oval on a dimension, the writer is crafting a piece for someone with whom he or she shares only limited understandings of the dimension or for an unknown reader. The writer either knows that he or she and the reader do not share knowledge or cannot assess how much he or she and the audience have in common. Therefore, the writer must develop a clearly focused topic, include sufficient relevant details, and organize the piece logically so that there are few gaps between what he or she is trying to convey and the presumed reader's understandings.

Defining the Four Dimensions of Our Communication Model

When we write to communicate ideas to others, "what counts is not simply what the text says but how what is said relates to what is already shared by writer and reader" (Nystrand, 1986, p. 71). Determining precisely what the writer and reader share is a key component of effective writing but also a task that can be quite formidable (Carvalho, 2002). We explore the writer–reader relationship by defining the four dimensions of our communication model: (1) world knowledge, (2) discourse knowledge, (3) time and space, and (4) sociocultural membership. These four dimensions are not discrete; they can and will overlap. We keep each one distinct, however, to illustrate unique characteristics of each dimension.

World Knowledge

World knowledge is what one knows about the world and how the world works. We define world knowledge as information that is stored in one's memory. Let's step back into Ms. Arnold's class for a moment to consider her students' world knowledge. The students certainly knew some things about salt before they began their investigation. They put salt on their food, swim in saltwater oceans, and witness the effects of salt on icy streets. Some students knew that salt is also referred to as *sodium chloride*. Few were familiar with the properties of sodium chloride. Through their class readings, discussions, writing experiences, and visits to Franklin Brook, they deepened their initial understandings of the role salt played in polluting the watershed. They were able to connect new information to their existing understandings and continually create new knowledge.

Discourse Knowledge

Discourse refers to extended, meaningful units of communication such as stories, reports, paragraphs, sentences, and phrases. Our discussion of discourse knowledge focuses on five related components: (1) genre knowledge, (2) organizational structures, (3) sentence construction, (4) word choice, and (5) conventions. In Chapter 8, "Reading to Evaluate Writing," we look closely at each of these components, but we pause here to define two of the major components: genre knowledge and word choice.

We begin our look at discourse knowledge by addressing genres. Intuitively you know texts are different: news reports, novels, obituaries, and sermons. You know the purpose of each and when you encounter them. Even young children recognize that stories and information texts are different (Donovan & Smolkin, 2002). They learn about different texts from situations at home, from teachers reading texts to them, and from their own reading of texts for specific purposes.

A long rhetorical tradition has described genres as specific text types with particular features or formats: description, narrative, explanation, instruction, and persuasion (Freedman & Medway, 1994; Grabe, 2002). These five types have been adopted by schools and state standards (Johns, 2002). For example, in language arts textbooks students are instructed how to write the five types of paragraphs. One difficulty is that the traditional view does not consider the situation in which the writing occurs or the purpose and audience for writing. Second, a type may appear in many different texts, such as description in information texts to describe the characteristics of geological formations and in fiction texts to describe the setting and characters. Third, the traditional view lends itself to formulaic rules—all narratives must describe the setting first—while variations abound, such as opening with an action: "Where is Papa going with that ax?" (the first line in *Charlotte's Web*; White, 1952, p. 1).

The new view defines genres as communicative actions developed in response to recurring situations (Coe, 2002; Miller, 1994). Genres have typical features and organizational structures that have evolved to suit the purposes of the authors' situations and the needs of the audiences. The features and organizations are typical because the situations recur but writers may change, invent, or modify them to fit specific audiences or situations. For example, think about the genre of TV situation comedy and how our society has changed from the 1950s to the 1990s. In the 1950s, *Ozzie and Harriet* portrayed a middle-class family of a mother, a father, and two sons, faced with noncontroversial, funny situations. Then, in the 1970s, *All in the Family* aired with controversial topics that exposed prejudice and racism in each episode. Yet the action was still within a family context (mother, father, married daughter, and son-in-law living in the same house) and the funny situations were resolved in a half hour. In the 1990s, a different relationship occurred when *Seinfeld* portrayed four single friends encountering situations about the most mundane issues—a sitcom about nothing. Each sitcom redefined the genre yet held to the basic features and organization—relationships in comic situations solved in the half-hour framework of TV.

In addition to features and organization, an important component of discourse knowledge is word choice. We describe word choice as the vocabulary writers use to support genres; for example, "Once upon a time" signals a fairytale. Similarly, readers would expect to see mathematical terminology when students write to explain their problem-solving processes. Students writing how-to directions should understand that transitional words play a key role in this genre: first, next, before, in 3 minutes. In all genres we encourage students to choose their words wisely including precise, definitive, genre-specific vocabulary.

Thus, we define genres as texts that purposely serve recurring communicative situations and so have acquired characteristics that serve the writers' and readers' needs. As teachers, we want to offer our students opportunities to experience a variety of purposes and situations so they learn the variety of genres that will enable them to communicate with audiences in a variety of discourses (Gee, 1996; Miller, 1994). We recognize that students may mix characteristics of different genres to form a hybrid text. For instance, they might include characteristics of informational texts (such as highlighting important words in bold) in a narrative text. Novice writers create hybrid texts because they do not yet have control over a particular genre. Experienced writers may purposefully create hybrid texts as they experiment with different genres for different effects.

Time and Space

Simply put, time refers to temporal distances between the writer and reader, while space refers to geographical distances. When considering time, writers acknowledge whether their readers are there with them to experience an action or event. When considering space, students must determine if they are writing for someone in their class, school, town, or if they are writing for a reader who is separated by hundreds of miles, an ocean, or perhaps even an imaginary galaxy. For example, pretend that students are writing letters to soldiers stationed overseas. They know the soldiers were not with them at the events they are writing about. They also know that the soldiers come from around the United States—not necessarily from their hometown. They are separated in both time and space. The greater the distance between writer and reader in either time or space (or both), the greater the need for precision in the way language is used and ideas are conveyed (Kaufer & Carley, 1994; Nystrand, 1986). Therefore, writers pay close attention to the details they include in order to situate their information in a temporal and spatial context that is clear for their readers to understand.

In our communication model, we merge time and space into one dimension. Unless writers and readers share mutual time and space, writers understand that their texts will be read outside the context in which they were written; therefore, they take care to contextualize their writing.

Sociocultural Membership

We are all members of various groups and organizations. These sociocultural groups or communities may be based on interest, occupation, ethnicity, culture, religion, family, or age, for example. Some communities are deliberate, formal, and well established (such as our classroom communities), while others are sporadic, informal, and spontaneous (such as the community of residents who frequent the local library). In every case, the community is part of a social network that has unique social languages, ways of thinking, and beliefs (Gee, 1996, 2001).

Let's back up for a moment and consider how students acquire membership in different communities. Each of us has a home community in which we are most familiar and comfortable. In our family community we learned language that expresses the beliefs, ideals, goals, and values of the family unit (Gee, 1996). As students come in contact with communities outside the family, they learn how those communities use language to express beliefs, customs, goals, and values. Students become members of structured communities that have been formed around sports, dance, music, theater, books, or teen idols. They also belong to less obvious communities that exist on school buses, in cafeterias, in skateboard parks, or in front of a local convenience store. One student, for instance, might concurrently be a member of a family community, a classroom community, a school community, a community of students who share a passion for science, a community of chess players, and various interactive online communities including blogs and Wikis. This student speaks and acts differently within each community.

Picture, for example, a soccer community. A soccer player would be comfortable using such words as *offsides, sweeper, striker, wing, pass back,* and *overlaps*—terms that reflect his or her membership in the community. Soccer players are also recognized by the clothing they wear: shin pads, cleats, spikes, and perhaps pinnies. They use nets, soccer balls, and scoreboards. Furthermore, protocols, routines, and rituals exist among members of this sociocultural group. They know, for instance, that before a game the captains meet with a referee who tosses a coin to determine which team has first possession of the ball. Soccer etiquette precludes players from running onto the field until the ritual is complete. The thinking and beliefs of teams may vary, depending on the members of a particular community. Some soccer communities, for example, might believe that winning is the primary goal; only the most proficient athletes compete. Other communities might deem it important for all members to get in to each game, regardless of a win or loss.

Communities exist to support the needs of their members, who typically adhere to implicit and explicit guiding principles. These principles signal membership within the sociocultural community. Because writing is a social act, we always write from within a particular sociocultural community. The participants in each community construct ideas about what writing is, what writing is for, and who writes within their community (Cairney, 2000; Gee, 1996).

The students in Ms. Arnold's class were learning new ways of using language while investigating the salt in their town's water supply partially because the students wrote for a variety of purposes and audiences. One group of students shared their findings at a town meeting with the local officials who originally sent out the report on the quality of the town's drinking water. You might think that the students and town officials all belong to the same community. They do when community is defined as a physical location; a town, for instance. In our model, however, community refers to one's membership in a sociocultural group—in this case, the group of people who participate in their town government.

As is the case in many towns, the officials regularly participate in public forums. They understand what language is appropriate (and not appropriate), what clothing is acceptable, and what procedures are customarily used to enter into a conversation. The students, who had never been to a public forum, had to acquire the same modes of speech, dress, and procedural behavior as the town officials in order to establish themselves within the sociocultural group. In short, the students needed to take on the town officials' ways of writing, thinking, talking, and behaving in order for their messages to be heard and taken seriously; they needed to earn acceptance and membership in this established sociocultural community of public meeting attendees.

All writers belong to different communities. They acknowledge the communities to which they belong and recognize that readers may or may not belong to these same communities (Sheehy, 2003). Stepping out of one's home sociocultural community to join a new sociocultural community can be a difficult goal to attain. We return to sociocultural membership (and the other three dimensions) throughout this book as we discuss learning to write effectively.

In the next section we build on the discussion of world knowledge, discourse knowledge, knowledge of time and space, and knowledge of sociocultural membership as we investigate the impact of distances between writers and intended readers.

WRITER–READER RELATIONSHIPS

Writers and readers pledge to uphold an implicit contract when they interact through written texts. The writer's role is to write clearly and engagingly for his or her purpose and audience so that the reader can interpret the writer's intended message. The reader's role is to use knowledge of the world and knowledge of how language works to comprehend the writer's intended message (Shanahan, 1990). When the distance increases between what the writer and the reader bring to this contract, communication may break down. Let's take a look at how we can use our communication model to depict distances in writer–reader relationships.

As we noted earlier in this chapter, when writing for oneself the author and reader are the same person. We indicate this on our communication model (see Figure 1.1) by placing all four stars in the center oval. More often than not, however, when we communicate through written texts, the writer and reader are not the same person, as we discuss next.

We began this chapter with a brief sketch of an expeditionary and interdisciplinary project completed by students in Ms. Arnold's class.

We return to this group to take a closer look at how the students used writing to express their ideas. For each of the four student groups identified below, we state the purpose for writing and the intended audience. We move the stars to mark the points along the dimensions that indicate distances between writers and readers. Then we provide a rationale for our decisions and consider what implications the distances between writer and reader have. The proximity or distance between writer and reader on each dimension has direct bearing on the choices writers make about what and how they write. Of course, this exercise is not an exact science and should not be. The point is to help students imagine their readers and make informed decisions about crafting their writing.

Students Writing for Their Teacher

Belinda's group sat at the watershed site, crafting written descriptions in their science notebooks of what they were observing. Before they left the site, they drew tentative conclusions based on their observations. Belinda's science teacher will read their observations and provide some feedback. Notice where we placed the stars in Figure 1.2. Then, read the rationale that follows to learn why we placed them where we did.

As you probably suspect, our rationale reflects the fact that Belinda's group and their science teacher share at least partial understandings

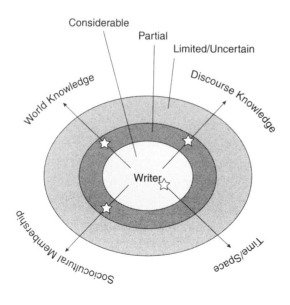

FIGURE 1.2. Belinda's group: Writing observations for their science teacher.

along the four dimensions of our communication model. The group is beginning to acquire relevant scientific knowledge (world knowledge) and knowledge about the genre of observational entries (discourse knowledge). In addition, they include the science vocabulary they have learned (discourse knowledge). However, since Belinda's teacher has considerably more world and discourse knowledge than the students do, we placed the stars in the *partial* oval for both dimensions. When evaluating time and space, we note that Belinda's group and their teacher did not stay right beside each other at the site, but because they were together in time and in close proximity to each other, we placed the star in the *considerable* oval. And, finally, Belinda's group is trying out the language of scientists, but the students still mix science language with conversational language to express what they are thinking and feeling. They remember to describe objective facts—the language practices of scientists (sociocultural membership) but feelings about the cold and mud creep into their descriptions. Again, because their teacher understands more fully than the students how scientists use language to organize and express concepts, beliefs, and values, we place the star in the *partial* oval.

What does all this mean for the students in Belinda's group—writers who are trying to communicate with their teacher? The students know they need to focus on the purpose of this writing assignment and use their science knowledge to determine the specific, relevant details they should include (world knowledge). With their teacher's instruction, the students are learning what is included in an observation entry and how it is organized. They strive to include the science vocabulary the teacher has taught (discourse knowledge). Since the students and their teacher share considerable contextual knowledge, they do not need to add more background information (time and space). Finally, to communicate with Ms. Arnold, a science teacher, students in Belinda's group continue to learn the language practices of scientists from Ms. Arnold's instruction and by reading notebooks and logs written by scientists (sociocultural membership).

Students Writing to Younger Students

Pablo's group has finalized its report on the Franklin Brook project. In the report, the students explained why there is a high level of salt in the water and why this is dangerous. They will be sharing his report with second graders in a nearby school (see Figure 1.3).

Over the course of this project, Pablo's group made several dozen on-site visits to the watershed and to the surrounding area. They conducted investigations, collected and analyzed data, and learned a great deal about salt and the watershed. The students in Pablo's group could

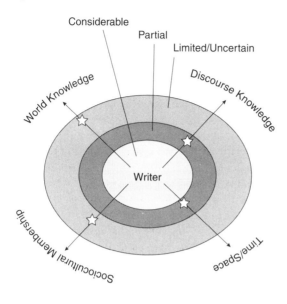

FIGURE 1.3. Pablo's group: Writing a report to second graders.

not be sure how much the second graders knew of the investigation or how much knowledge they had about salt, but they probably shared only a *limited/uncertain* amount (world knowledge). By eighth grade, most students have written several science reports and are somewhat familiar with the genre (discourse knowledge). Second graders probably have had some experience with reports, documenting the life cycle of butterflies or observing how seeds become plants. Since the discourse knowledge of the students in Pablo's group is more sophisticated than that of the younger audience, they share *partial* understanding. Even though the second graders were not present when Pablo's group conducted the investigations (time), they were quite familiar with the physical area around the school (space). Therefore, we place the time/space star in the *partial* oval. Finally, Pablo's group's experiences on the project have bolstered their understanding of what scientists know and how they think and express themselves. Because the young audience has not yet had the breadth of scientific experiences that Pablo's group has had, they share *limited/uncertain* sociocultural membership.

What does this mean for the students in Pablo's group—writers who are trying to communicate with second graders? The students in this group know what information about salt and the watershed they want to convey to the 7-year-olds. Anticipating little knowledge, they know to focus on the key ideas and connect the new knowledge to what the children already might know (world knowledge). As a result of conferences with their teacher, the students in Pablo's group are aware that they need to organize the report clearly and engagingly, define science vocabulary, and express their thoughts in sentences that are not too complex for the younger students (discourse knowledge). From their teacher's feedback, they have learned to set a context for the investigation (time and space). They don't worry about being too explicit, however, because the group and their audience already share some knowledge of where the investigation took place. Finally, Pablo's group is learning to sound like a scientist, but at Ms. Arnold's suggestion, they modify their language to make the scientific concepts accessible for the second graders (sociocultural membership).

Students Writing to Town Officials

Julia's group was excited. They were revising a report they would share with the town officials who issued the original statement about the quality of the town's water supply. They would be reporting the students' findings and trying to convince the officials to fund additional research at Franklin Brook (see Figure 1.4).

When marking distance on the world knowledge dimension, we envisioned that some officials knew about the scientific basis of the students' findings while others knew very little. Since the students in Julia's group could not be certain about the amount of shared world knowl-

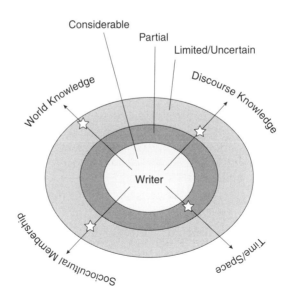

FIGURE 1.4. Julia's group: Writing a report for town officials.

edge, the star appears in the *limited/uncertain* oval. Like the students in Pablo's group, these students have written reports before, but they are learning about the rigor of scientists' reports (discourse knowledge). They are learning to explain the investigation, the results, and the conclusions thoroughly and clearly for an adult audience. However, since Julia's group was unsure of the town officials' knowledge of scientific writing and vocabulary, we moved the star just into the *limited/uncertain* oval. Again, like Pablo's group, Julia's group knows the officials were not present during their investigations (time) but are probably familiar with the geographical context of the study (space). Therefore, we placed the star in the *partial* oval. Finally, the town officials were members of a social community that differed from the sociocultural community of the students. The students are learning to adjust their writing, speaking, and behavior to be heard and appreciated in the public forum community that is new to them. Thus, we placed the star in the *limited/uncertain* oval.

What does this mean for students in Julia's group—writers communicating with town officials? Julia's group knows to present their scientific findings with purpose and audience in mind: They want to use the research to convince the town officials that a problem needs to be addressed. Informed by Ms. Arnold that they will have a limited amount of time in the public forum (sociocultural community), they seek to focus their remarks to the major findings and use specific data to support their claims (world knowledge). Since Ms. Arnold and Julia's group think most officials are nonscientists, they decide the group must show data, use scientific vocabulary accurately, and pause to clarify when necessary (discourse knowledge). In addition, Julia's group learns that they need to set a context for their report or the key points they are trying to convey could be lost. Since the town meeting members likely know the area, their description does not need to be comprehensive (space), but they need to accurately report when different results occurred (time). Finally, the students know they are unfamiliar with the customs of public meetings. With help from their teachers, they prepare their report so that they sound both like scientists and like respectful young people speaking publicly to unknown adults (sociocultural membership).

Students Writing to Unknown Students

Michael's group is writing a report that will provide a brief overview of the Franklin Brook project. The students' intended audience will be other middle school students from the eastern part of the state who have gathered to share their science investigations at a middle school science conference. You will probably notice immediately when looking at Figure 1.5 that three of the four stars for Michael's group reside in

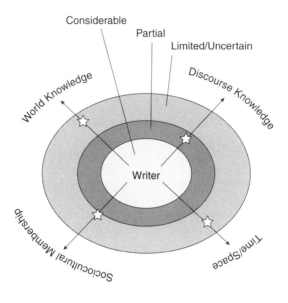

FIGURE 1.5. Michael's group: Writing for an "unknown" audience of middle school scientists.

the *limited/uncertain* oval. Can you predict our rationale even before you read it?

As you probably predicted, since the students in Michael's group could not determine how much they and their audiences share in world knowledge, time and space, and sociocultural membership, we placed those stars in the *limited/uncertain* oval. Since all the students were presenting science reports, they probably had common discourse knowledge; so we placed the star in the *partial* oval.

What does this mean for students in Michael's group—writers writing for distant, unknown readers? In the report, Michael's group knows to provide a clear purpose, emphasize key points, and include relevant details to support its points. The students at the conference may share different kinds of scientific knowledge, so Michael's group writes so that every student will understand the information they are trying to communicate (world knowledge). Since their readers are fellow scientists, they are likely to share some discourse knowledge of scientific reports, although Michael's group has no definitive way of knowing. So, with the teacher's feedback and instruction, the students take care to include genre-specific features and vocabulary, organize the report effectively, and use sentence constructions and conventions that serve their purpose and engage their readers. Michael's group learns from their teacher that they need to include background information about when and where that establishes a clear context for the investigation for their readers (time and space). Finally, since they all share membership in a community of middle school students who are interested in science, Michael's group is learning to sound like scientists in their report (sociocultural membership).

The writing situations featured above focus on expository writing or writing to explain. Regardless of purpose, audience, or genre, however, writers need to become aware of the four dimensions of our communication model. As students move through the grades and into the work force, they will be expected to apply what they know about writing for specific situations. They need to understand the situation in which they are writing as well as the expectations of their intended readers (Beaufort, 2006). Teachers at all grade levels can help prepare students to write for unknown audiences by providing them with real-world opportunities to write for distant readers. Distant writing can be explored when students:

Send letters to favorite authors.
Write to students in another grade.
Connect with e-pals.
Plan a fund-raiser.
Create brochures for local civic groups.
Write to local newspapers.
Enter writing contests.
Advocate for others who live in their community or in other parts of the world.
Correspond with college preservice teachers.
Prepare for standardized tests.

We encourage teachers and students to determine what they want to accomplish through their writing (i.e., set their purpose) and then judge the commonalities that exist (or do not exist) between themselves as writers and their intended audiences.

CHAPTER SUMMARY

Our communication model acknowledges the relationship between writers and their audiences. We hold that writers and readers are members of sociocultural groups that share some degree of world knowledge, discourse knowledge, and time and space. When writers write they consider these four dimensions, which are the dimensions of our communication model, and try to determine whether knowledge shared by themselves and their anticipated audiences is considerable, partial, or limited/uncertain. When writers consider the world knowledge of their intended audiences, they think about the types and amount of content information to include in their texts. Considering their purposes and the situations in which they are writing, writers make decisions about discourse knowledge. They choose from among genres, text organizations, and specific words. Thinking about time and space, writers include the amount of contextual information audiences need to bridge temporal and geographical differences. Finally, writers judge whether they have shared memberships in sociocultural communities with their audiences—similar or different social languages, ways of thinking, and beliefs. Writers learn to write to audiences within and outside of their sociocultural communities.

We want students to use their varied situations in and out of school so that they write for real purposes to a variety of audiences while gaining practice in judging the world knowledge, discourse knowledge, time and space, and sociocultural memberships they might share with their readers.

In Chapter 2, "A Writer's Cognitive Processes," we continue to explore the relationship that exists between writer and reader as we look at how writers write.

APPLICATION BOX

Select one writing assignment that a student is currently working on (or will work on shortly). Using our communication model, mark the writer–reader relationship. Where would you position a star on each dimension? If the stars come close to the center, think about an audience and purpose that encourages the student to write for a more distant reader. After you and your student have picked a distant reader, place the stars on our communication model and discuss how much world knowledge, discourse knowledge, understanding of time and space, and similarity of sociocultural memberships the reader might share (or not share) with the student. Choose another audience; then discuss whether the student would change the position of the stars. If so, why?

Chapter 2

A Writer's Cognitive Processes

Have you thought about *how* you write? Most of us concentrate on *what* to write without thinking about *how* we write. Yet, *how* is the process that allows the *what* to get written. Think about what you do when you write a newsletter to parents, an e-mail to friends, a poem for your students, or a letter to the editor. Do you compose the same way regardless of purpose, audience, or genre? We think your processes are basically similar, but the ease with which you proceed through the tasks might differ depending on your purpose for writing and your intended reader. Your processes might be on automatic pilot when you write a school newsletter because you know the content, the audience, and the genre well. Using our communication model, you easily communicate to parents because you:

- Write about classroom events (world knowledge).
- Write in a newspaper genre (the five W's) and use everyday words, not educational jargon (discourse knowledge).
- Include details so that parents who were not there can understand the events (time and space).
- Adopt a friendly, conversational voice (sociocultural membership).

However, when you write a letter to the editor to unknown audiences, you may be metacognitively aware of your processes and consciously think about the differences between you and your readers in the four dimensions of our communication model. You probably:

- Think about the facts to support your position and maybe even research facts (world knowledge).
- Decide how to organize your argument and use precise terms (discourse knowledge).
- Consider what background information is needed (time and space).
- Recognize different perspectives on the issue and use the convincing voice of a concerned citizen (sociocultural membership).

Thus, especially when writing to unknown audiences, writers intentionally think about the four dimensions of our communication model. Their processes for writing are not automatic; they are very deliberate.

Writing processes, like reading processes, are difficult to figure out because all the work occurs inside the writer's head; we only see the product—not the processes. To try to describe writers' processes, researchers have asked writers to think aloud as they write (Emig, 1971; Flower & Hayes, 1981), have interviewed students as they write (Calkins, 1983; Graves, 1983) or have given writers different writing tasks to carry out (Bereiter & Scardamalia, 1987; Graham & Harris, 2005; McCutchen, 1994, 2006). Although the researchers differ in their descriptions, they agree that the processes are not static. Instead, writers recycle through a number of processes when thinking about their purposes and audiences at varying points. We have adapted the work of these researchers to present our model of a writer's cognitive processes, which will help teachers better understand their students' writing habits and better design instruction that will support students.

In this chapter, we:

- Present our model of a writer's cognitive processes and concurrently describe Sam, an experienced sixth-grade writer.
- Provide an Inquiry Guide to a Writer's Cognitive Processes and concurrently describe Melissa, a struggling sixth-grade writer.
- Define the writer's task environment.

Before we describe our model of a writer's cognitive processes, we introduce you to Sam, a competent sixth-grade writer.

Sam's teacher just announced that *Stone Soup* magazine is sponsoring a writing contest. Searching his brain for an idea, Sam flips the pages in his writer's notebook to the lifeline assignment his teacher had the class complete at the beginning of the year. He reviews the events, such as his little sister's birth, T-ball in first grade, the death of Uncle Andy, and stunt kite flying. The contest calls for a memoir about an event—not an autobiography—like the memoir writing the class did in September. Thinking about the memoirs he and his classmates read and wrote in September, Sam wonders whether he should revise his earlier memoir on T-ball or start a new one. He decides to write about his hobby of stunt kite flying. We follow Sam's writing experience as we introduce our model of the writer's cognitive processes in the next section.

A WRITER'S COGNITIVE PROCESSES

What do writers do when they compose texts? Unfortunately, there is no simple answer to this question. What we do know, however, is that if we are to help students learn to write, we need to investigate how they compose—not just evaluate their finished pieces. Basing the cognitive processes on past research (especially Flower & Hayes, 1981; Hayes, 2004; McCutchen, 2006), we crafted a model of writing that includes three writing processes: *planning, producing text*, and *reviewing* (see Figure 2.1). When authors write, they do not proceed in a linear fashion from planning to reviewing. Instead, based on their purposes and audiences, authors monitor or keep track of how the writing is going and decide which process is needed.

Now, we describe the writer's cognitive processes and return to Sam to see how he navigates these processes. As we discuss each process, remember that purpose and audience are central to communicating a message.

Planning

Planning is preparing to write (see Figure 2.1). Effective writers think about purpose, audience, ideas, and genre when they plan. Writers usually start with a message and purpose they want to communicate to an audience and then figure out how to communicate or what genre to put it in. At other times, writers think about message, audience, and genre together, for example, writing directions. Because Sam is entering a contest, he is given a specific genre (a memoir) and audience (unknown judges). His task is to figure out the content.

Because his teacher has emphasized planning, Sam spends time brainstorming ideas. Knowing a memoir is about experiences in his life, he examines his lifeline to locate the stunt kites topic and then brainstorms ideas for the topic:

- Visiting the kite shop with his dad.
- Learning to fly stunt kites.

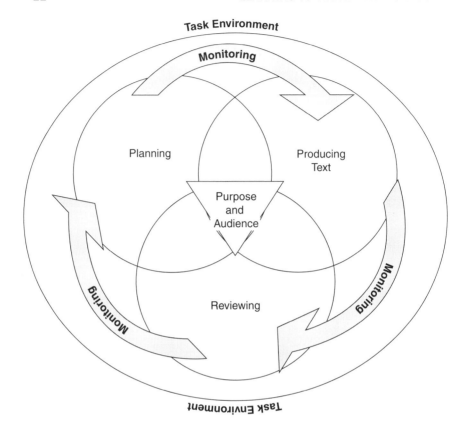

FIGURE 2.1. A writer's cognitive process.

- Starting to design kites.
- Mom teaching him to sew the kites he designed.

In the midst of his brainstorming, Sam realizes the judges of the contest, like many of his classmates, won't know what stunt kites are and will think they are ordinary one-line kites that first graders fly. So, he adds *describing or defining stunt kites* to his brainstorming list. Sam keeps thinking and adding to his list in his writer's notebook until the end of the period. The next day, Sam surveys his brainstorming list and adds numbers to organize his stunt kite events, monitoring both the amount and quality of his ideas in his plans. Deciding he has enough ideas, Sam begins to produce text.

You can see that Sam plans well because his teacher has emphasized planning strategies. However, as you will see in the next section—producing text, Sam had to return to planning.

Producing Text

When producing texts (see Figure 2.1), writers engage in two tasks: (1) generating the language (words in sentences) for ideas and (2) transcribing those words and sentences onto paper or a computer screen.

Generating Text

Generating text is thinking of the specific words and sentences that can be written to communicate ideas. When writers have many ideas, are familiar with the genre, and have decided on the organization of their piece during planning, they often can convert their ideas easily into words and sentences. At other times, writers think they know what they want to say, but when it comes to turning those ideas into words and sentences, they struggle.

Transcribing Text

Transcribing is the physical act of turning oral language into a written form. Some writers prefer a specific tool—a special pen or the computer—and even a special location. When writers have handwriting and spelling under reasonable control, generally they can transcribe their ideas into written text easily. If they have a difficult time with handwriting or spelling, their thinking resources go into the physical transcription of their message rather than into generating text (De La Paz & Graham, 1997). We recommend the computer programs listed in Appendix 2.1 at the end of this chapter; several are designed to assist writers who struggle with transcribing texts.

Even though he numbered the events on his list, Sam is unsure about how to begin; how to turn his ideas into words and sentences. He realizes that a time sequence—from his discovery of stunt kites to now—would be boring. He knows he has to define or describe stunt kites early but again a definition would be dull. Sam circles *describe stunt kites* and looks over his flying events in his list. He decides to start with flying stunt kites with his dad at the school's playground and then renumbers the other events on his list. Noticing that the classroom computers are being used by others, Sam flips to a blank page in his writer's notebook and begins to change his ideas into sentences:

> Hey, Sam, grab your kite! Let's go flying calls Dad.
> We head for the playground next door and begin to put our kites together thread the struts through the sleeves, attach the two strings with their handles. We stand our kites on edge and back away letting out the strings from the handles. Then yanking down

on the handles, the kites rise gracefully into the air. We steer them left and right with the handles. Soon, Dad and I are in our usual dog-fight or kite-fight which is sort of like the Quiditch matches that Harry Potter plays. As usual, Dad downs my kite, although I did dodge his kite for longer and got in a couple of charges myself.
 Tada! Better luck next time says Dad.

Looking over Sam's shoulder, Matt, his classmate, says, "You'd better draw a picture. I'm not sure what stunt kites look like." Sam quickly sketches a picture of the stunt kites flying to use as a plan to refer to when he fixes the description later. Deciding to continue writing his draft, he refers back to the renumbered events on his brainstorming list, rereads the text-so-far, and continues producing the draft.

You can see that Sam concentrates on producing text, although he interrupts himself to review his text-so-far and returns to planning by drawing a picture to assist with later revisions. Thus, Sam freely moves among the processes of planning, producing text, and reviewing because he is continually monitoring his text in light of his purpose and audience. When he has finished a rough first draft, Sam turns to reviewing.

Reviewing

Reviewing (see Figure 2.1) has three components—evaluating what was written, revising the text, and editing. Some authors delay reviewing until a complete first draft is produced because the end often affects the beginning; they do not stop to make changes. Other writers evaluate while producing a first draft and stop to revise and edit before they finish the draft. Writers may post drafts online to receive reviewing help from peers or even strangers.

Evaluating

A key part of reviewing is the evaluation of what has been written so far. Writers evaluate their texts (during or after producing texts) and monitor by keeping their purposes, intended audiences, and plans in mind. We discuss evaluating again in Chapter 8.

As Sam reviews his draft with Matt, they both realize that Sam needs to describe stunt kites better—not only what they look like but how they fly. They refer to Sam's drawing and discuss whether to describe how to get the kites in the air or just to begin with the kites already in the air. To help Sam focus his draft, his teacher asks, "Is this a memoir about stunt kites or getting to know your dad?" Sam looks at her, stunned, "I don't know." As Sam heads to the computer to revise, his teacher adds, "Well, work on the description and think about it."

their motivation and behavior during writing (termed *self-regulation* by Graham & Harris, 2005). In all three writing processes, Sam consistently engages in monitoring:

- He decides whether he has enough ideas in his plan to begin producing text.
- He discovers he has to include a better description of stunt kites.
- He thinks about the focus of his memoir—his dad or flying stunt kites.
- He keeps track of his purpose and the distance between himself and his unknown audience in terms of world knowledge, discourse knowledge, time and space, and sociocultural membership—our communication model.

Learning from Sam

Let's summarize what we can learn about the writer's cognitive processes from Sam, an experienced sixth-grade writer.

1. Writers engage in different processes—planning, producing text (generating language and transcribing), and reviewing (evaluating, revising, and editing).
2. Experienced writers rarely work in a linear fashion proceeding from planning straight through to editing.
3. Instead, experienced writers move among the processes as needed, perhaps reviewing while producing text or revising while editing.
4. Writers monitor their processes in order to decide which processes will help them accomplish their purpose.
5. Writers monitor purposes and audiences, thinking about the dimensions of our communication model, especially when they plan and review.

Let's look more closely at how Sam uses our communication model. When Sam plans, he thinks that his unknown audience will most likely have little world knowledge about stunt kites, will need a context for stunt kite flying (time and space), and will not be a part of the stunt kite community but will have discourse knowledge of memoirs. When producing text, Sam only briefly thinks about his unknown audience's lack of world knowledge; instead he is concentrating on his own world knowledge. By beginning with a description of stunt kite flying, Sam is trying to bridge the time and space and sociocultural membership differences between himself and his readers, although he is unsuccessful in his first draft. During reviewing, Sam is keenly aware that he needs to provide for the unknown audience's lack of world knowledge about stunt kites, lack of presence when flying stunt kites (time and space), and lack of membership in the stunt kite community (sociocultural membership). In addition, Sam focuses the theme of his memoir on his relationship with his dad (discourse knowledge).

If you were Sam's teacher, how would you learn about his processes? You could observe him listing ideas or discussing his draft with Matt, for example. You could ask him questions such as "Is the draft about kites or your dad?" You could compare his early draft to his final memoir for effective revisions. While we have evidence of Sam's processes, for other students, especially students who struggle, we may need to inquire into how they write. To help teachers inquire into their students' processes, we have created an Inquiry Guide to a Writer's Cognitive Processes, in which we address the cognitive processes of planning, producing text, and reviewing, as well as the process of monitoring.

AN INQUIRY GUIDE TO A WRITER'S COGNITIVE PROCESSES PLUS MONITORING

As teachers we are always searching for ways to examine our students' writing processes more closely in order to make the best instructional decisions we can. Using the final product alone would not highlight a writer's cognitive processes or pinpoint processes in need of instruction. Therefore, we propose an inquiry guide to analyze a writer's cognitive processes and monitoring.

Using the Inquiry Guide

Gathering evidence of a writer's cognitive processes is one of the hardest things we can do as teachers, especially in busy classrooms. We do not recommend that a teacher examine all of the writer's cognitive processes on the guide with *every* student *every* time students write. Instead, we encourage you to try using the guide with a student who interests you or about whom you are curious or puzzled.

The inquiry guide asks an overall question for each of a writer's cognitive processes (planning, producing, and reviewing) as well as an overall question for monitoring (see Figure 2.2). For each overall question, we provide a list of *Things to Observe* and a list of *Things to Ask* to assist your observations and conversations with students. After some information is gathered, we recommend that you refer to the *Potential Issues* box in which we suggest possible reasons a student might be struggling. Finally, glance through the *Things to Try* box for instructional suggestions. Over time, you can probe each overall question and look at an individual writer's cognitive processes across writing tasks. Let's see how

Planning	Things to Observe	Things to Ask

• Does the student show evidence of planning?	• Identifies a topic.
	• Organizes ideas.
	  ○ List
	  ○ Map
	  ○ Discovery draft
	• Selects a genre that matches purpose.
	• Uses mentor texts or other resources (e.g., Internet, writer's notebook, person).
		• What is your purpose for writing?
		• Who is your audience? What do you know about your audience?
		• Why did you choose this topic?
		• Why did you choose this genre?
		• Why did you use these resources?
		• Do you know more about this topic?
		• Which is the beginning idea on your plan?

	Potential Issues	**Things to Try**
	• Writes immediately without planning. • Ignores purpose. • Disregards audience. • Knows only a few genres or selects inappropriate genre. • Selects the same strategy every time or selects an ineffective strategy. • Lists ideas randomly without organization. • Uses full sentences in plans and thinks the plan is a draft. • Has difficulty thinking of ideas. • Has meager or incomplete notes. • Overlooks additional resources.	• Engage student in activities to formulate ideas for writing. • Teach different strategies for planning. • Have students interview each other to formulate more ideas. • Model and explain decisions about purpose and audience. • Teach features of genre using a graphic organizer and mentor texts. • Introduce a variety of resources. • Introduce planning software, such as Draft Builder.
Producing Text	**Things to Observe**	**Things to Ask**
• Can the student turn ideas into words and sentences to produce text?	• Refers to plans while producing text. • Selects preferred writing tool (e.g., computer, pencil). • Writes fluently and with ease. • Pauses while writing. • Uses a resource: word wall, dictionary. • Produces thoughts fully and effectively.	• How are you using your plans to write this text? • Do you know more that you could write? Tell me. • Why did you choose this tool to write? • Do you want to try another tool? • Why did you pause? • What resources would help you?
	Potential Issues	**Things to Try**
	• Ignores plan. • Switches to new topic not on plan. • Copies from list or graphic organizer. • Has difficulty making word choices to carry out purpose. • Attends more to conventions than ideas. • Uses less than optimal writing tool. • Transcribes laboriously. • Produces unreadable text.	• Discuss why writers use plans. • Model and explain how to use a plan when producing text. • Teach strategies to elaborate on important ideas. • Emphasize content and deemphasize conventions in the first draft. • Try a different transcription tool. • Provide a variety of transcription tools. • Encourage student to use a talking word processor to hear text-so-far, such as Co:Writer. • Find a scribe.

(continued)

FIGURE 2.2. An inquiry guide to a writer's cognitive processes plus monitoring.

Reviewing	Things to Observe	Things to Ask
• Can the student evaluate and revise the text? Does the student edit the final piece?	• Rereads text. • Pauses. • Rereads and marks text to change. • Rereads and changes content (e.g., adds details, cuts cluttering details). • Uses arrows or numbers to show where to change organization. • Compares text to plan. • Consults resources for additional content. • Makes word-level changes to the text while reading out loud (e.g., fills in missing word(s)). • Edits for conventions. • Uses resources for help with spelling, grammar, and punctuation.	• When you reread, do you think about your purpose and audience? • What do you know about your audience? • What were you thinking during that long pause? • What are you planning to change or what did you change? • Why will/did you make the change? • How will/did this change improve the quality of the piece? • Can you find a resource for additional information? • Would additional (or different) punctuation help your reader understand your message? • What resources could you use for help with spelling, grammar, and punctuation?
	Potential Issues	**Things to Try**
	• Needs to learn why to reread. • Is unwilling to reread. • Needs to learn what to evaluate in text. • Evaluates based on length and conventions. • Ignores plan while reviewing. • Substitutes big words for common words without regard to meaning differences. • Changes only conventions. • Needs to learn effective revision strategies. • Uses a tool that makes it cumbersome to revise.	• Model and explain rereading texts to evaluate meaning and effectiveness. • Teach to evaluate and revise one specific element (e.g., details, organization, voice). • Teach strategies for revision. • Provide mentor texts to use as resources for specific elements. • Teach editing skills as communicating with an audience. • Provide software that allow students to easily revise and edit, such as Write Out Loud.
Monitoring	**Things to Observe**	**Things to Ask**
• Does the student indicate where he or she is in the writing process and what he or she needs to do next?	• Returns to a planning strategy or revisits original plans when necessary. • Seeks out resources throughout the processes (e.g., texts, teacher, another student, computer). • Sustains a piece of writing for a period of time. • Rereads text-so-far. • Pauses. • Marks text for potential changes.	• Do you keep your purpose and audience in mind when making decisions? • Where are you now in your writing processes—planning, producing, or reviewing? • Do you need to switch to another process? • What are you thinking when you pause or reread? • What are you going to do next on this piece? • Do you have any more ideas for this piece?

(continued)

FIGURE 2.2. *(continued)*

Potential Issues	Things to Try
• Starts new pieces often instead of sustaining a piece. • Pauses frequently because distracted. • Leaves place where writing because distracted. • Needs to learn when to use a process (e.g., when to begin producing text, when to evaluate).	• Model and explain determining a purpose. • Explain decisions you make while writing, why you make them, and how they help you achieve your purpose and meet the needs of your intended audience. • Model and explain why switching from one process to another. • Provide reminders to reread to monitor the work. • Pair students with writing partners. • Try different task environments—alone, computer area, cluster of desks.

FIGURE 2.2. *(continued)*

Sam's teacher uses the inquiry guide to trace the cognitive processes of Melissa, a struggling student.

Melissa, like Sam, is also writing a memoir for the magazine contest. Melissa remembers that memoirs focus on one key life event. She goes to the classroom library to find Tomie dePaola's *26 Fairmont Avenue* (1999) series to see if they remind her of events in her own life. Overhearing her teacher tell other students to return to their lifeline for ideas, Melissa rereads her lifeline. Although her special education teacher often helps her plan, Melissa knows she needs to start planning on her own now. Using her lifeline, she writes in one column the events that remind her of when she was younger. In a second column, she lists a detail about each one of these lifeline events.

> Things from when I was yunger
> I did Reading   books I liked
> Tricia at camp   slept in same cabin
> I learned to Write   liked using markers
> Campping with YMCA
> New skool   Moved when 7

The next day, Melissa takes out a blank piece of paper. Bypassing the plans she made the day before, she immediately begins to write:

> When I was yungr I did many things. I played with my puppy. my baby bruthr was brn

After 20 minutes, Melissa puts her writing away and tells her neighbor she's done.

Surveying the Inquiry Guide, Melissa's teacher begins with the overall question for Planning: *Does the student show evidence of planning?* Pondering this question, she skims the *Things to Observe* box and remembers that yesterday Melissa found dePaola's memoir series and used a planning strategy (the two-column chart). Today, she observes that Melissa started writing right away without looking at her plan.

Skimming the *Things to Ask* box, she decides to interview Melissa. After asking to see Melissa's plan and the writing she has done on her memoir, her teacher asks Melissa for a one-sentence summary (Elbow, 1973). Melissa responds, "When I was younger." Noticing that Melissa's plan and writing do not match, she asks her to read what she wrote, but Melissa has a hard time reading and remembering what she wrote. "Tell me about learning to write," her teacher probes. With her teacher as scribe, Melissa enthusiastically reveals many more events than she has on her planning chart and then says, "I remember using markers and even one time writing on the wall in my bedroom. My mom was really upset with me." Melissa's teacher encourages her to write a memoir about the marker incident, and suggests reading *A Grain of Wheat* by Robert Clyde Bulla (1985), a memoir about learning to write. In addition, she reminds Melissa to ask her writing partner to take notes for her, and to use the Co:Writer program on the computer (see Appendix 2.1 at the end of this chapter). Although Melissa knows her partner is a good friend who can help her, she reluctantly turns to him for support.

Observing Melissa reading Bulla's book, her teacher wonders if Melissa will pick a new topic like struggling writers often do. Seeing Melissa talking to her writing partner, she hopes Melissa will begin a draft about writing with markers on her wall.

During lunch, Melissa's teacher glances down the *Potential Issues* box and finds *Has difficulty thinking of ideas*, which seems to be Melissa's main problem and often results in her meager planning. Glancing down the *Things to Try* box, she finds some suggestions listed: *Have students interview each other to formulate more ideas* and *Introduce a variety of resources*.

Melissa's teacher then turns her attention to the section on Producing Text: *Can the student turn ideas into words and sentences to produce text?* (see Figure 2.2). She recalls that Melissa did not refer to her original plan while producing text. Even though the plan was incomplete and unfocused, she did get some ideas down on paper. In addition, Melissa's teacher remembers Melissa bore down on her pencil and lacked fluency. She looks at the *Potential Issues* box and sees at least two concerns that apply to Melissa—*Ignores plan* and *Transcribes laboriously*. Referring to the *Things to Try* box, she notes that she reminded Melissa to *Find a scribe* (her writing partner), and to *Use the computer* (the Co:Writer program). The guide affirms decisions she made. She decides that going forward she needs to *Discuss why writers use plans* with Melissa.

Melissa's teacher knows she will need to observe and talk with Melissa again. For now, however, she decides to concentrate on the two areas of greatest concern for Melissa: her inability to plan effectively and her struggle to produce text. The inquiry guide helped Melissa's teacher look beyond *what* this sixth grader was writing (the product) and focus on *how* this sixth grader was writing (her cognitive processes). Realistically, Melissa will probably continue to struggle with writing. However, with her teacher's, writing partner's, and the computer's help Melissa can learn to plan and produce a draft.

Learning from Melissa

Melissa has learned from previous writing situations but is unable to apply what she has learned independently. We see that Melissa exhibits both strengths and needs (Troia, 2006).

- She recalls that memoirs focus on one event but lists several events from her lifeline.
- She refers to mentor texts for ideas but may change her topic.
- She knows to plan but is unable to supply elaborative details about one event.
- She works with determination at transcribing text—tight pencil grip—but forgets to use the computer.
- She knows to talk with a scribe but is reluctant to bother Sam.

Although she is motivated to enter the writing contest, Melissa's resources are clearly stretched when engaged in the complex task of writing (McCutchen, 2000, 2006). She remembers what she has learned (memoir) and what she has experienced (her life events) but struggles to access her stored memories and learned knowledge independently. Although she knows to plan, Melissa does not monitor her processes; she does not recognize that her planning is incomplete. When she does have an idea, she struggles to hold on to it while she writes. Melissa puts all of her efforts into transcribing, leaving few resources for generating ideas while producing text.

In other words, Melissa cannot juggle two tasks much less handle the multitasking required in writing. In urging Melissa to read a book on the same topic, to talk about her ideas with a partner who will ask her questions, and to plan and transcribe on the computer, Melissa's teacher seeks to divide the complex task into more manageable, though not easy, parts. If we evaluated only Melissa's first draft, we would see a struggling writer who produced a meager product. However, by thinking about a writer's cognitive processes, we can see her emerging strengths as well as where she struggles and needs support and instruction.

Given Melissa's inability to multitask, we should not be surprised that she does not think about the four dimensions of our communication model. Struggling with accessing her own world knowledge, she gives little thought to the unknown audience's lack of knowledge about her youth. She exhibits minimal discourse knowledge—memoirs are about one past event—but she plans for several events without any detail; thus not meeting her reader's discourse expectations. However, her audience is not the primary focus for her or her teacher now. Both are concentrating on accessing world and discourse knowledge to use in her first draft.

We suggest teachers use the inquiry guide when working not only with struggling writers like Melissa but also with any student about whom you are curious. Although we have only presented two diverse learners who typify students in today's classrooms, we could have described bilingual writers or reluctant writers, for example. Since today's students are so diverse, we need to investigate their writing beyond their products; we need to investigate their processes, too, in order to provide robust instruction. We like to watch what particular students are doing, to talk with them, to try to determine what is working or not working, and then to provide them with the support and instruction they need to use the writer's cognitive processes effectively. We know observing writers in the act of writing takes time and practice, since writers' cognitive processes are not uniform; students are diverse in many ways including their writing cognitive processes. We suggest you take one guiding question at a time and observe one writer closely. You may be surprised by what you learn.

You have probably noted that Sam and Melissa's teacher provided different support for each student based on that student's particular needs. Before we leave a writer's cognitive processes, let's consider the task environment, in this case the classroom that surrounds these writers.

TASK ENVIRONMENT

The task environment consists of the *physical* and *social* conditions in which writers complete their writing (Flower & Hayes, 1981; Hayes, 2004). Consider the high-stakes test environment of your state's performance measures versus the daily classroom community environment. Writers are sensitive to environmental differences in those two situations! Writers can be particular about their physical environment. Many published authors prefer to write in a particular room or in a studio outside their home. Some have favorite tools—pads of paper, special pens, computer keyboards, and screen size. The second component of the task environment is the social environment or the interaction and communication among people—peers, teachers, or parents for students, other writers, and editors for published authors—that occurs when writers write and receive feedback on their writing whether in person or online.

Returning once more to Sam, let's take a look at the task environment that supports his writing. First, Sam's physical environment is conducive to writing. The classroom has different writing tools, a variety of paper, and a library of books. He moves freely between his writer's notebook and the computer. His desk and other students' desks are grouped together so that they can converse and help each other write. Yet, the classroom also has quiet nooks in corners for students who need to concentrate without distractions.

Second, Sam's social environment is a classroom community that supports writing tasks. Most importantly, Sam's class engages in real-world writing tasks with meaningful purposes and intended audiences that are sometimes outside of the classroom and school. In addition, his teacher explicitly teaches the class the memoir genre by having them read several memoirs, discuss and identify the characteristics of memoirs, and then write their own memoir. She scaffolds Sam's writing— teaching him to use a writer's notebook, teaching him how to use the planning strategies of a lifeline and a brainstorming list, conferring about his focus, and assisting in editing. Furthermore, his classmates talk about their reading and writing. Matt reads and evaluates Sam's draft and then suggests the planning strategy of drawing a picture to assist writing a description. Although Sam is an experienced writer, the social environment—a community of writers—helps him learn to write better than he would on his own.

We touch upon the task environment here because the physical and social conditions in which the writing takes place plays a pivotal role in what writers compose and the cognitive processes they use. In Chapter 3, we take another look at the task environment of the classroom community by delineating features that support both writers' cognitive processes and the dimensions of our communication model.

CHAPTER SUMMARY

Examining a student's product seems easier than examining cognitive processes because we can look at a hard copy of text but cannot peer inside a writer's head. However, if we only look at products, we cannot help students produce more effective products. How students write affects what they write.

Our adaptation of researchers' descriptions of writer's cognitive processes—planning, producing text (generating and transcribing), and reviewing (evaluating, revising, and editing)—plus monitoring is designed to help you think about processes. When writers plan they gather ideas for their messages while thinking about their purposes, audiences, and what genre they could use to best convey their messages. Having sketched ideas, taken notes, and devised graphic organizers, writers begin producing texts. They turn those plans into words and sentences (generate ideas) and put words and sentences on paper or computer screen (transcribe). Having a partial or full text produced, writers then review their texts. First, they evaluate the text for how it meets their intended messages and audiences. Second, they revise to better meet their purposes and audiences to get their intended messages across. Finally, they edit to ensure their messages can be read easily by audiences. While we describe these processes in a linear fashion for our audiences' understanding, writers move flexibly among the processes— editing as they produce text or revising their plans.

Following an articulate, experienced writer like Sam through a piece of writing allows us to observe and discuss a writer's cognitive processes and the monitoring of the task. We look for not only evidence of processes in a text but for those pauses, stares, and conversations with peers. We also ask writers, "What are you thinking and why did you...?" Through observations and conversations, we seek to understand different writers' cognitive processes, expecting differences among our diverse students. Our Inquiry Guide was created to assist you in examining a writer's cognitive processes. While we used the guide to inquire into Melissa's struggle to write, we could have used it with an experienced writer. The key is using observations and conversations to uncover what is happening inside a student's head.

Understanding a writer's cognitive processes leads to instructing students how to write—not just what to write. In subsequent chapters, we present ideas for supporting students' cognitive processes through instruction. In Chapter 3, we discuss how features in a teacher's classroom support students' learning about cognitive processes and our communication model.

APPLICATION BOX

Select a student who struggles when transcribing text. Notice what writing tool the student uses and how much text is produced. For example, if the student writes with a pencil and paper, how many words are written when the student writes on a topic of his or her choice? Ask the student to choose another writing tool such as a marker, the computer, an Alpha Smart, or an adaptive software program, and write on another topic of his or her choice. Compare how fluently the student writes and the quantity of text produced. Discuss with the student which tool was easier to use and why. Which tool allowed the student to focus on his or her ideas more easily?

Technology Tools to Support the Writer's Cognitive Processes

The proliferation of new technologies over the past few years has provided students and teachers with tools that can support all students, especially those who struggle with writing due to physical or learning challenges. The technology tools we describe below allow writers to produce text more easily than with pencil and paper and help them focus on their messages rather than the transcription of ideas. When evaluating the match between a technology tool and students, we suggest you consider four factors. Does the technology tool:

- Allow writers to focus on their messages rather than on the transcription of writing?
- Allow writers to write fluently, thereby increasing the text produced?
- Provide writers access to their text-so-far in print and through speech?
- Allow writers easy access for viewing and manipulating their writing?

Categorized by processes, even though some programs work across processes, we present technology tools that we have found to be the most useful and flexible in working with a diversity of writers, situations, and teachers. In most cases, the tools are designed to interface with adaptive equipment, such as scanning arrays or an alternative computer mouse, that support alternative access for students with special needs.

Planning

- Inspiration by Inspiration Software Inc. (*www.inspiration.com*). The well-known Inspiration and its companion software for students in grades K–5, Kidspiration, allow writers to proceed from graphic organizer/web/outline formats to writing texts by using premade templates or by designing their own free-form webs. The software offers features such as audio support, symbols/pictures, and dictionary/thesaurus.
- Draft Builder by Don Johnston Inc. (*www.donjohnston.com*). Draft Builder is a writing organization tool that supports students as they plan, organize, and draft a text. The software has three major components: an easy-to-manipulate outline; a place to take notes that can then be dragged into the outline; and a space for writing a first draft from the notes. Students can input text from the Internet or other digital texts. The tool also has speech output so students can hear their text as they are writing, if they wish to do so.
- Noteshare by Aquaminds (*www.aquaminds.com*). Noteshare is an electronic notebook that allows writers to keep, annotate, and organize notes, videos, pictures, and hyperlinks to websites. Students can organize materials by projects, topics, or in a daily diary format. Since portions of the electronic note-

book can be made public and shared across users, the tool can support students working collaboratively on projects.

Producing Text

- Co:Writer by Don Johnston Inc. (*www.donjohnston.com*). Co:Writer predicts what the writer is trying to type by selecting from words the writer has previously used. Compatible with most word processing programs, the software converts invented spelling into conventional spelling and provides writers with word choices that fit semantically and syntactically into the sentences they are creating. In addition, Co:Writer has speech output for individual words or full texts that teachers can activate.
- My Own Bookshelf by Softtouch (*www.softtouch.com*). My Own Bookshelf is designed to make texts that can be published electronically or printed out. The software enables writers to import pictures from the Internet, digital libraries, or one's own collection of photos and to hear one's own writing. Books can be organized by individual students on separate electronic bookshelves, arranged thematically, or compiled by class, allowing students to read each other's books.

Reviewing Text

- Write Out Loud by Don Johnston Inc. (*www.donjohnston.com*). Write Out Loud is a word processing program with a text-to-speech feature that highlights the text as it is read aloud. Students can control the amount, the pace, and the volume of the reading. In the spell check feature, the program reads aloud choices for the highlighted misspelling, allowing the writer to select the correct word for the given context.
- ReadPlease and ReadPlease Plus by Read Please (*www.readplease.com*). ReadPlease and ReadPlease Plus are similar pieces of software that can read aloud digital text or websites. ReadPlease and ReadPlease Plus can only be used with Windows operating systems but can read text from the Windows clipboard or by cutting and pasting from any word processing program. You can download ReadPlease free from the website or purchase ReadPlease Plus, a version that contains additional features.

Chapter 3

Creating a Community of Writers

"Do you think I should say 'woof' and 'warp' or just say 'up and down and crosswise'? I want people to know what I mean," says Tanisha to her tablemate, Isabella.

The two girls are drafting the text for a PowerPoint presentation on making clothes during colonial times. As part of a unit of study in social studies, all the students in this fourth-grade classroom have been considering the question: What was daily life like for people during the colonial period of American history? Tanisha and Isabella, like other groups of students in the classroom, have identified an area of personal interest for further research.

"Well, I think those words are interesting. Maybe there's a way we can tell people what they mean?," replied Isabella.

"Do you mean do something like in the Lemony Snickett books and put the meaning right there?"

"I don't know ... sometimes that really annoys me when I'm reading if I already know what the word means."

"I don't think too many people will know what woof and warp mean."

"I guess we could make a glossary at the end like our social studies book has. Remember how Mr. Frank did that when he was writing his book on sailing boats?"

"Yeah, but that was a book—how would that work with Power-Point?"

As he circulates throughout the room, checking in with his students about their projects, Mr. Frank overhears this exchange and offers a suggestion.

"I agree that it's important for your readers to hear the words that the colonists would have used to describe their weaving. You're using PowerPoint, right? I wonder if there is a way to create a link that would provide your readers with a definition if they need it. You know how on some websites you can click on underlined text and a box pops up with more information? I'm not sure if or how you can do that in PowerPoint, but let's invite Ms. Jackson, the library media specialist, into the classroom to show all of us how to do this."

"Okay. That sounds good. For now, I'll write in woof and warp. I can work on the definitions later," Tanisha decides.

Isabella looks thoughtful. "You know, Mr. Frank, I was thinking … it seems like it was an awful lot of work for the colonists to get their clothing. We can just go to the store and buy it."

"Do you know where the clothes in the store come from?" asks Mr. Frank. "That might be interesting for you to find out. You could do some more research and compare the ways that clothes are made today with the way they were made in the colonial period. We don't make our own clothes, but somebody makes them."

After talking with the girls, Mr. Frank steps to the side of the room and pauses for a moment to survey his class as they work. As he heads toward students who look as if they could use assistance, he ponders how diverse the students are, varying in their interests, cultural backgrounds, native languages, and performances on standardized tests. Mr. Frank has worked hard to establish cooperative working groups and he is generally pleased.

While Tanisha and Isabella draft their PowerPoint presentation, other groups are hard at work on their writing projects. Jason, Max, and Alicia are writing a script to dramatize a town meeting and are also constructing a chart that compares the colonial governance process to that of their own town. Omar, Alex, and Joaquin are compiling brief biographical entries on key figures, focusing on why and how these people decided to move to America. Mr. Frank has been encouraging them to think about the reasons that people continue to immigrate, legally and illegally, to America today. Omar, an English language learner (ELL), has firsthand experience with immigration, since his family has recently come to the United States from Pakistan. Jen, Sharmane, and Sandra are struggling to make an alphabet book about colonial life that will be shared with their Kindergarten Book Buddies. Having selected a key concept for only 10 letters of the alphabet, Mr. Frank sees they will need help completing their book; maybe the class can generate ideas for them. Carrying forward their research on explorers, John and Tony are composing a report and chart that discusses the relationships between the colonists and native peoples. Mr. Frank has been working closely with the boys to find texts the fourth graders can understand.

As a culmination to their study, the students in Mr. Frank's class will host a Colonial America evening at their school. The students are eagerly anticipating this opportunity to share what they have learned with their relatives, fellow schoolmates, and community members.

The vignette above provides a view into a classroom community where writing plays a central role in the learning process. Based on our combined experiences in classrooms and with teachers, we now explore what teaching and learning is like in classrooms where the features of effective writing communities exist.

In this chapter, we:

- Discuss how Mr. Frank's classroom functions as a writing community.
- Discuss how teaching moves from explicit instruction to independence.
- Identify classroom features that support writers' cognitive processes.
- Discuss teaching with the dimensions of our communication model in mind.

THE WRITING CLASSROOM COMMUNITY

When teachers work with students to become cooperative members of a writing community, students come to view writing as a communicative act—a vehicle for them to express their learning to audiences (Chapman, 2006). While they write, they learn to consider the needs of their audience, carefully thinking about their writing decisions and how their choices will affect their readers' abilities to construct meaning from their texts. Students talk with one another and with their teacher about the goals and options they have as writers and their responsibilities to their readers. Students learn that writing occurs over time and recognize that writers can revise their content in order to better convey their meaning to a reader.

At the beginning of the year in Mr. Frank's classroom, each student arrived with different ideas about what writing is, what writing is for, and who writes. From their multiple community memberships (Gee, 1996), such as family community, neighborhood community, religious community, and sports community, students have different experiences with purposes of writing and the processes of writing. Each is more or less comfortable with different ways of using words in different sociocultural communities (Heath, 1983). Mr. Frank's goal is to help students expand their knowledge of the range of purposes, audiences, and genres of writing, while simultaneously establishing a classroom community that honors students' understandings.

Here are three snapshots of students in Mr. Frank's class:

- Tanisha's family has two computers on which they e-mail their extended family to keep in close touch about events in each other's lives. Using abbreviated language forms and sentence fragments rather than conventional grammar, they communicate life's events to make other family members feel as if they were experiencing the event, too. Tanisha hurries home from school to check her e-mail; she especially loves hearing from her brother Malcom who is stationed in Iraq. She tells him about her friends and little brother and always ends with "LYLMY," which stands for "love you lots—miss you." In Tanisha's family, writing is a way to maintain family ties by sharing daily experiences despite distances in time and space.
- Isabella's father is a published poet. Even with many books at home, Isabella and her two sisters regularly go to the library for more books to read with each other. Isabella's family talks about interesting vocabulary words and notices the rhythm and sounds of language. Everyone in this family can recite poems by heart and cite books when an event reminds them of a story they have read. When the girls were young, their father recorded the dictated stories that accompanied their drawings. Isabella keeps a journal and claims that she wants to be a writer when she grows up. In Isabella's family, writing is viewed as a means of artistic expression and enjoyment.
- At the home of Jason, his mother and father communicate by leaving notes for one another because they work two different shifts: "kitchen sink leaking, please call plumber." Jason sometimes leaves notes, too: "Dad, soccer game on Saturday at 10:00." Since their weekday time together is limited, Jason and his family also leave notes that are expressions of affection. Jason especially likes to find on the kitchen table a funny sketch with the message, "Only three more days till the weekend! Love, Dad." Writing is functional and affectionate, while ensuring that the household runs smoothly.

We described these three family communities to illustrate different understandings of writing and its purposes. For some children, their family experiences have prepared them to meet the teachers' expectations. Other students need to expand their conceptions of writing and its purposes and take on practices that are unfamiliar to them (Gee, 1996; Heath, 1983).

While influenced by the conceptions of writing that students bring to the classroom, the classroom writing community is largely shaped by the beliefs and assumptions of the classroom teacher (Lipson, Mosenthal, Daniels, & Woodside-Jiron, 2000). As teachers design their instruction and conduct their teaching, they express their beliefs about literacy and learning (Johnston, Woodside-Jiron, & Day, 2001). Their beliefs are reflected in the talk they encourage in the classroom, the texts that they use for instruction, the activities in which students engage, and the assessments they use. Their choices and actions communicate to their students what they value about writing and writing processes. To illustrate this point, let's revisit Mr. Frank's and Ms. Arnold's classrooms.

Mr. Frank's Class: Writing to Learn and to Share Your Learning

Think back to Tanisha and Isabella pausing to discuss their word choices for their readers. The interaction, though brief, reveals how Mr. Frank and the students in this writing community have constructed an understanding of writing and its purposes. Their writing is purposeful and arises from their content-area study. The students know their message will reach an interested audience besides their teacher. Since these two writers are engaged in drafting and revising their presentation, writing is also being constructed as processes in which writers plan their writing, produce initial ideas on paper, reread, evaluate, and revise their writing with their purposes and audiences in mind. Students seek the support from their classmates and teacher as they write, discussing their writing decisions, processes, and products.

Ms. Arnold's Class: Writing as Inquiry and Action

To Ms. Arnold and the students in her eighth-grade science class, writing was the means by which they explored their hypotheses, recorded their observations, and communicated their findings about salt content in water to a variety of stakeholders. Students learned that they needed to use language differently depending on whether their audiences were town officials, fellow middle school students, or second-grade students. As you will read in Chapter 7, the students in Ms. Arnold's class learned that their writing had the power to spur action within their local and state community. Writing for Ms. Arnold's class was constructed as processes in which writers explored their thinking and learning and in which writers called for action by officials.

In classroom writing communities, the primary goal of writing instruction is to increase students' communication repertoire to effectively communicate for a variety of purposes and to a wide array of audiences. In the next sections of this chapter, we discuss features of classroom practice that lead to the development of the kind of writing communities that we think best support students' growth as writers in their cognitive processes and as communicators who use the four dimensions of our communication model. We begin with an overview of instruction.

TEACHING: FROM EXPLICIT INSTRUCTION TO INDEPENDENT APPLICATION

Perhaps you are familiar with the Gradual Release of Responsibility model (Pearson & Gallagher, 1983) or Self-Regulated Strategy Instruction (Graham & Harris, 2005). Both delineate a deliberate shift of responsibility over time, beginning with teacher modeling and explicit instruction, to guided teacher support and practice, and finally leading to student independence. We next explain the shift using Mr. Frank's classroom.

Mr. Frank taught the girls and their classmates strategies for writing informational text in a series of lessons. He began by posing his inquiry question—"What was literacy like in colonial times?"—and then he *modeled his own writing processes* by composing his informational text with them. Talking about why the inquiry question was of interest to him, he listed subquestions, such as: What books were available to the colonists? How did colonial children learn to read and write? To complement his modeling, Mr. Frank also engaged in *explicit teaching*. He explained how his questions would guide his research and for one subquestion he explicitly instructed how to take notes using information he found on the Internet. In addition, Mr. Frank and the students read informational books as mentor texts to see how authors wrote and speculated about the inquiry questions authors' might have asked.

After his modeling and explicit instruction, the students engaged in *guided practice*; they asked their inquiry questions and subquestions while Mr. Frank circulated, commenting and questioning the students. When students' questions were asked and resources were found, Mr. Frank supported the students' note making for their subtopics. When the students were taking notes, they again turned to mentor texts and examined the details authors included for their subtopics.

Over the next few weeks, as he researched his topic, organized his information, and composed his text, Mr. Frank worked in front of the students, thinking aloud about his processes of planning, producing, and reviewing text. He continued to provide explicit instruction and guided practice as the students worked on their research and writing. During their continuing experiences of *teacher modeling, explicit teaching,* and *guided practice,* some students were ready to *apply* their learning as they worked *independently* or in pairs, like Tanisha and Isabella, while Mr. Frank gave guided support to other students.

Students learn from their teacher's explanations of how and why pieces of writing are planned, generated, transcribed, evaluated, revised, and edited. A lesson on planning might feature a graphic organizer to plan arguments and evidence for a persuasive piece. A lesson on producing text could focus on turning the planned ideas on a graphic organizer into sentences and paragraphs. Students' reviewing skills are honed when the teacher provides a lesson on using lively verbs to add interest and precision. While all students benefit from teacher modeling and explicit instruction (Graham & Perrin, 2007), these teaching strategies are particularly effective for struggling writers and students with learning disabilities (Englert, Raphael, Anderson, Anthony, & Stevens, 1991; Graham & Harris, 2005; Graham, MacArthur, & Schwartz, 1995).

As you continue to read this book, you will find several additional examples of teachers engaged in instructional practices that explicitly model and explain, support students' writing, and encourage independent application. In the next section, we look at the defining features that teachers incorporate into effective classroom environments—first that support the writer's cognitive processes and second that teach with our communication model in mind.

SUPPORTING THE WRITER'S COGNITIVE PROCESSES

A classroom community of writers supports all writers as they plan, produce, and review their texts by incorporating the following classroom features.

Student-to-Student and Student-to-Teacher *Talk* Is Encouraged

The teacher and the students of a writing community engage in frequent conversations focused on writing products and processes (Englert, Mariage, & Dunsmore, 2006). They study and discuss books and authors, share their evolving ideas, confer about their writing processes, and provide feedback to each other (Graves, 1983; Hillocks, 1995). While the teacher is a strong presence and the coordinator of activities, the teacher does not dominate talk in the classroom. As students plan, produce, and review their writing pieces, they confer with one another. Remember how Sam was prompted to revise his description of stunt kite flying based on feedback from his classmate? Peer support and feedback increases students' awareness of the audiences for their writing (Kos & Maslowski, 2001), encourages their willingness to engage in revision (Dahl, 1988; MacArthur, Schwartz, & Graham, 1991), and improves the quality of their writing (Olson, 1990). The opportunity to talk with others exposes students to alternative perspectives and deepens their understanding of the topic of study (Wells & Arauz, 2006).

Students Are *Decision Makers* in the Classroom

What do I want to say? To whom do I want to say it? How do I want to say it? Have I done enough planning? Is it time to start producing text? Should I review what I have written so far? These are just a few of the many monitoring questions that writers ask themselves while they undertake a writing project (Hayes, 2000). Take a moment to think about the decisions Sam made when writing his memoir, from his decision to write about stunt kite flying to his final proofreading. With the goal of fostering student independence and increasing student engagement, teachers provide opportunities for students to take charge of their own learning (Turner & Paris, 1995; Wells & Chang-Wells, 1992). Within the broad content curriculum, students choose the topics, purposes, and readers for their writing pieces. They learn how to decide when to move among the writer's cognitive processes, such as from planning to producing texts.

Teachers Build on the Strengths of a Diverse Group of Students with *Flexible Instructional Formats*

In today's classrooms, students vary in their social and cultural experiences, their academic skills, their facility with the English language, their learning processes, and their personal interests and motivations. Teachers employ a variety of instructional formats including whole-class, small-group, and individual instruction to meet their students' needs. In the whole-class format, teachers introduce a new revision strategy or reinforce the characteristics of a genre, for example. Needing to differentiate instruction, teachers form small groups of students to explore the writer's craft in mentor texts and practice imitating sentences in journals. Responding to individuals, teachers offer topic choices in purposeful writing activities and target instruction to specific needs so that learning can be transferred to future writing, such as narrowing the topic of memoirs or how-to directions.

Teachers Employ a *Flexible Classroom Schedule* That Allows Students to Progress through Writing Processes

In a classroom community focused on writing for a variety of purposes, the teacher recognizes that the amount of time required to complete a writing task differs according to the students' familiarity with the task and the particularities of the writer. Teachers recognize that writing letters to family members will likely require less planning, producing, and reviewing and less instruction than writing a letter to a congressional representative. Even with the more familiar letters to friends, some students will require more time and support. To allow for this variation, the teacher maintains a schedule that is flexible, while keeping in mind that students, like all writers, do need deadlines to complete a project!

Classrooms Include Many *Tools* for Writers to Use

Do you prefer to write longhand or on the computer? Would you rather dictate to a tape recorder or to a computer with speech recognition? Many of us have particular writing tools that help to facilitate the process of transcribing text. A productive writing classroom includes a wide range of tools for writing: a variety of types and sizes of papers, notebooks, and sticky notes; pencils, pens, markers, and art materials; and technology including audio recording devices, computer and Internet access, word-processing tools, and software that aids students in their composing processes (Lowther, Ross, & Morrison, 2003). (Refer back to Appendix 2.1 in Chapter 2 for technology tools.) Teachers guide students to become aware of how writing tools can facilitate their processes for producing text (Willis, 1993). Teachers model the possible uses of tools for writing and offer students choices to facilitate student independence in selecting helpful writing tools.

Teachers *Assess* Students' Writing Processes and Products

Effective classroom assessment is ongoing and focused on growth. Teachers observe students' composing processes using guides like the Inquiry Guide to a Writer's Cognitive Processes that we introduced in Chapter 2. Using the guide, teachers can determine whether students need support in planning, producing, or reviewing. In addition, they examine students' writing products to determine what elements or qualities of good writing are present or need instruction (see Chapter 8 for a discussion about evaluating products). Because students' strengths and areas for improvement may change depending upon the purpose, audience, and genre, teachers assess students across a range of writing experiences.

Supporting students' cognitive processes is one aspect of effective classroom communities. When students write for a variety of readers, teachers instruct students how to consider the four dimensions of our communication model.

Teaching with the Dimensions of Our Communication Model in Mind

The features of effective classroom writing instruction, listed below, are framed by the four dimensions of our communication model. We describe each feature and reflect on it in the context of Mr. Frank's fourth-grade classroom.

World Knowledge

Teachers who link writing instruction with content learning view writing as an instrument that students can use to track their own learning and to convey their new knowledge to others. The following features describe classrooms where students are building and communicating world knowledge.

- Students engage in writing that is *empowering*. When teachers ask students to complete authentic writing tasks rather than skill–practice exercises, students view writing as a communicative instrument with the power to influence thought and action (Dahl & Farnan, 1998; Duke, Purcell-Gates, Hall, & Tower, 2006; Hiebert, 1994). With their teacher, students explore the wide range of writing people use in their everyday lives. They engage in writing that requires them to use their world knowledge and to think about the needs of real audiences. A sense of responsibility to their audience motivates them to communicate what they have learned accurately and clearly.

- Teacher and students value *inquiry and the process of inquiry* across content areas. Inquiry is the process of asking and investigating a question with an unknown answer (Short, Harste, & Burke, 1995). In an inquiry-oriented environment, writing is used to explore ideas across the curriculum (Graham & Perrin, 2007; Hillocks, 1982). Both teachers and students have a questioning disposition and an eagerness to seek answers. Students record questions and wonderings, document research, express evolving understandings, and report findings (Bangert-Drowns, Hurley, & Wilkinson, 2004; Shanahan, 2004; Vacca & Vacca, 2000). As students engage in the work of readers, writers, mathematicians, social and physical scientists, and artists, writing is a primary means for learning and expressing their world knowledge. Recall that Mr. Frank's students asked questions about colonial clothing, government, and immigration.

- Students use multiple types of *resources* in the process of content learning. To build their world knowledge, today's students draw upon many different types of resources, such as books, Internet, multimedia, primary sources, people, and firsthand experiences. Teachers and students evaluate the accuracy, usefulness, and appropriateness of different sources, especially Internet resources. Mr. Frank's students read trade books, watched videos, browsed relevant Internet sites, and visited Plimoth Plantation in Plymouth, Massachusetts, to experience colonial-style living firsthand. Each different resource contributed information to their world knowledge of the colonial period.

Discourse Knowledge

Discourse knowledge refers to students' understandings about genres—their purposes, characteristics, vocabulary, and conventions. The following features describe classrooms where students are developing their discourse knowledge.

- Through the study of *mentor texts in different genres*, students learn how text characteristics, vocabulary, and conventions vary. Teachers and students deliberately examine mentor texts—good models of the writer's craft written for specific purposes (Ebbers, 2002; Graham & Perrin, 2007; Pantaleo, 2007). Together students and teachers closely study the structure of the text as well as the word choices and conventions used by the author. They discuss how authors shape texts to be appropriately matched to their purposes and intended audiences. As they plan their curriculum, teachers recognize opportunities that arise to teach specific genres (Purcell-Gates, Duke, & Martineau, 2007). The students in Mr. Frank's classroom composed in a wide array of genres, realizing that different genres serve different purposes.
- As students engage in *wide reading*, they acquire incidental learning about genres. In addition to explicit instruction provided by their teacher, as they read students acquire information about how writers use genres, organize text structures, and choose words (Langer & Flihan, 2000). The more they read, the more they know about how texts function and how authors shape their texts. Tanisha and Isabella referred to embedded definitions in Snickett's books and to the glossary in their social studies textbook—familiar models from their reading.

Time and Space

In order to fully understand how to shape their writing to address the differences that exist in time and space between themselves and their readers, students need experiences writing for many different audiences—not just their peers and teachers. Through practice and with teacher support, students learn to include the right amount and type of background and contextual information for their familiar and unknown audiences.

- Students write to a *variety of audiences*. Too often in school, students write for the same audience in assignment after assignment—their teacher or peers. Since students know that their teacher and classmates share their experiences and understand what they mean even when gaps exist, the students often do not see a clear need to provide contextual information. When teachers seek out other audiences for their students' work, both proximate and distant (Kaufer & Carley, 1994), they provide opportunities for students to explain the conditions that surround an event, using the amount and type of detail that each reader warrants. In writing to entertain, students focus on time and space when describing the setting in a story; when writing to inform, students provide contextual information about the methods of a science investigation. Because Mr. Frank's class wrote for other classes, relatives, and community members, students provided background information about the colonists.

Sociocultural Membership

Teachers engage students in conversations about various perspectives and language practices within sociocultural memberships.

- Students practice using the *language of different communities*. Students begin to understand variations in language use in different contexts by asking the questions: Why have these people come together? How do they talk to one another? Are they using a specialized vocabulary or "lingo"? Heath and Mangiola (1991) describe a teacher who sent her students out into the community to record language use in various contexts—on the street, at the bank, on a children's playground, on the radio, and in the newspaper, for example. After they discussed the grammatical structures and specialized vocabulary found in different social situations, the students became more aware of their own use of language and began to think about how they could "use language more effectively to get things done" (p. 32). Explicit study of language use in social contexts opens up the opportunity for students to try out different voices in their writing in order to be heard by diverse audiences. Moving beyond their home languages and the language of their classroom, students practice writing in different voices, using the language of the content-area disciplines (e.g., scientists, mathematics, historians, artists) and the language of community groups (Chapman, 2006; De La Paz, 2005; Lea & Street, 2006). Mr. Frank's students incorporated the vocabulary of colonial people in the dialogues of characters and in referring to artifacts.
- Teachers encourage students to consider *multiple perspectives or viewpoints*. As we learned in Chapter 1, language reflects the values of different sociocultural groupings (Gee, 1996; Heath, 1983). In Chapter 7, you'll read that students often need teacher support to consider multiple perspectives on an issue when writing persuasive letters. In Mr. Frank's class, one group's research about immigration during colonial

times spurred conversations about current views on this topic. Omar, in particular, who recently immigrated, had firsthand experience understanding different perspectives on this topic. When students share perspectives or viewpoints, they learn how to offer, accept, and value different opinions and ideas.

The classroom characteristics described above function in an integrated fashion to create a classroom community that fosters students' ability to write for a variety of purposes and audiences. Together they create an environment that is flexible, responsive, and supportive of all writers.

CHAPTER SUMMARY

Recognizing that students come into the classroom with different conceptions of what writing is and does, teachers work to build a community of writers working together to write effectively. First and foremost, teachers explicitly instruct as they model and explain their writing strategies and give students guided practice, aiming for independent application.

Second, teachers build classroom communities that support the writer's cognitive processes by incorporating specific features: encouraging student talk; allowing students to decide and choose topics, purposes, audiences, and genres; forming flexible instructional formats and schedules; providing a variety of writing tools; and assessing students' processes and products for growth.

Third, teachers build classroom communities with the dimensions of the communication model in mind. To build students' world knowledge, teachers emphasize inquiry projects using multiple resources, and thus empower students through authentic learning and writing situations. Teachers and students study mentor texts in different genres and engage in wide reading to increase their discourse knowledge. Writing for a variety of audiences provides situations when students need to learn to account for time and space differences. And finally, engaging students in learning about differences in language use and differences in perspectives helps them recognize their own and other's sociocultural memberships.

Thus, through their explicit instruction, guided practice, and provision of independent opportunities, teachers build communities that support students' cognitive processes as they write and that support students' recognition of how writers need to account for the dimensions of our communication model. In this chapter we discussed the two models—a writer's cognitive model and our communication model—to describe classroom writing communities. In the next chapter we fuse the two models to describe students' progress in writing.

APPLICATION BOX

We invite you to reflect on the writing community in your classroom. Who are your students? What conceptions about writing do they bring to the classroom? How do you define writing? How do your students define writing?

Use a tape recorder to capture one or several writing lessons. Listen to the tape to analyze the kind of talk that occurs during a lesson. First consider, Who talks? How often do you talk? How often do the students talk? Which students talk?

Then, consider the kind of talk that occurs during the lesson. How would you describe the talk? What kinds of questions do you ask and what kinds of answers do students give? Do you and your students talk about the processes of writing? Are you and your students talking about purpose and audience for writing? Do you introduce and discuss the dimensions of our communication model?

How does the quantity and quality of talk in the classroom inform your instruction?

Chapter 4

The Writers in Our Classrooms
Recognizing Student Diversity

Take a moment to think about the students in your classroom. Chances are, when you think about them, you exclaim what a diverse group they are! Your students vary in their cultural backgrounds, by their family structures and economic resources, in the languages they speak, by their social abilities, personality traits, hobbies and interests, and by their academic strengths. The teacher's challenge is to orchestrate classroom instruction and activities so that the students know they are part of a learning community in which they can grow—academically, socially, and emotionally. Whew!

One goal for the writing teacher is to design classroom instruction to support all students' expanding writing repertoires—to develop their competencies to communicate their messages for a variety of purposes to a wide array of audiences including those whose background experiences are very different from their own. You will meet our communication model in this chapter as we describe diverse students' writing growth.

A second goal for the writing teacher is to increase students' facilities with the writer's cognitive processes—planning, producing text (generating and transcribing), and reviewing (evaluating, revising, editing). An additional aim is for students to monitor where they are and when to move freely among the processes in order to meet their purposes for writing. You will meet those processes again in this chapter as we describe diverse students' writing growth.

In this chapter, we combine the dimensions of our communication model and the cognitive writing processes into a developmental continuum for writing. Specifically, as we discuss student diversity in relation to writing instruction, we:

- Portray the diversity of the students' concepts about writing through a return visit to the classroom of Mr. Frank.
- Introduce a developmental continuum that will help you map your students' writing growth.
- Examine how you can use the developmental continuum for instructional planning.

We begin with a return visit to the fourth-grade classroom of Mr. Frank.

STUDENT DIVERSITY IN A FOURTH-GRADE CLASSROOM

How does a teacher encourage writing growth for diverse students in a classroom setting? How can the cognitive processes of writing and an understanding of the relationship between writers and readers (our communication model) inform instructional planning? Let's visit Mr. Frank's classroom once again to see how he plans in response to the diversity of students.

Mr. Frank, like most teachers during the first month of school, is still getting to know his students. His beginning-of-the-year activities included opportunities for students to talk and to write. Students write in journals to reflect on their daily learning: to respond to read-alouds and independent reading, to record mathematical understandings and scientific inquiry questions, and to capture potential topics in their writer's notebooks. Mr. Frank often asks students to volunteer to read some of their journal entries aloud to the class and more and more students raise their hands to share. Mr. Frank decides it is time for his students to create an extended piece of writing because he wants to observe their cognitive writing processes.

To introduce the extended piece of writing, Mr. Frank writes the following question on the white erase board: What makes a good classroom? and engages the class in a discussion. They talk about the kind of working environment they prefer (e.g., noise level, work surface, preferred writing tool, proximity to others), whether they should have classroom rules and, if so, what they should be, how they would like to be treated by their classmates, and what their learning goals are for the year. While students share their responses, Mr. Frank keeps his own opinions to himself. He is working to establish a classroom culture where open discussion is valued and students see one another as learning resources.

Before he sends his students back to the classroom tables to work, Mr. Frank reviews the purpose and audience: They are to write him a letter describing the classroom they would like to have this year. He also explains that he will respond to each letter and will share the students' ideas in a future class discussion of guidelines for the classroom.

Mr. Frank has two primary goals for this assignment. First, he wants to find out what his students' learning goals are and how they think they work best. Second, Mr. Frank wants to learn about his students' writing processes. Observing them closely, he will note how they plan, produce, and review their letters, as well as whether they monitor their writing processes and move back and forth among the processes.

With a clipboard in hand for note taking, Mr. Frank walks around the room as his students work, his eyes and ears tuned to their spoken and written words, their facial expressions, and the writing tools in their hands. Here are examples of what he notices about his students' writing:

- Tanisha is making a list of items that she wants to include in her letter. She writes down ideas as they occur to her, one after another in a vertical column. She is having no trouble planning content for her letter.

- Alimushtaba has begun his letter and is writing ideas in the body of the letter as they occur to him. He has not yet included a greeting in his letter and his ideas are expressed in statements that begin with "I want...." Ali's written language use reflects the fact that he is learning English as a second language. While he writes, he sometimes pauses mid-sentence, looking up toward the ceiling. Mr. Frank wonders if he is trying to recall the English word he wants.

- Alice has a blank piece of paper in front of her. She twirls her pencil between her thumb and forefinger and looks worried as she steals glances around the room at her classmates. She whispers to her neighbor, "I can't think of anything to write." Approaching the class chart, she copies an idea onto scratch paper. Returning to her seat, she begins her letter on good paper, "Hi Mr. Frank" and writes the copied idea.

- William is seated at one of the classroom computers, talking into a microphone. As he talks, his words appear on the screen. He is listing a series of points he wants to include in his letter. William's educational plan specifies that he should use the computer and voice-recognition software for his writing projects.

- Jason is up and down out of his seat visiting other students to see what they are writing. On his paper he has written one idea. He begins his letter "Dear Mr. Frank" and writes his idea.
- Aisha had sharpened her pencil and a backup pencil and fussed a bit with getting her desk set up—pencils and paper laid out in perfect order. Now she is writing away steadily. Her letter reads: "Dear Mr. Frank, Thank you for asking me to tell you what my ideal classroom is like. It is very nice to have a teacher who is interested in kids' opinions. In this letter I will tell you how I work best, what I want to learn, and what I think our classroom rules should be."

Over the next couple of days, Mr. Frank provides additional time in class for students to work on their letters. He continues to observe their writing processes and asks them questions to begin to understand what they are thinking about as they write. As he observes his students, Mr. Frank makes anecdotal notes, listing the students' names and details about their writing pieces and their writing processes. As students produce their letters, Mr. Frank notices many differences in how they work.

You probably noticed, just from the brief descriptions above, that Mr. Frank's students vary widely in their approaches to and capabilities with the writing task. Mr. Frank faces the challenge that most teachers face—how to design classroom experiences that help *each* student to move forward from different starting points. In addition to learning how each individual student writes, Mr. Frank needs to consider how he will use small-group and whole-class instruction to support his class's writing growth. To plan his instruction for the next several months, Mr. Frank will use a developmental continuum that outlines progressive descriptors for student understandings and performance.

A DEVELOPMENTAL CONTINUUM FOR WRITING

To help you see where your students are and where they should aim, we provide a developmental continuum with two purposes in mind. First, we connect our communication model with the writer's cognitive processes. The descriptors on the continuum illustrate how students may be thinking about their purposes for writing and the needs of their audiences as they plan, produce, and review their texts as well as whether they monitor their writing. Second, we describe the writing behaviors of students as they develop increasingly sophisticated understandings about writing. We created the descriptors that appear in the continuum based on research and our cumulative experiences in working with student writers and teachers. The continuum that appears in this chapter is a general continuum. In Chapters 5, 6, and 7, you will find more specific continua that have been customized to the genres explored in each chapter.

Our developmental continuum is presented in three figures, one for each of the writer's cognitive processes (planning, producing text, and reviewing). For each process, we provide descriptors of writers along each dimension of our communication model (world knowledge, discourse knowledge, time and space, and sociocultural membership). For example, look at Figure 4.1, which considers the process of planning. We describe how students are able to plan their writing while considering the potential differences between themselves and their readers. You will notice that monitoring appears first in the vertical axis because a writer's awareness of the dimensions of our communication model is determined by his or her ability to reflect upon the cognitive processes he or she is using.

For each of the three processes, we map growth in student understanding of the processes of writing and how to craft writing to match purpose and audience. You probably notice right away that we have not included ages or grade-level references in our developmental continuum. Instead, each dimension contains three sets of descriptors. The first describes a novice (N) understanding; the second set a developing (D) understanding; and the third set an experienced (E) understanding. Writers characterized as novice in a particular category demonstrate little understanding for that dimension of our communication model and require teacher instruction. Writers characterized as developing are learning how to account for that dimension of the communication model but still require teacher support. Writers who are characterized as experienced in a category are able to demonstrate how that dimension can be accounted for in the writing process, although they probably are not fully accomplished. Remember that these terms (novice, developing, and experienced) are not connected with grade levels. A sixth-grade student may have a novice understanding of aspects of the communication model, or a fourth-grade student may demonstrate an experienced understanding.

By considering the continuum, we think you will better understand and respond to the diversity of students in your classroom. These days our students come to us with a variety of labels attached to them. They may be English language learners, learning disabled, have attention deficit disorder, be physically challenged, or have a sensory integration disorder (and the list goes on and on). The reasons for which your students have been given these labels bring with them a particular set of challenges in relation to writing instruction. Regardless of the label,

Monitoring the Process	World Knowledge	Discourse Knowledge	Time and Space	Sociocultural Membership
N: Does not plan without instruction. May be unaware of purpose. Is unaware of audience.	**N**: Is unaware of own knowledge of the topic. Does not consider audience's knowledge of topic in plans.	**N**: May think about familiar genres, vocabulary, and organization structures.	**N**: Assumes the audience shared the experience.	**N**: Is unaware that differences exist between own experiences and those of others.
D: Plans with teacher support. Has limited planning strategies. Begins to plan for purpose. May begin to be aware of audience.	**D**: Uses some of own knowledge of the topic in plans. May need help to find resources. Has some awareness that audience's knowledge of topic may differ from his or her own.	**D**: Is aware of different genres, vocabulary, and organizational structures. Needs guidance to select genres and vocabulary that meet purpose and audience needs.	**D**: Recognizes that audience may not have shared the experience but does not include background information in plans.	**D**: Has beginning awareness that audience may have a different background. Needs instruction to think about voice for purpose and audience.
E: Plans independently. Has an increasing range of planning strategies. Plans with purpose and audience in mind.	**E**: Is able to assess own knowledge of topic. Finds resources/strategies to augment knowledge of topic. Represents knowledge of topic in effective plans. Plans for differences in audience's knowledge of topic.	**E**: Has knowledge of an increasing range of genres, vocabulary, and organizational structures. Plans to match genre, vocabulary, and conventions to purpose and audience.	**E**: Anticipates that the audience will need contextual information if they did not share the experience. Includes background information in plans.	**E**: Has an increasing awareness of how own cultural background and social experiences influence how one writes about a topic. Uses teacher support to think about voice.

FIGURE 4.1. Developmental continuum: Planning. N, novice; D, developing; E, experienced.

our job as teachers is to help to identify our students' strengths and to teach and support students with aspects of learning that are challenging. We think that an understanding of the cognitive processes and how a writer communicates to readers helps teachers to develop the capabilities of their diverse student population. The continuum addresses a range of factors that impact students' performance in writing and will prove a useful tool for thinking about *all* your students, regardless of their learning classifications.

Later in the chapter, we describe how Mr. Frank uses the continuum and suggest other uses. Now, we take a closer look at writing growth represented in the developmental continuum beginning with the writer's cognitive process of planning.

Planning

In Figure 4.1 we describe the process of planning. Usually, planning occurs when the writer begins the task of writing, but it may also occur throughout the writing when the author's evaluation of the text-so-far indicates that more planning is needed. Surveying the chart, you will notice that writers' sophistication with planning progresses as we move from novice to developing to experienced. Let's first examine monitoring and then each dimension of our communication model.

Monitoring the Process

With instruction, students become cognitively aware of the value of planning and learn to plan for their purposes and audiences. They also develop a repertoire of planning strategies and purposefully consider when and how to use these strategies.

World Knowledge

Novice writers do not recognize the amount of knowledge they have about their topics (Bereiter & Scardamalia, 1987), may use the first resource they find, and may not evaluate resources (Coiro, 2003). However, with instruction and practice, students become better equipped at determining their own world knowledge, anticipating what knowledge readers need, and learning when they need to acquire more information in order to create effective plans.

Discourse Knowledge

As students become more sophisticated writers, their plans reflect a choice of genre that suits their purposes and audiences. Their plans also reflect their growing understanding of how genres are organized, such as stories versus reports (Donovan, 2001; Donovan & Smolkin, 2002; Langer, 1986).

Time and Space

With instruction and experience, students become better able to anticipate the amount and type of background and contextual information (e.g., who, what, where, when) they will need to include in their plans.

Sociocultural Membership

Writers learn to consider how their personal background and experiences may differ from those of their readers—the most challenging aspect of bridging distances between writers and readers. When planning, only experienced writers may think about different voices (e.g., personal voice vs. objective scientific voice) to potentially use in their writing.

Now, we turn to the developmental continuum for producing text.

Producing Text

In Figure 4.2 we describe the process of producing text. As students become more proficient in producing connected text, their attention shifts from the physical act of transcribing their thoughts to a greater focus on their messages (McCutchen, 2006). They use their plans to produce texts that match the demands of purposes and audiences.

Monitoring the Process

Increasingly, as students become more fluent writers, they think about how they can effectively use their plans and which tool will best serve their production of text.

World Knowledge

Often, novice and developing writers use ineffective strategies for producing text, for example, thinking of what's next while writing (Bereiter & Scardamalia, 1987) or writing the most interesting facts instead of the most informative (Many, Fyfe, Lewis, & Mitchel, 1996). As writers gain experience, they transform their plans into connected texts that fully represent their knowledge of their topics.

Monitoring the Process	World Knowledge	Discourse Knowledge	Time and Space	Sociocultural Membership
N: Relies on one writing tool. Transcribes haltingly. Focuses on getting words on paper. Does not refer to plans when writing.	**N**: Represents topic knowledge incompletely in written words. May include irrelevant information.	**N**: Uses familiar genres, vocabulary, and organizational structures. Uses oral language and everyday vocabulary. May use conventions haphazardly.	**N**: Records ideas without consideration of contextual differences between self and audience.	**N**: Records ideas without thinking about difference between own experience and audience's. Records ideas without consideration of voice.
D: Tries using a variety of writing tools. Transcribes with increasing fluency. Refers to plans while writing. Works on conventions.	**D**: Represents topic knowledge in written words with some gaps. Begins to consider knowledge needs of audience.	**D**: Uses knowledge of familiar genres and organizational structures. Needs teacher support for unfamiliar genres. Mixes everyday vocabulary and content vocabulary. Uses conventions inconsistently.	**D**: Is aware of the need to provide contextual information to account for differences between self and audience. Is unsure of how to provide contextual information.	**D**: May consider how own experiences differ from audience's. May use own voice. Needs instruction to develop voice.
E: Uses different writing tools flexibly. Is aware of best writing tool(s). Transcribes fluently. Refers to plans. Recognizes when additional planning is needed.	**E**: Represents topic knowledge in written words fully. Keeps knowledge needs of audience in mind while writing.	**E**: Transforms ideas and plans using characteristics and organizational structures of chosen genre. Uses content-specific vocabulary. Uses conventions fluently.	**E**: Includes contextual information to account for differences between self and audience.	**E**: Generates text with differences of own experience and audience's in mind. Uses teacher support to develop voice.

FIGURE 4.2. Developmental continuum: Producing text. N, novice; D, developing; E, experienced.

Discourse Knowledge

With continued instruction, students produce texts that reflect the characteristics of the genre. For example, novice and developing writers differentiate between stories and reports but do not connect story events (Donovan, 2001; Langer, 1986) or subtopics in reports (Donovan, 2001; Donovan & Smolkin, 2002; Langer, 1986; Many et al., 1996; Spivey & King, 1989). They may produce hybrid texts—texts that mix characteristics from different genres, such as a story about doing a science investigation rather than a report about the investigation.

Time and Space

Reflecting the amount of information in their plans, writers differ in the amount of background information they write. For example, they may not situate their science investigation in a context that allows someone else to understand or replicate the experience or they may not provide adequate information about the setting in a story to build background for the plot.

Sociocultural Membership

With teacher support, students develop their own voices (Ball, 1992) and learn to try voices that speak to readers of varied social memberships and disciplines (Kamberlis, 1999).

Students increasingly use their plans to produce texts that, while not perfect, can be reviewed—evaluated, revised, and edited. We now look at the developmental continuum for reviewing.

Reviewing

In Figure 4.3 we describe the processes of reviewing. As students grow as writers, they read more critically in order to evaluate whether they conveyed their message so that their intended readers could easily understand. They also recognize that revising involves making meaning changes, whereas editing focuses on surface feature changes, such as, spelling. (We discuss evaluating text in Chapter 8 and strategies for revising and editing in Chapter 9.)

Monitoring the Process

Most novice writers do not understand the reviewing process (MacArthur, 2007). As writers develop, they recognize that first drafts typically

Monitoring the Process	World Knowledge	Discourse Knowledge	Time and Space	Sociocultural Membership
N: Does not understand need to reread, evaluate, and revise for purpose and audience. Believes the first draft is the final draft.	**N**: Does not make changes to content. Thinks that included information is complete.	**N**: Does not make changes to organization. Makes small changes in words and conventions (e.g., spelling, punctuation, grammar).	**N**: Does not include necessary contextual information.	**N**: Assumes the reader has the same background knowledge and experiences as self. Uses own voice.
D: May reread focusing primarily on editing. Needs support to evaluate for purpose and audience. Knows a few revision strategies.	**D**: Needs support to evaluate coverage of topic. Begins to identify some areas of content that need revision. Has only a few strategies to revise content.	**D**: Needs support to evaluate the effectiveness of the genre, organization, vocabulary, and conventions. May make some changes to wording and conventions.	**D**: Needs support to evaluate whether enough contextual information is included. Attempts necessary revisions with support.	**D**: Needs support to consider potential differences in audience's knowledge and experiences. Lacks strategies to revise voice.
E: Rereads to evaluate whether writing meets needs of purpose and audience. Assesses need for further text generation or planning. Considers revisions based on purpose and audience's needs. Has a repertoire of revision strategies.	**E**: Rereads critically to evaluate the content. Determines if writing includes the right amount and type of information. Makes revisions to improve the content.	**E**: Rereads critically to evaluate whether the chosen genre, organization, vocabulary, and conventions meet the needs of purpose and audience. Makes revisions to improve the organizational structure, vocabulary, and conventions for the chosen genre.	**E**: Rereads critically to evaluate for adequate contextual information. Makes revisions to provide needed contextual information.	**E**: Attempts to critically reread to evaluate for potential differences in audience's knowledge and experiences. Attempts revisions of voice for purpose and audience.

FIGURE 4.3. Developmental continuum: Reviewing; N, novice; D, developing; E, experienced.

need to be revised and edited before they are written well enough to convey their intended messages. Critical reading or evaluating one's text is difficult to learn (Beal, 1990). However, with instruction, students learn how to detect places that need work and acquire a repertoire of strategies for revising and editing their writing.

World Knowledge

As writers become more sophisticated, they are better able to determine whether they have included the right type and amount of information for their purposes and audiences. Gradually, their repertoire of revising and editing strategies increases, providing them with concrete actions they can use to improve the quality of their content.

Discourse Knowledge

Following a developmental progression, writers revise for mechanics and conventions before they revise for genre organization and vocabulary. They learn the characteristics of stories and reports gradually (Donovan, 2001; Donovan & Smolkin, 2002; Langer, 1986), whereas characteristics of persuasive genres are rarely exhibited (Crowhurst, 1990: Ferretti, MacArthur, & Dowdy, 2000; Nippold, Ward-Lonergan, & Fanning, 2005) unless teacher support or instruction is given (De La Paz, 2005).

Time and Space

Only experienced writers, who have been cognizant of time and space differences between themselves and their intended readers, evaluate, revise, and edit to ensure that the writing is situated in a framework for the reader. Knowledgeable and skilled writers evaluate whether they have included adequate background and contextual information, especially for readers who were not with them to experience an event. With instruction, they learn how to integrate the information effectively into the text.

Sociocultural Membership

With practice and teacher guidance, students become increasingly aware that their writing reflects their worldviews and begin to evaluate whether someone with different social experiences would be able to understand their messages. Over time, they attempt to evaluate and revise their voice for varied communities and content-area disciplines. However, we think even adult writers struggle with this dimension.

Most students find reviewing a difficult process to conquer. Learning to read one's writing critically continues for a lifetime. That is why authors have peers and editors read their drafts.

We predict that the students in your class will present mixed profiles across these charts. For example, a student who struggles with fine motor skills may be able to fully represent his or her content knowledge in planning—and thus be classified as experienced in planning and world knowledge—but may be unable to physically produce connected text that expresses the ideas represented in the plan—and thus be classified as novice in producing text and world knowledge. Furthermore, as we remind you in Chapters 6 and 7, students may be experienced writers in one genre and novice in another. We propose the general continuum to allow you to follow your students' incremental and sometimes uneven growth.

You may be wondering if Figures 4.1–4.3 are rubrics. We do not think they are. We believe rubrics are scoring guides that allow teachers to evaluate how well students achieve a defined outcome. Although Figures 4.1–4.3 are formatted like rubrics, they were designed as developmental continua because we emphasize students' growth and teachers' potential instruction. See Chapter 8 for a fuller discussion of rubrics. Now, having described the developmental continuum, we suggest how teachers can use the continuum in their classrooms.

USING THE DEVELOPMENTAL CONTINUUM: MR. FRANK'S INSTRUCTIONAL PLANNING

In the beginning of this chapter, we described Mr. Frank's methods for gathering information about his students' writing processes. His purpose was to learn about his students individually, as well as the class as a whole, in order to guide his teaching of writing over the next couple of months. To begin, Mr. Frank started writing his observational notes on a copy of the Developmental Continuum: Planning (see Figure 4.4).

As the students settle in, Mr. Frank notices that most of them simply begin composing the body of their letter without making any plans at all. Rather than trying to squeeze many names next to the descriptor on the continuum, he jots "most of the class" next to *Does not plan without instruction.* Tyrone, Tanisha, and Kate are exceptions—they each used a listing strategy to plan for their writing. Since it is the beginning of the year and Mr. Frank is not sure what other planning strategies these students have in their repertoire, he jots down their names in between *Has limited planning strategies* and *Has an increasing range of planning strategies.* He also notices that Alice and Jason have trouble getting started

Monitoring the Process	World Knowledge	Discourse Knowledge	Time and Space	Sociocultural Membership
N: Does not plan without instruction. Class May be unaware of purpose. ~~Nola~~ Is unaware of audience.	**N:** Is unaware of own knowledge of the topic. Jason Alice Does not consider audience's knowledge of topic in plans.	**N:** May think about familiar genres, vocabulary, and organization structures.	**N:** Assumes the audience shared the experience.	**N:** Is unaware that differences exist between own experiences and those of others.
D: Plans with teacher support. Has limited planning strategies. Tyrone Tanisha Kate Begins to plan for purpose. May begin to be aware of audience.	**D:** Uses some of own knowledge of the topic in plans. May need help to find resources. Has some awareness that audience's knowledge of topic may differ from his or her own.	**D:** Is aware of different genres, vocabulary, and organizational structures. Needs guidance to select genres and vocabulary that meet purpose and audience needs.	**D:** Recognizes that audience may not have shared the experience but does not include background information in plans.	**D:** Has beginning awareness that audience may have a different background. Needs instruction to think about voice for purpose and audience.
E: Plans independently. Has an increasing range of planning strategies. Plans with purpose and audience in mind.	**E:** Is able to assess own knowledge of topic. Finds resources/strategies to augment knowledge of topic. Represents knowledge of topic in effective plans. Plans for differences in audience's knowledge of topic.	**E:** Has knowledge of an increasing range of genres, vocabulary, and organizational structures. Plans to match genre, vocabulary, and conventions to purpose and audience.	**E:** Anticipates that the audience will need contextual information if they did not share the experience. Includes background information in plans.	**E:** Has an increasing awareness of how own cultural background and social experiences influence how one writes about a topic. Uses teacher support to think about voice.

FIGURE 4.4. Mr. Frank's notes. N, novice; D, developing; E, experienced.

Revising

Revising is closely linked with evaluation. The decisions the writer makes while evaluating are implemented during revising. Revising text involves making content changes to the text—topics, events, details, organization, sentences, and words—with purpose, audience, and genre in mind. We discuss revising and editing again in Chapter 9.

During the next language arts period Sam reviews his draft again and thinks about his teacher's remark. He decides to cut out a section about his mother teaching him to sew and to concentrate on his dad and himself. Evaluating and revising the dogfights and the kite-flying contests, Sam realizes he learned his dad was a friend who liked a friendly rivalry and new challenges just like he did. Sam concludes that he got to know his father as a person while flying stunt kites together.

Editing

Editing refers to the conventions of writing—spelling, punctuation, grammar, and usage. Writers edit texts so their pieces conform to established customs (conventions), thereby helping any audience read it easily. As is the case with revising, some writers edit as they produce drafts; others ignore errors until they have finished their drafts.

Reading his revised memoir to his teacher, Sam stops to fix a few mechanics, like quotation marks. Together they polish some sentences and refine his word choices. Sam then heads to the computer to input his changes, prints his memoir, and gives it a last proofread for silly errors, like mixing up *to* and *too*, which spell check would miss. After mailing his memoir into the contest, Sam wonders who the judges will be and what they will think; at least his classmates liked it.

Sam exemplifies reviewing in the experienced writer. Reviewing is not simply fixing a text after the writing is over; instead reviewing is critically rereading during the whole writing activity. Throughout his writing, Sam monitors his plan and text-so-far to evaluate whether his text meets his purpose and his audience's needs. Let's examine monitoring more closely.

Monitoring

Experienced writers are metacognitively aware: they know what they know (their knowledge) and how they write (their processes). Because they are metacognitively aware, they monitor or keep track of how their processes and their tasks are proceeding. While consistently monitoring both the text and the processes, they move among planning, producing text, and reviewing. Struggling writers may need instruction to monitor and then both write one idea in their letters. He writes their names with a question mark next to *Is unaware of own knowledge of the topic.* He wants to remind himself to ask them what ideas they remember from the class discussion and about their own knowledge of classrooms.

As his students continue to write over the next two days, Mr. Frank switches to the Producing Text and Reviewing developmental continua to record his observations and comments:

- Four students have varying degrees of facility with the English language, which affects their fluency in generating their ideas and transcribing on paper (*transcribes haltingly: novice in Monitoring the Process on Producing Text continuum*).

- Half of the students have incorporated all of the standard characteristics of the friendly letter genre into their writing and half have not (*novice and developing in Discourse Knowledge on Producing Text continuum*).

- Five of his students provide some background information to explain past experiences in classrooms and the rest just list classroom preferences (*novice and developing in Time and Space on Producing Text continuum*).

- A couple of students do reread their letters to edit them—they make spelling changes and fix some punctuation (*makes small changes in words and conventions: novice in Discourse Knowledge on Reviewing continuum*).

- The majority of his students do not reread their letters when they have finished (*believe first draft is the final draft: novice in Monitoring the Process on Reviewing continuum*).

As he makes notations about his students on the continuum, Mr. Frank knows that his notes and conversations about letter writing do not present a full picture of each student as a writer. Unconcerned that every student's name is not on the continua, he is satisfied with a rough picture of where the students are—enough information to guide his instructional decisions. By surveying the notes by the descriptors, Mr. Frank sees a map of similarities and differences in students' understanding of writing. To learn more about his students' competencies to respond to greater distances across our communication model, Mr. Frank will need to incorporate additional writing projects for varied audiences. But for now, he has gathered enough information to plan his writing instruction.

Mr. Frank cannot set one course of instruction for all students because they have different needs. He realizes that his instruction will need to provide a mix of whole-class, small-group, and individualized instruction to ensure that all his students make progress.

Whole-Class Instruction

As he reviews his notes on the developmental continuum, Mr. Frank first thinks about the class as a whole, looking for patterns. Noticing "most of the class" written next to *Does not plan without instruction,* he confirms that the majority of his students do not go beyond the class discussion to plan what to write and how to arrange their ideas. He wonders if perhaps some students think letters are similar to e-mails, a familiar genre that never requires a plan before writing. Based on the class's general lack of planning, Mr. Frank decides that it will be a focus of his next instruction for the whole class. He then will model his own process by creating a plan for a personal narrative or memoir. As he plans, he will think aloud to explain the decisions he is making about purpose and audience as well as the dimensions of our communication model. He may ask Tanisha how she would plan since she created her friendly letter.

Mr. Frank also intends to provide explicit instruction in a variety of planning strategies throughout the year as they write in different genres. Last year, he prepared tiered graphic organizers (Tomlinson, 2004) to accompany several of his genre projects. For example, after providing whole-class instruction on writing book reviews, he created three different planning organizers. On the basic organizer students were asked to name and summarize the book. Mr. Frank provided specific space on the organizer so students could write what happened in the beginning, middle, and end of the book. Students also recorded their reaction to the book. At this level, Mr. Frank gave the students quite a bit of support. Students working on the middle-level organizer recorded the same information as students using the basic organizer did. In addition, they included evidence to support their reaction. Finally, on the most challenging organizer, students were expected to not only complete the task of the middle group, but also compare or contrast the book to something else they had read. Although all children were introduced to the same concept, when they began to plan their book review, they worked on a graphic organizer at a level that was just right for each one. Mr. Frank designed the organizers so they all looked equally demanding, but the level of cognitive activity increased with each level. He has not yet created tiered graphic organizers for the letter-writing genre, because he wants to see how students plan on their own. When needed in other genre studies though, he will introduce tiered graphic organizers.

Small-Group Instruction

Mr. Frank also reviews his notes on the developmental continuum to plan for some small-group instruction. First, he sees that six students had difficulty fluently producing text. While these students will benefit from the whole-class focus on planning strategies, they also need to develop some additional strategies for jump-starting their own ideas. Mr. Frank plans to meet with these students in a small-group setting to get them talking together as they plan and produce their next writing pieces—personal narratives. He thinks the opportunity to share their ideas orally in a small group will help not only the bilingual students but also Jason and Alice who had only one meager idea in their plans and texts. For students who need extra support, Mr. Frank will record a few of their ideas on sticky notes and read aloud the notes to them as a way to recap key points before he sends them off to continue planning independently.

Second, Mr. Frank plans to meet with Tanisha, Kate, and Tyrone to determine whether they have any other planning strategies beyond listing. While the whole-class planning instruction may show them more strategies, they might benefit from the jump-start that small-group instruction could provide.

Individualized Instruction

Mr. Frank also thinks about several students who need some individual attention. He is particularly concerned about Jason and Alice, who relied on other students' ideas to produce one idea in their letters. Making a mental note to find time to talk with each of them about their interests and experiences with writing, he suspects that each student has ideas but may have difficulty accessing those ideas. Mr. Frank also wants to find time to talk with Juan, who is an English language learner. He was impressed that Juan attempted to express the differences he has noted between his new American classroom and his old Ecuadorian classroom, showing an awareness of differences in sociocultural membership. Mr. Frank wants to learn more about how he can ease Juan's transition to a new classroom culture and language.

Mr. Frank knows he cannot provide all the whole-class, small-group, and individual instruction tomorrow or even over the next few days. He decides to begin with whole-class instruction in planning. Over the next couple of weeks, he will work on instruction with small groups. He can casually slip in conversations with Jason, Alice, and Juan while the class is writing. In addition, he will introduce them to technology and software, for example, AlphaSmarts, which might motivate them to write more. Throughout the remainder of the school year, Mr. Frank will continue to use the developmental continuum to plan his instruction and to assess student growth over time. As he and his students write for varying purposes and audiences, the continuum will help Mr. Frank better understand what his students know about the functions and processes of writing.

The general developmental continuum is an introduction for you to consider how the diverse students in your classroom write. While Mr. Frank used the full continuum to gain an overview of his class, you could use a single chart to map a composite of the whole class—for example, just use the Planning chart. Or you could use the continuum to identify the strengths and areas of needed instruction for an individual student who intrigues you. The descriptors on the charts may help you understand how to instruct the individual. We build on this continuum in subsequent chapters.

CHAPTER SUMMARY

Although our classrooms have always enrolled students with different family structures, as well as varied academic, language, cultural, and socioeconomic experiences, in the past we did not always recognize explicitly that diversity or alter our instruction to meet students' diverse needs. Today's teachers not only recognize that their students are diverse in many characteristics but seek to match their instruction to a range of needs. Based on their home and school experiences, students bring diverse understandings about and approaches to writing tasks. We created a developmental continuum to help teachers document their students' diverse understandings about writing.

Bringing our communication model together with the cognitive processes and monitoring, we describe writing growth of novice writers, developing writers, and experienced writers. For the process of planning, we describe progressive growth first in monitoring and awareness of the planning process. Then, we describe how writers increasingly include information about their world knowledge, discourse knowledge, time and space context, and sociocultural membership in their plans. Similarly, for the process of producing text, we describe how novice, developing, and experienced writers increasingly monitor their processes of generating and transcribing and include the information about the four dimensions of our communication model into their drafts. And for the process of reviewing, we describe the increasing capabilities of writers to monitor and to evaluate, revise, and edit their texts for the four dimensions so that they increasingly account for the differences between themselves and their audiences.

We do not expect even growth; instead, a writer could be novice in planning but developing in producing text. Furthermore, since a fifth grader could be experienced and an eighth grader novice, we purposely have not assigned grade levels to our descriptions.

We recommend several uses for the developmental continuum. Teachers could take one section, like planning, and write students' names next to the behaviors observed. With a composite picture of students' understandings, teachers can plan whole-class instruction and identify small groups of students for targeted instruction. Teachers could also use the continuum to inquire how an intriguing student plans, produces, and reviews a piece of writing.

We hope you find the developmental continuum interesting and useful both for understanding your students and for planning instruction. Instruction becomes the focus of the subsequent three chapters. In the next chapter, "Writing to Explore," we present journals as vehicles to practice producing text and describe a developmental continuum for journals that is based on the comprehensive continuum introduced in this chapter.

APPLICATION BOX

We invite you to explore the use of the continuum to look at individual students. Select a student in your class whose writing process intrigues or puzzles you. Observe the student closely as he or she plans, produces, and reviews a piece. Make notes on a copy of the developmental continuum— one process at a time—to determine which descriptors on the developmental continuum fit your student. Remember that you may not be able to definitively pick a descriptor in all categories. Based on the information you find, what instruction will you plan?

You may want to continue to observe this student across several pieces of writing. What can you learn about this student as a writer? Do you see growth in this student's ability to consider how much shared world and discourse knowledge, understanding of time and space, and sociocultural memberships exist between the writer and intended readers? Do you see changes in the student's writing processes? Based on the information from several pieces of writing, what instruction will you plan?

Chapter 5

Writing to Explore

People often write to explore their learning and thinking. They might jot down their ideas on scraps of paper that they tuck into a special box, open a particular file on a computer where they pull together their thoughts, or use a more traditional journal to capture their ruminations. Many authors keep a writer's notebook to collect ideas, observations, conversations, events, and reflections. Scientists, such as Darwin or Lewis and Clark, keep journals in which they carefully record data and their thoughts about the data. Historians (such as Delores Kearns Goodwin) also carefully record their data from documents, interviews, and artifacts. Artists (e.g., Leonardo DaVinci) keep sketchbooks to explore their ideas. Even some athletes keep records of their performances. For example, Curt Shilling, an inactive baseball pitcher (as we write) for the Boston Red Sox, recorded his pitches so that he could analyze them for the next time he met the same batters. As you can see, people write to explore what they are learning and thinking in many diverse ways; yet, in each instance, the writer is writing for oneself.

When writing for themselves in journals, students usually explore their world knowledge or what they know and are learning in our content areas. In addition, we use journals to explore learning about the other three dimensions of our communication model. Students benefit from exploring the dimensions in the safe environment of their journals before they write extended pieces for known and unknown audiences.

In this chapter, we:

- Discuss using journals based on our communication model and suggest exploratory activities that explore world knowledge across the curriculum, expand discourse knowledge, provide contextual information including time and space, and investigate the voices of diverse sociocultural communities.

- Specify a developmental continuum for journal writing.
- Discuss journals as sites for planning extended pieces of writing.

We use the general term *journals* to encompass all the specific types of writing to explore, such as science field notebooks, learning logs, math process journals, and literature response journals; however, we do make an exception for writers' journals. Since most current books call them *writers' notebooks*, we, too, refer to writer's journals as notebooks. Journals, as we are defining them, do not include diaries because diaries contain private thoughts and emotions that are too personal. Regardless of what you decide to call the specific journal your students use, they should record both the information they are learning and their thinking about that information (Fulwiler, 1987).

In discussing what students are learning and how they are learning, we are less concerned with conventions—grammar, spelling, punctuation—and more concerned about the free expression of ideas (Britton et al., 1975). Yet, we agree with Buckner (2005), who expects students to use what they know about conventions and grammar when writing in journals. Students may write like they talk, may ramble, may use codes or abbreviations, may doodle, diagram, graph, or draw, may make lists, and may use phrases or sentences. We want students to practice generating their ideas and transcribing those ideas into written text. With practice, our goal is for students to fluently produce written text, but that text need not be conventional sentences or paragraphs.

If students are to produce text fluently, they need to transcribe with the best tool for them. Some students require a voice-activated computer; others like a red marker, while still others prefer keeping e-journals or blogs. Therefore, students need to have available not only pens and paper, but markers, computers, pencils, graph paper, drawing paper, sticky notes, digital cameras, tape recorders, and video cameras—a variety of tools.

We invite you to explore your learning about writing and teaching in a journal as you read this book and as you incorporate our ideas into your teaching. (See the Application Box at the end of this chapter.) Now, we begin with writing to explore world knowledge across the content areas.

JOURNALS: A PLACE TO EXPLORE
WORLD KNOWLEDGE

Exploring students' growing knowledge about the world is a primary objective for keeping journals whether in social studies, math, science, or

English language arts. You may have encountered programs or articles advocating "writing to learn" or "writing across the curriculum." The assumption behind writing to learn programs is that the act of writing produces learning (Graham & Perin, 2007; Ochsner & Fowler, 2004). Even though many teachers attest to gains in students' learning (ourselves included), gains may depend upon the type of writing the students complete (Bangert-Drowns et al., 2004; Langer & Applebee, 1987). To explore their world knowledge, students need not only to record data, ideas, and concepts, but they need also to write about their thinking or how they are learning (Bangert-Drowns et al., 2004). Students tend to use their journals simply to record information unless they are taught how to use them for different purposes. Showing them a speculative entry, or actually speculating in front of them, might encourage them to try out contemplating possibilities based on evidence at hand in their entries. Thus, when you incorporate journals into a content area, you will want to explain and demonstrate the thinking you want students to exhibit in their entries (based on Fulwiler, 1987, and Mayher, Lester, & Pradl, 1983):

1. To record—writes the information learned, the observations seen, the text read, the data collected.
2. To connect—links content to prior knowledge, prior experiences, and/or prior readings.
3. To question—asks questions and/or expresses wonderings or doubts about the content and one's understanding.
4. To consolidate—summarizes or synthesizes content and the understanding of the content or finds relationships or patterns among ideas.
5. To speculate—wonders about future content, events, or results.
6. To invent—creates new ideas, events, or inferences.
7. To analyze—reflects on the learning processes and strategies used or tried.
8. To digress—departs from initial intent or focus to include disparate ideas which may or may not become fruitful in the future.
9. To reread—revisits past entries and considers whether ideas and thoughts have changed and/or patterns are apparent.

In Table 5.1, we look at a sampling of purposes for using journals to enhance world knowledge in different content areas. You'll notice that we list not only purposes, but also the different types of thinking writers might tap into for different purposes. Through different purposes and types of thinking, students explore their world knowledge. To encourage their explorations we suggest exploratory activities.

TABLE 5.1. Journals across the Curriculum

Type	Overall purpose	Format	A sampling of possible purposes
Social studies journals	• To explore living in a historical period or a geographical area	• Diary form with dated entries. • Description of historical event or geographical location. • Description of life in era or location and personal reaction.	• Rehearses ordinary person's role in events in era or location. • Digresses to describe ordinary life events. • Invents point of view and reactions of person. • Speculates about outcomes or future events.
Math process journals	• To document how solves problems as well as the solutions	• Dated entries: • One section for problem and solution. • Second section reflects on processes or strategies and degree of understanding.	• Records how solved problem. • Connects to other problems. • Questions about concepts not understood. • Summarizes concepts understood. • Analyzes processes or strategies used.
Science lab notebooks or field notebooks	• To record observations of experiments or natural events • To analyze, question, or reflect on observations	• Dated double-entry journal: • One section for data. • Separate section for reflections on the learning experience.	• Records observations and/or measurements. • Consolidates data into charts or graphs. • Connects data to prior knowledge. • Speculates about results or outcomes. • Analyzes what and how learned. • Rereads to compare current data to earlier data.

Type	Purpose	Contents	Processes
Reading response journals	• To record personal reactions and reflections	• Dated entries. • Title or section of book. • Text of interest quoted or noted. • Reactions and reflections on content, author's craft, genre.	• Records a snippet of text in response. • Connects to own experiences, life in general, other books and authors. • Speculates about upcoming chapters. • Analyzes personal reactions to book, author, or craft. • Questions character actions or own understanding of motives. • Invents own version.
Writers' notebooks	• To collect ideas, observations, and thoughts that may or may not use in other writing pieces • To collect examples of writer's craft • To try out the craft of writing	• Dated entries. • Lists of ideas or titles to write. • Quotes of conversations heard. • Descriptions of people, places, events observed. • Quotes or copies of texts read. • Diagrams of ideas. • Drawings of characters or places. • Notes from interviews. • Experiments with writer's craft trying out (metaphors, dialogue). • Free writing on any topic or idea. • Record of craft ideas practiced.	• Records what experienced, observed, heard, or read. • Connects ideas on topics to books, life, or previous entries. • Rehearses new genres, language usage, or author's craft. • Invents ideas, events, characters. • Digresses, especially when free writing, to disparate ideas. • Reflects on thinking in entries. • Analyzes own writing process and what works or doesn't work in pieces. • Rereads to find topics to communicate.

Note. Based on Fulwiler (1987) and Mayher, Lester, and Pradl (1983).

Exploratory Activities

Although the list of possible journal activities to enhance world knowledge is infinite, we offer a few specific journal activities to help students deepen their understanding of world knowledge in social studies, mathematics, science, and English language arts.

Social Studies

KWL CHART

Referring to the *Curriculum Standards for Social Studies: Expectations of Excellence* (National Council for the Social Studies, 1994) suggestion to build on students' prior knowledge, we recommend using a KWL chart. At the beginning of an Africa unit, a sixth-grade class first writes what they *know* (K) about Africa—their background knowledge gained from any source. Second, they write questions about *what* (W) they want to learn about the continent or about particular countries. The social studies teacher asks the students to compare life in Africa to their life in the United States. As they research the geography of Africa in general and then focus on one country, they create notes in their journals about the similarities and differences between lives in the two countries, recording what they *learned* (L) and their own thoughts about what they learned.

INTERVIEW AN ADULT (ORAL HISTORY)

Again referring to the National Council for the Social Studies standard of Time, Continuity, and Change (1994) to build an understanding of historical perspectives, students could interview an adult who lived during the era they are studying. Or for Black History month or Women's History month, students could interview adults about their lives. In March, one fifth-grade class interviewed their mothers, learning not only about their mothers' childhoods but learning about their mothers as adult women. Other classes have interviewed senior citizens about what life in town was like when they were young. Students recorded possible interview questions in their journals and then audiotaped or videotaped answers and on-the-spot questions asked. Thus, students explore firsthand knowledge of a historical era.

Mathematics

One of the first organizations to publish standards, the National Council of Teachers of Mathematics (2000) advocates students not only solve mathematical problems, but also be able to explain how they solved them and justify or prove why their processes were appropriate. Consequently, tracking one's mathematical processes is a common practice in math journals. Students detail how they arrived at their answers, reflect on their understandings, try out new vocabulary, and develop fluency in mathematical writing. (Countryman, 1992; McIntosh & Draper, 2001). We suggest the following activities to explore mathematics knowledge.

PONDERING MATH PROBLEMS AND PROCESSES

Pose the following questions:

- What questions do you still have about your math homework?
- What part of this process is still puzzling for you?
- What discoveries did you make about _____ (concept students are learning)?
- In your own words, tell me what the problem is asking you to do.
- Describe what you did when you got stuck on a word problem.

CREATE A NEW PROBLEM

To recognize that mathematicians solve problems in the real world—not algorithms in textbooks, math problems include real data and students create new, similar problems for situations they experience. If students can apply their mathematical world knowledge in new problems in their journals—through words, numerals and symbols, and/or visuals—they probably have a solid grasp of the concepts.

Science

Science journals can serve two important purposes: They can help students foster an understanding of scientific thinking, concepts, and skills; they can also provide information for formative assessments (Fulwiler, 2007). Before, during, and after investigations, students can record their growing science knowledge in journals.

PRIOR TO A SCIENCE INVESTIGATION

Fulwiler (2007) suggests that prior to the beginning of an investigation, students can write entries that explain what they expect to happen, provide a rationale for the investigation, or include a question (hypotheses) they will address during the investigation (Shepardson & Britsch, 1997). They also can include their prior knowledge about the investigation.

DURING A SCIENCE INVESTIGATION

While engaged in an investigation, students can include the procedures or methods of investigation, their observations, data, charts or graphs, and their reflections on what they are finding.

DURING AND AFTER A SCIENCE INVESTIGATION

Throughout and at the conclusion of an investigation, students can focus their journal entries on answers to their questions, their emerging results, predictions generated from data they have analyzed, and ideas for future investigations. (Shepardson & Britsch, 1997). Both Fulwiler (2007) and Jablon (2006) want students (and teachers) to appreciate that journal entries are places where students can practice formulating ideas and communicating their content knowledge—two essential skills for scientists of all ages.

English Language Arts

In English language arts, teachers are no longer satisfied with just literal comprehension of literature. Instead, teachers probe students' understanding of and reactions to the texts they are reading (Langer, 1995; Rosenblatt, 1938/1995) through the use of reader response journals. Students use reader response journals to record their insights, reactions, and questions about the texts they are reading. When students begin reading a new text, they may have more literal questions because they may be figuring out who the characters are or in what time period the action is occurring. Soon, however, they can react to the characters, predict possible plot events, contrast characters' motives, and compare the text to other texts they have read. Teachers may ask students questions to move their responses beyond summary statements (Berger, 1996) to reactions that are personal and yet grounded in the text (Spiegel, 1998). Some teachers have students keep partner journals, in which they dialogue with classmates about open-ended questions or clarify points in the texts they are reading (Brannon et al., 2008). Other teachers use Wikis, software that allows multiple students to read, contribute to, and edit a text, as a safe place for students to share responses to literature collaboratively online.

English language arts teachers also have students keep writers' notebooks serving as places for them to collect ideas. While some ideas will be "recycled" into future pieces, others will be captured in their notebooks but never incorporated into other texts. Writers' notebooks are also sites to explore and practice the craft of writing—a purpose we consider in the following section of this chapter when we discuss discourse knowledge. For now, we concentrate on how writers' notebooks can be used to collect ideas and extend the writer's world knowledge. Teachers can help students begin to live a writer's life (Fletcher, 2001) by teaching them how to record ideas and observations that might otherwise be forgotten.

LIST OF TERRITORIES

Students create a list of territories (Atwell, 1998) or topics that a writer knows about and might one day be interested in writing about. Teachers share their personal list of topics, for instance, their pets, the books they're reading, their recent vacations, and their interests in wildlife, pausing after reading a few items to allow students to add ideas to their lists of territories. Periodically through the year, students return to these lists to update and expand their territories. Teachers direct students back to their territories when they struggle to find a topic for their writing.

EXCERPTS FROM PUBLISHED TEXTS

Writers use notebooks not only as records of their own ideas and observations but also as sites to collect ideas from published texts or online sources using Noteshare (see Appendix 2.1 in Chapter 2). They never know when these "promising ideas" (Mueller & Reynolds, 1990) or "seeds" (Angelillo, 1999; Calkins, 1991) may become fodder for future writing. Students may paste articles from the newspaper, cartoon drawings, and magazine ads into their notebooks. These sources contain topics or situations they might one day write about, or may provide background information for a draft.

COLLECTION OF SMALL ITEMS

Periodically, the teacher (or students) brings in small items to tape into the notebooks—a birthday candle, a candy wrapper, a photograph of someone special, a sticker, a Monopoly $20.00 bill. Then the students spend 5 or 7 minutes writing a list, narrative, web, sketch, or poem about whatever thoughts the item triggers for them. At a later time, students can return to these exploratory entries to add to them or to reread when searching for a new topic. Until then, they remain seeds that are temporarily dormant.

POSITIVE AND NEGATIVE LIFELINE (RIEF, 1992)

The students draw a lifeline from the age of their earliest memory to the present. Above the line, students record positive events, memories, people, and places, while below the line they record negative ones. The distance from the line indicates how joyous or unfortunate the memory is. Students survey their lifelines for important memories to write about. They may discover that one type of event has recurred, such as moving to new schools, and decide to write about how that experience has changed over the years. You recall that Sam in Chapter 2 reviewed his lifeline to find a topic for the memoir contest.

ARTIFACT OF SIGNIFICANCE

Students, or families, may have objects that hold particular importance to them. Students may cherish a sports medal, a beloved stuffed animal, or even a favorite book. Families may have a recipe they always make, a birthday ritual they always keep, or a scanned picture of an object from an ancestor. Students brainstorm words that describe the artifact, ideas that explain its significance, and how they came to have an attachment to the artifact.

We spend a considerable amount of time experimenting with exploratory entries when we initiate journals in the content areas. While exploring world knowledge is important in every content area, journals also offer a site to experiment and practice discourse knowledge, especially if the genre is new.

JOURNALS: A PLACE TO EXPLORE DISCOURSE KNOWLEDGE

Although we think of journal writing across the curriculum as being directed first and foremost to the development of content knowledge (world knowledge), journals can also be used to enhance discourse knowledge. Early entries may express learning in a home genre (a story) with everyday vocabulary (crackling noise). Later entries may contain the students' learning of content-area vocabulary (static) and genre (report). Although hybrid genres can be expected in entries, students can use content-area journals to explore how discourse is practiced in the disciplines.

Think back in this chapter to our discussion of journals in social studies. When students completed the KWL on Africa, they organized their new information by their questions or *what* they wanted to learn. They also practiced using geographic vocabulary for locations and land formations. When they interviewed an adult, they were learning about the genre of biography and structured their interviews chronologically.

Science journals are sites for trying out scientific writing by gaining practice in organizing science concepts and using scientific vocabulary clearly (Fulwiler, 2007). Students record data, organize data into cause and effect or problem and solution, speculate about results or outcomes, and draw conclusions. In addition, they express data either mathematically or pictorially in charts, tables, graphs, and diagrams. In other words, they practice the genre characteristics of science reports.

Consider the discourse knowledge in which students engage when they keep mathematics journals. They use the journal to practice explaining and justifying how they solved problems—the discourse of mathematics. Students might mix familiar and math vocabulary as they explain their understanding of math concepts.

Looking at reader response journals in English language arts, students can practice analyzing the strengths of the text, such as the characters, plot, and theme, or comparing the strengths of the text to other texts. They can also practice expressing their opinion or recommendations to other readers. In other words, they can use their reader response notebooks to practice the elements of the review genre.

Finally, we think of writers' notebooks as safe places in which to practice the craft of writing and to study mentor texts to learn more about how other writers across the curriculum create meaningful texts (Dorfman & Cappelli, 2007). Students might tape, glue, or staple into their notebooks copies of excerpts from mentor texts and then analyze one small feature of the author's craft (Buckner, 2005), marking the text—circle words, underline phrases, or write marginal notes. Students may collect endings of stories, figurative language in sports articles, or phrases with captivating words. In these instances, students are preserving the author's language—discourse they might imitate in their own writing.

Exploratory Activities

We can enhance students' discourse knowledge through the following three journal activities.

Exploring Mentor Texts for Conventions and Sentences

Students and teachers can explore mentor texts examining when and why authors conform to and violate the conventions of writing (grammar, punctuation, and spelling). Anderson (2006) explains that he "zooms in and out." When he zooms in, he has the students look closely at a target convention such as the semicolon, identify the pattern, and try out semicolons in their notebooks. Then, he zooms out to the text level where students apply what they have learned in their writing. Students might also examine specific sentence structures, like complex sentences. Noticing authors' complex sentences, they practice imitating the structures and also rearrange the phrases or clauses. In addition to practicing the conventions and sentences, students should note or discuss how the meaning changes with each change.

Outside and Inside of People

People are central to several genres: fiction, biography, news reports, and feature sports articles; yet students tend to concentrate on plot or events and not the people who are motivated into action. Using the sports page as a mentor text, students can notice how a player and physical actions are described (the outside), and then what the descriptions lead the sports writer to conclude about the athlete's ability, personality, or motivation (the inside). Students, for example, can practice thinking about the outside and inside of people or characters by observing younger students at an area of the playground, like the jungle gym. They can describe the children on the jungle gym and the actions they used to climb around—the outside. Did each child hop on the jungle gym the same way? How did a child climb up to the top? Did a child hang upside down? Then, students would interpret the child's actions to create a personality—the inside. Was the child adventurous or timid? Was the child a loner or gregarious? Finally, the students can choose one child to characterize or compare different children. This activity can be adapted to different content areas and different genres, such as biographies in social studies.

Record a Local Event

Students can attend a performance, sports event, or art exhibit. They can describe the event, the performers, players, or art works, interview other attendees about their opinion of the event and, if possible, interview a person who was in the event. If teachers set up classroom blogs, they can give students access to the blogs at various times during the day and create "community daybooks" or journals (Brannan et al., 2008). The classroom blogs enable students to share data they've collected and ask questions to extend each other's thinking. Events in and out of school allow students to practice the discourses found in newspaper writing—reporting on events and reviewing events.

We return to discourse knowledge, especially planning strategies for text organization in Chapters 6 and 7. Now, we consider how journals can support writers' understandings of time and space.

JOURNALS: A PLACE TO ACCOUNT FOR TIME AND SPACE

When considering the dimension of time and space in journals, we think about two purposes: the student rereading previously written entries and the student providing contextual information for potential readers.

For both purposes, we assume students date their entries; however, we know reminders are sometimes needed.

First, we encourage students to reread their entries to discover how their knowledge and thinking may have changed over time, to review a process they previously used (e.g., how they solved a mathematical problem), to find ideas for a new piece, or to remind themselves of how a writer crafted a piece. While we choose not to belabor the point, if students are to reread, then the entries must be minimally legible. (You've probably had difficulty deciphering a note to yourself at least once!) Furthermore, students need to include sufficient content (world knowledge) so that they have useful information in the future. Providing an authentic purpose and class time for rereading previous entries will help students realize they need to have legible and thorough entries in order to use them later.

Second, we encourage students to practice writing the contextual details that they will need to provide when writing for audiences beyond their classroom—when and where they learned the information. In science journals, they record the context of their investigations—the procedures or methods of data collection. In math journals, they describe when to use their problem-solving procedures. In social studies journals, students include the historical period, the specific year, the geographical location, and maybe even the mood of the times behind the events (the furor over the tea tax, for example). In reading response journals, students reference or quote specific text that caused their reactions or opinions. And finally, in writers' notebooks, students practice writing the setting or weaving in setting details when they write stories and practice providing background information when they write reports.

Exploratory Activities

Here are two activities to use to explore time and space.

Turf Map of My Place

Students draw a map or diagram of a place they consider their very own. For some students, their turf is the bedroom; for others it's a hideout in the woods, a basement clubroom, or a corner of the roof above their apartment. Students draw the contents of the place and record events that occurred there as well as people who visited the place. Students can make notes regarding the uniqueness or oddity of their turf. Students may try writing a paragraph describing the setting for an event that might occur on their turf. They may also try to write a fictional event and weave in details about the setting or their turf when the details become significant to the action.

Tape Record the Sounds in Your Neighborhood

We are so accustomed to using our eyes that we often ignore our other senses; or we are in our own enclosed world, listening to our iPod. Since neighborhoods, homes, playgrounds, streets, and corner stores are filled with sounds, students can quietly record the cacophony of sounds and identify the place and the origin of the sounds. For example, at the local convenience store, the student could record the sound of the store door opening, the lottery machine cranking out tickets, the sucking sound of the refrigerator door opening and slamming shut. Listening to the sounds later, the student can try different ways to describe each sound. Students can practice incorporating sound descriptions into lines about characters' actions or lines of poetry describing a place. Describing sounds, or other senses, enlarges students' views of how to specify a space and maybe even time, if sounds occur only in the morning, for example.

Although we haven't mentioned it, we assume you would also have students search mentor texts to explore how writers provide the contextual information of time and space for readers. How do they weave into their texts necessary background knowledge? How do they show (instead of tell) the environment in which the action occurs? How do they refer to characters or events so readers understand to whom writers are referring? As we analyze mentor texts, we look to see how writers convey ideas to readers who have not shared the same experiences as the writer.

Now, we turn to the most difficult dimension for writers, teachers, and students—the sociocultural dimension. In the section that follows, we discuss how journals can provide a risk-free space for students to approximate the voices associated with various sociocultural communities.

JOURNALS: A PLACE TO INVESTIGATE SOCIOCULTURAL COMMUNITIES

Journal writing can help students begin to think about how their social and cultural experiences influence what they write and how they write— the beliefs and values they convey, the language they use, and the voice they choose. In journal entries, students can explore their own voice and begin to take on the voices of other sociocultural communities. Because the concept of voice is complex, we spend time discussing it here. We think that journals, as low-risk settings for writing, are the ideal sites for students to practice using different voices. Therefore, in content-area journal writing, we encourage students to begin to adopt the voices of the disciplines as they engage in the work of scientists, historians, mathematicians, literary critics, and writers.

So what does it mean to practice the voices of the discipline? Each discipline has more than one voice because discipline experts match the voice in their writing to their purposes and audiences. For example, a doctor's voice would change depending on whether he or she is explaining medical information to other doctors or to a patient. Although purpose and audience influence voices of disciplines, they are connected because all voices express the values, beliefs, processes, and understandings common to the discipline.

Voices across the Curriculum

Studying mentor texts written by experts in the field will help to make the concept of voice more concrete to your students. Gathering several sample texts, we discuss the authors' language choices and how the language communicates the authors' understandings, processes, and values. To help orient you in your study of mentor texts within the disciplines, we discuss the ways of thinking and writing in each discipline (informed by our review of the literature and conversations with experts in the fields) and provide mentor text examples in the sections that follow.

Voices of the Social Scientist

The social scientist engages in inquiry to learn about the human world past and present. Although our students may think of history as a set of indisputable fixed facts, historians see the study of human experience as a process of interpretation. VanSledright (2000) describes the processes of the historian as: "analyzing primary and secondary sources, drawing inferences from sometimes thin and inconclusive data, plunging deeply into historical contexts, and creating narratives about the past" (unpaged). When students read historical texts, they can investigate how historians describe their sources, explain their interpretations, and weigh conflicting perspectives. Students can practice techniques for setting the context, for reporting and interpreting events, and for making their findings interesting to the reader (making the text come alive), when recording either historical or current events.

We suggest *The Lost Colony of Roanoke* by Jean Fritz (2004) to examine the voice of the historian. In the last section of her book, Fritz describes various theories proposed to explain the vanishing of the colonists. She explains the research process of anthropologist Lee Miller, who examined state papers from the time of Queen Elizabeth that tied a statesman to the disappearance of the colonists. Since archaeologists continue to search for physical clues to solve the mystery, Fritz suggests our understanding of the events may change with new discoveries. In the back of the book, she includes source notes that tell where she made inferences from available information. For example, she notes that while no document verifies that Sir Walter Raleigh ever laid his coat over a puddle for the queen to walk upon, sources indicate that he was likely to have made that type of gesture. In other mentor texts, such as *What You Never Knew About Beds, Bedrooms, & Pajamas* by Patricia Lauber (2006) and *Pompeii Lost and Found* by Mary Osborne and Bonnie Christensen (2006), writers reveal their source information within the text, describing the artifacts that have been found and the conclusions that have been drawn from them. Through each text, we follow how the authors narrate the past using voices of historians.

Voices of the Mathematician

The language of mathematics is characterized by its use of mathematical symbols, clear description of problem and solution, and an emphasis on logic, precision, and brevity (Umland & Hersh, 2006; Walshaw & Anthony, 2007). As they write in their mathematics journals, students develop their abilities to clearly explain their problem-solving processes, building an argument for the logic of their solutions. Students also explain how mathematics helps them to understand and solve problems in their everyday world (National Council of Teachers of Mathematics, 2000).

Voices of the Scientist

Members of the scientific community are linked by their methods for observing, analyzing, and reporting the phenomena of the world around us. Their investigative processes include observing, describing, questioning, evaluating, concluding, arguing, classifying, and comparing (Cervetti, Pearson, Bravo, & Barber, 2005). Using technical terms, scientists objectively document results often reported in charts, graphs, tables, or diagrams, emphasize causal relationships, and provide evidence-based conclusions in their texts (Lemke, 1990, 2004).

In the children's nonfiction text *Dinomummy: The Life, Death and Discovery of Dakota, a Dinosaur from Hell Creek* (2007), paleontologist Dr. Phillip Lars Manning describes the discovery of a mummified hadrosaur in South Dakota. He defines technical terms, such as *overburden, soft tissue,* and *lidar,* within the sentences and includes diagrams to illustrate the internal skeleton of the hadrosaur. Throughout the text, Manning states his questions and hypotheses about the dinosaur and explains how he determines causes and effects through his testing processes. This mentor book sheds light on the voice of a scientist who provides evidence to substantiate the conclusions he draws.

Voices of the Literary Critic

As students write in reader response journals, they take on the voice of the literary critic. In addition to using their personal voice to describe their reaction to the text, students can evaluate the text through a discussion of the elements of literature: plot, setting, characterization, style, theme, point of view, text organization, accuracy, authenticity, content, and perspective (Kiefer, 2007), and the qualities of good writing (see Chapter 8).

Students also exemplify voices of a literary critic when they write book reviews. Examples of book reviews written by students and adults can be found in magazines for students, such as *Merlyn's Pen* and *Stone Soup*, and in online sources, such as *www.kidsreads.com, www.spaghettibookclub.org, www.teenreads.com, www.schoollibraryjournal.com*, and *www.bookhive.org*. Browsing published reviews, your students can create a list of criteria for useful book reviews and collect exemplary reviews to use as mentor texts.

Voices of the Writer

In the writers' notebook, the writer has the luxury of experimenting with multiple voices. Writers can explore their positions or perspectives on issues or try out alternative perspectives, rehearse the voices of fictional characters, or take on the voice of a contemporary or historical person of interest; the possibilities for experimentation are endless.

In fiction books authors give characters their own distinctive voices. Sara Pennypacker endows third-grader *Clementine* (2006) with a spunky voice as she describes her "not so good of a week" (p. 1). Jack Gantos gives Joey Pigza an exuberant voice as he experiences mishaps and successes in *Joey Pigza Swallowed the Key* (1998). In her third-person narration of the Newbery-award *Criss Cross*, Lynne Rae Perkins (2005) bestows a different voice on each of her characters. Students can discuss how voice is expressed not just through the characters' words, but also in their actions, thoughts, and the reactions of others.

While we have referred to fiction books as mentor texts, we assume you recognize that every reader-engaging text (e.g., poetry, graphic novels, informational books, and biographies) can serve as mentor texts for a writer's voice. The sociocultural dimension of our communication model is probably the most challenging one for all writers, making exploratory activities useful practice zones.

Exploratory Activities

Learning to step outside our comfort zone to consider how people with different social and cultural experiences view the world or learning to take on the different voices of the content-area disciplines is not easy. You might want to try the following three journal activities to explore different voices of disciplines.

Record Conversations in the Cafeteria

Authors use dialogue to define characters and so they listen to how people talk. Recording how different people talk in natural situations gives students practice in gaining an ear for dialogue. For example, in the cafeteria, students can note who is talking and describe the person's body language as well as the words used. They can describe how the listener responds, noting the second person's body language and the words used. Do they speak in complete sentences? Do they interrupt each other? In other situations, students can also listen to how people of different ages talk and how a person talks differently in different settings or with different people. Do they use language that connects them with a specific sociocultural community? Students can work on voice while writing out conversations of real and fictionalized people.

Interview an Expert

Everyone has expertise in an area or has a particular interest or hobby; first graders are experts in everything. Students can interview each other, younger students, or a person in their neighborhood or family. Students can find out what the person is really interested in, how the expert became interested in it, why the expert finds it fascinating, what the expert is learning about it now, and what the expert wants to do in the future. Recording the expert's voice allows students to hear the language, cadence, and inflections in the expert's voice again and again.

Shift One's Perspective

Judith Viorst's poem *If I Were in Charge of the World* (1984) details changes she would like to have happen: no Mondays, no sisters, shorter basketball nets. Students can draft the changes they would make from their perspectives. Then, they can outline the changes their pets, their teachers, or that grumpy man below in the first floor apartment might make. Each activity provides students with opportunities to consider an idea from a different perspective and different voice.

Although the writing students produce for their journals is primarily for their own use, journals can also be used by teachers to help them determine student growth in world knowledge, discourse knowledge, understanding of time and space, and appreciation of variations among members of different sociocultural communities. In the next section of this chapter, we adapt the developmental continuum in Chapter 4 to journal writing.

JOURNALS IN THE CLASSROOM: A DEVELOPMENTAL CONTINUUM

In this chapter, we adapted the Developmental Continuum from Chapter 4 so that it provides specific indicators for journal writing (see Figure 5.1). You will notice that unlike the continuum in Chapter 4, this one focuses only on Producing Text. Remember journals are places to freely and fluently explore and practice the dimensions of our communication model—in other words, to produce text. No one really plans in detail what to write in journals. Writers do reread and evaluate earlier entries, but then they usually produce new entries with new thinking rather than revise the earlier entries.

Writers increasingly Monitor the purposes for writing in journals. As they become more reflective, students recognize that journals are not written for the benefit of the teacher; rather they understand that journals benefit their own learning.

When we survey World Knowledge, we see a gradual increase in amount and completeness of ideas explored in journal entries. By talking with peers or their teacher, developing writers may tell more than they've written and learn to add more to their entries. Only experienced writers make connections among prior knowledge, current learning, and past entries.

Referring to Discourse Knowledge, we know that a journal entry in mathematics will probably be organized differently than an entry in English language arts or in a science journal and will definitely contain different vocabulary. With instruction, students learn different formats for different disciplines and recognize that the content they are exploring in their journals impacts how they organize the information in the journal.

In order to be useful in a "distant" Time and Space, students' entries need to include meaningful ideas, contain relatively complete thoughts, and be written legibly enough to be easily reread. As students progress, they are more likely to reread entries for different purposes, such as to find a topic to write about, to review a writer's craft, or to examine how ideas have changed.

	Monitoring the Process	World Knowledge	Discourse Knowledge	Time and Space	Sociocultural Membership
Producing Text	**N:** Records for the teacher. Does not reflect on learning. Produces text haltingly with same tool.	**N:** Produces meager entry about an idea.	**N:** Relies on one format (e.g., a story or a list). Uses everyday vocabulary. Is unaware of writer's craft.	**N:** Writes entries that may not be decipherable later. Does not reread entries.	**N:** Uses own voice.
	D: Knows journal is to explore own ideas but still usually writes for the teacher. Needs support to reflect on learning. May produce text fluently with a variety of tools.	**D:** Generates one or two ideas in entries. Needs support to elaborate. May be able to tell more than writes.	**D:** Follows teacher's model for journal entries. Mixes everyday and content-area vocabulary. May collect writer's craft ideas if directed to.	**D:** Needs support to write complete entries that can easily be reread later. Needs teacher's encouragement to reread entries.	**D:** Experiments occasionally with another voice.
	E: Knows the journal is for one's thinking and exploring ideas. Is aware of what and how learning. Reflects on process easily. Produces text effortlessly with a variety of tools.	**E:** Explores extensively several ideas. Connects prior knowledge to newly learned ideas.	**E:** Uses teacher's model but is inventive for own purposes. Incorporates content-area vocabulary into entries easily. May add diagrams or drawings as appropriate. Practices short pieces of writer's craft (i.e., dialogue).	**E:** Periodically rereads for different purposes. Knows ideas may have changed. Searches for patterns in learning. Seeks ideas for other writing pieces.	**E:** Experiments with the voices of the disciplines.

FIGURE 5.1. Journals in the classroom: Developmental continuum.

In Sociocultural Membership, writers experiment with voices so that the differences in language, beliefs, customs, and values of the disciplines are evident in the journal entries. After they have had opportunities to develop their own voice, writers can experiment with different voices. For example, students may explore a reporter's voice for a historical event and a personal voice of a citizen living through the event.

We encourage you to think about how you might use the journal continuum in your classroom. First, you might decide that the continuum helps you anticipate what your students might do when writing in journals. The continuum may guide your thinking about particular students in the class—which students you will challenge and which students need your support. Second, you might decide to use the continuum, as Mr. Frank did, to obtain a class profile for planning future instruction in journal writing. And third, you may decide to use the continuum to help you pinpoint a student's process when that student writes in a journal. Does the student have difficulty generating ideas or transcribing words and sentences fluently? Most of all, we encourage you and your students to experiment with using journals to explore.

JOURNALS: SITES FOR PLANNING EXTENDED WRITING PIECES

Throughout this chapter, we have characterized journals as sites to explore writers' world knowledge, discourse knowledge, time and space, and sociocultural membership. Writers' explorations may remain in their journals—never refined for another audience. On the other hand, writers can use their notebooks as resources for ideas and craft when writers have purposes for communicating to an audience. Rereading entries for topics, for patterns of thoughts, or for poignant images from mentor texts, writers mine their journals when they write extended pieces.

However, you recognize that going from an idea or message to an audience beyond oneself and actually producing that text is a huge leap sometimes. Even when you have explored your world knowledge, you usually take an intermediate step—a planning strategy—before you produce a draft. But, students, especially novice writers, often jump right to producing a draft without any planning. Both novice and developing writers need teacher support to plan.

Think back to Sam, the experienced writer in Chapter 2. Using his writer's notebook as a resource, his lifeline only gave him the idea; he needed to brainstorm his world knowledge about stunt kite flying by making a list of events and then to number the events to organize the ideas—his planning strategy. While notes for every communication dimension were not written in his plan, Sam did think about the discourse of memoir, time and space distances, and sociocultural membership differences. He obviously made mental plans to address his readers' needs. You remember he did need to revert back to planning after he began to write because his text was not a clear description of stunt kites; maybe he should have written more in his plans. Brainstorming and organizing notes of main ideas in a list is a common planning strategy for many pieces.

Although writers often brainstorm lists as a planning strategy, there are many other effective strategies. Earlier in this chapter, we suggested that students interview adults in social studies in order to acquire first-person accounts from someone who has lived through a specific era or local event. In order to plan for the interviews, students would generate the questions to ask the adults and arrange them in a logical order prior to the interview. Some students might create a web, a graphic organizer, or a semantic map to arrange the questions and leave room to take notes.

As you can see, so far, we've identified two broad planning strategies:

- Brainstorming ideas and then organizing the list.
- Organizing ideas in a graphic organizer, such as a flow chart, Venn diagram, semantic map, or seasonal cycle (see Inspiration in Appendix 2.1 in Chapter 2).

In other cases, students may return to what they've begun in exploratory drafts and use one of the following planning strategies to help them think through how they will rework the exploratory draft into a more developed text for another reader or readers:

- Organize ideas by the characteristics of the genre, such as a story grammar (setting, problem, resolution) or argument (position, pros and cons).
- Outline ideas by sections or subtopics.
- Talk with peers.
- Use technology such as the manipulative outline in Draft Builder.
- Sketch, diagram, and graph information, ideas, or data.
- Record questions to research.

By completing plans in journals, students can refer to earlier entries as resources and then expand on their entries in their plans. In many plans, students primarily consider world knowledge or the topic and details to write about, and discourse knowledge or the genre they will use. We find this to be particularly true if students use graphic organizers that outline the characteristics of the genre. For some purposes and genres, students consider time and space distances in plans, for example, how and when science experiments were done. For some purposes and genres, students plan for sociocultural membership differences. For example, they may plan for differing perspectives or opinions on an issue when planning a persuasive piece. In Chapters 6 and 7, you will read how teachers support their students' planning for different purposes, audiences, and genres.

In addition to planning in journals, writers could begin to draft pieces of writing that will eventually develop into extended texts. One benefit of having students draft and revise their pieces right in their journals is that everything except the final draft is in one place. Students can draft on the right side of their journals and leave the left side for revisions (Angelillo, 1999).

Whether students use journals as resources in which to explore ideas that remain in their journals or as sites for planning and drafting longer pieces of text, their entries provide opportunities for them to practice using the dimensions of our communication model in order to more effectively communicate what they are learning about themselves and the world in which they live. Journal writing provides students with time to think, write, review their thinking, and then have thoughtful ideas to share with others (Spiegel, 1998).

CHAPTER SUMMARY

Although thinking on paper or the computer screen can take different forms, writers often use journals as a safe place to explore what they are thinking and how they are learning. In journals, students can practice producing texts fluently, without the constraints of full grammatical sentences, correct spelling, or standard punctuation. Furthermore, students can think about ideas in different ways—not just recording data but also speculating, questioning, analyzing, or consolidating their thoughts about data.

We encourage teachers to incorporate journals across the curriculum and provide opportunities for students to investigate the dimensions of our communication model. First, in every content area, students can explore the new content or world knowledge they are learning as well as how they are learning, such as new math concepts and how they solved the problems. Second, in content-area entries, students can practice the particular discourse knowledge of the discipline—genres, text organizations, and vocabulary—such as interviewing neighbors who lived during the Vietnam War for a biography. Third, students can learn the importance of noting the details of time and space in entries, such as how and when science data was collected. Fourth, students can try out the sociocultural dimension by practicing their own voices or collecting the voices used in different disciplines from mentor texts, such as the voices of fictional characters. For each of the dimensions, we suggest exploratory activities, which teachers can use to teach students to explore their ideas.

Building on the developmental continuum in Chapter 4, we discuss a specific developmental continuum for journals. While writers may think about what they will write in an entry, they really only produce text and never revise an entry; they write a new entry. Therefore, we only discuss students producing text in the continuum.

Finally, we encourage teachers and students to use journals as a site to plan and draft pieces of extended text for specific purposes and audiences. Students can mine their journal entries for worthwhile ideas, use one of the planning strategies suggested, and safely begin to produce extended pieces that may actually reach known or unknown audiences.

Writing to explore in journals is a place to safely experiment with generating and transcribing ideas into text. Before writers produce extended texts, they usually explore ideas to find a specific message and purpose, to decide upon an audience, and to choose a genre. In the next chapter, we begin discussing different genres with writing to entertain and present classroom scenarios of students who explore ideas and then write to entertain known audiences.

APPLICATION BOX

As you read this book, you probably discovered several new ideas: our communication model, the writer's cognitive processes, or the developmental continuum. We suggest that you keep a journal to explore your ideas about teaching writing as you read:

- What thoughts or reactions do the ideas in this book generate?
- How could you incorporate the ideas in this book into your classroom?
- What do you question or wonder about?
- Can you speculate about your students' processes (Chapter 2)?

- What connections can you make to the classroom characteristics we suggested that support the writer's cognitive processes (Chapter 3)?
- How might you use the overview developmental continuum in Chapter 4 or the one for journals in this chapter?
- How could you incorporate journals into your classroom (Chapter 5)?

Chapter 6

Writing to Entertain

Families have been entertaining each other since the beginning of time. Your family probably has stories that have been handed down for generations, such as the story of one author's grandma—"The day little Laura fell asleep in the strawberry patch." We tell jokes and riddles, sing songs, recount daily events and gossip, and retell TV programs. We entertain because we have a joy (or tragedy) and we want our audience to share our emotions. Usually, our early attempts to entertain occur at family or friend gatherings where we recount experiences, stories, and jokes to our known audiences. We learn to anticipate how our family and friends are similar to us: their world knowledge, their discourse knowledge, their time and space knowledge, and their sociocultural memberships. Most of us only entertain known audiences in social gatherings. However, a few of us turn class clown antics into late night TV for unknown audiences (Jay Leno) or early story attempts into a blockbuster novel read by millions of unknown readers (Dan Brown's 2003 *Da Vinci Code*). Then, anticipating the unknown audience's world knowledge, discourse knowledge, time and space differences, and sociocultural memberships is difficult. (You have likely heard a failed joke from Leno.) In this chapter, we present entertainment situations in which the audiences are familiar—peers or students within the school—because the students are learning to entertain. However, we suggest venues for unfamiliar audiences when students want that challenge.

Writing for the purpose of entertaining audiences includes three genres: (1) personal experiences, (2) fictional and imagined events, and (3) poetry. The three genres really have more than one genre. For example, you know the genre of fictional and imagined events contains many different genres, such as myths, fantasy, historical fiction, and comics. We suggest a range of genres for you and your students to explore in both reading and writing. When students are familiar with a variety of genres, then they will know which genre to choose for the specific situation they're in. In Appendix 6.1 at the end of this chapter, we list mentor texts that can serve as examples of the genres that entertain.

For each genre, we present a classroom scenario that represents how we teach writing. The teacher first recognizes when a situation occurs that provides an opportunity to teach a specific genre (Purcell-Gates et al., 2007). Second, the class reads mentor texts to explore genre characteristics either through direct teaching or through an inquiry investigation. Third, the teacher and students support each other while they plan, produce, and review (evaluate, revise, edit) their pieces. They discuss how similar their audiences are to themselves and evaluate their drafts for characteristics of the genre. And finally, the teachers observe and question students about their processes thereby noting how the students are developing as writers.

We begin this chapter with the genre of personal experiences; then, discuss the fictional or imagined events genre, and end the chapter with the poetry genre. For each genre, we:

- Introduce the genre.
- Provide genre characteristics.
- Present a classroom scenario for teaching that incorporates our communication model, supports the writer's cognitive processes, and evaluates specific text characteristics.
- Describe a developmental continuum.

As you read this chapter, we encourage you to explore the genres in the journal you began in Chapter 5. You may use the journal to explore ideas for possible drafts or find an idea that you'd like to turn into an extended piece worthy of sharing with an audience. In our classroom scenario for the personal experiences genre, you will read about a teacher sharing her writing with her fourth graders.

PERSONAL EXPERIENCES GENRE

One advantage of the personal experiences genre is that students have world knowledge—their past experiences, although their classmates may or may not have had similar experiences. Students' discourse knowledge of personal narrative may vary widely depending upon whether they have been writing personal narratives since first grade (Graves, 1983). Because the events are from the past, both reader and writer differ in time and space, requiring the writer to recreate the context for the reader. Finally, the students may come from diverse home sociocultural communities and so may be relating different experiences to their readers. While these communication differences will vary from classroom to classroom, the personal experiences genre allows us to celebrate the differences and create a classroom community.

In Table 6.1 we have brainstormed a sampling of personal experiences genres. You might want to have your class brainstorm the oral and written genres that they use and the audiences they entertain with stories from their lives. In Appendix 6.1 at the end of this chapter, we recommend mentor texts appropriate for a range of reading levels. You and your middle school students might like to read *I Thought My Father Was God* by Paul Auster (2001), a poignant collection of short memoirs written by ordinary citizens and sent into National Public Radio.

Although each genre tells about true past or present experiences in the writer's life and are written in the first person, distinctions among the genres can be confusing, especially among personal narrative, memoir, and autobiography. You may remember the scandal of *A Million Little Pieces* by James Frey (2003) that was billed as a memoir but turned out to be fiction. Since definitions differ, we offer you our definitions:

- Personal narrative—story about one past or recent event in one's life.
- Memoir—story about one significant past event in which the writer reflects on the meaning of the event from the perspective of a later time.
- Autobiography—story of a series of events from one's entire life or from a segment of one's life, such as childhood.
- Diary—commentary on personal events and relationships and one's reaction to them, often an emotional reaction.
- Family stories—story about family member(s) or event(s).

We teach personal narratives and memoirs together because students may not have the perspective to reflect on events in their lives. Yet, some students might reflect on the meaning of the experience (Daiute, 2000). You recall Sam in Chapter 2 who began writing about kite events with his dad—a personal narrative—until his teacher asked him "Is this a story about kites or your relationship with your dad?" Then, he revised

---

TABLE 6.1. Sampling of Personal Experiences Genres

- Personal narrative
- Memoir
- Autobiography
- Diary
- Family stories
- Personal letters, pen-pal letters, greeting cards
- E-mails, text messages

his piece into a memoir about the significance of kite flying with his dad.

A variation of personal narratives is the telling or writing of family stories. In a bilingual classroom, students interviewed parents, composed, and reviewed their stories to publish an English and Spanish family storybook (Dworin, 2006). A national project to collect family stories is StoryCorps, modeled after the 1930s Works Progress Administration that employed people to collect oral histories from ordinary people, for example, accounts of former slaves. Anyone can make an appointment to record a family story when one of the mobile booths comes to his or her town or request the Door-to-Door or Outpost options to record a memory. If asked, trained facilitators can assist people in recording their memories. In 2006, StoryCorp launched the StoryCorp Griot Initiative to collect interviews from African American citizens, especially those who have lived during World War II and the Civil Rights era. You and your students might want to investigate the website of StoryCorps (*www.storycorps.net*) to listen to the ordinary people tell their family stories and memories.

Audiences for the personal experiences genres usually begin with oneself (diary) or friends, schoolmates, and family. However, we encourage students to write for unknown audiences, too. Magazines such as *Ink Blot* and *Stone Soup* accept personal narratives from students (Rubenstein, 1998). Some town newspapers occasionally have special sections in which they publish students' personal narratives.

Now let's turn to a classroom scenario in order to show how we teach not only personal narrative and memoir but how we teach all genres. We begin each genre with a section describing how teachers prepare to teach and then detail how students and their teacher explore ideas, plan, produce, and review their texts. As you read, notice the classroom characteristics discussed in Chapter 3: (1) explicit teaching, guided practice, and independent application, and (2) the inclusion of our communication model.

Classroom Scenario: Personal Narrative and Memoir

Ms. Alverez considers classroom situations, purposes, and audiences that are appropriate for the genre (Purcell-Gates et al., 2007). She teaches personal narrative and memoir in September because each September students are thrust into new classroom situations in which they may not know everyone. Sharing important personal events or family stories will acquaint or reacquaint students with each other. Furthermore, since Ms. Alverez is also writing about a personal event, everyone is learning about everyone else—becoming a familiar audience. Therefore, her purpose is not just to entertain classmates, but also to build a sense of community among her fourth graders. She aims for the fourth graders to write about one event that is important to them and that they are willing to share with classmates.

Preparing to Teach

Ms. Alverez collects mentor texts to read aloud to students and for them to read themselves. She reads several herself to ensure she understands the characteristics used in the personal narrative/memoir genres.

Supporting Students' Exploring Ideas

Assuming that the genre is unfamiliar to the students or at most ill defined, Ms. Alverez reads a mentor text aloud. In addition, the students choose mentor texts to read independently. She directs the students to notice how the memoirs are different from other books they have read so that they can discover the characteristics of the genre.

While they read mentor texts, the class gradually identifies characteristics of the genre:

- Focuses on one important and real, not imaginary, event.
- Focuses on one event per chapter if writing about a time period, like childhood.
- Uses "I."
- Describes the event with many details.
- May include a picture to accompany the event.

In addition, occasionally a student recalls an event from a fiction book by Roald Dahl, for example, that is similar to an event in his personal narrative, *Boy: Tales of Childhood* (1986).

While the class continues to read, Ms. Alverez and the students begin to explore their own lives. Ms. Alverez has the students compose a lifeline of positive and negative events, people, and places that they had experienced in their lives (Rief, 1992). She models her lifeline so students can see how to set up the lifeline and the types of events she includes. Students talk with each other about events, helping their neighbors to remember more incidents (see Lucy's lifeline in Figure 6.1). Ms. Alverez encourages students to share their lifelines with their families to help them remember events they might want to add.

Supporting Students' Planning

After three days of exploring ideas in their lifelines, Ms. Alverez asks the students to choose one or two events that are important to them

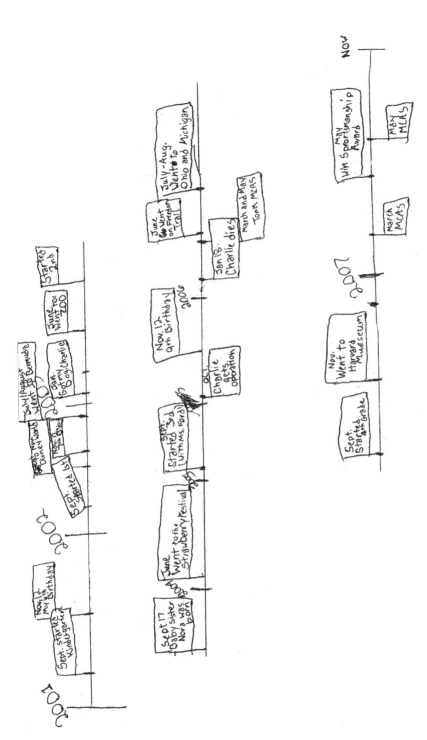

FIGURE 6.1. Lucy's lifeline.

and tell them to a partner. Then, Ms. Alverez first shares her childhood lifeline from age 3 to 14 years old and then shows her brainstorming web where she has written details only about second-grade
events. Using her brainstorming web, she asks the class to think about
her audience—"What do you, my students, need to know?" Everyone
remembers their second-grade experiences: learning to read, playing at
recess, doing phonics, and math work (world knowledge). They remark
that not all them had the same teacher or even went to the same school.
Since the students are her audience and they were not with her when
she was a second grader, she tells them she will need to describe her
second-grade experience (time and space). She also reminds them that
they know what memoirs are like because they've been reading them
(discourse knowledge). Finally, Ms. Alverez tells them that she will try
to write as the shy, little second grader she was (sociocultural membership).

Next, she asks them to brainstorm on a web all they remember
about one event in their lives—the people, the place, what happened.
Ms. Alverez circulates to observe students' lifelines and webs noting who
has focused on an important event. Stopping by students with few events
on their lifelines, she asks questions about the events they have and suggests other events to think about adding.

Supporting Students' Producing Text

While the class continues to read and discuss mentor texts, Ms. Alverez
explains how she produces her text from her brainstorming web. She
explains that she reread items, thought about how she might arrange
them, and numbered the items so she'll remember how she wants to
sequence them. She explains that the better organized her notes are
before she begins to write, the easier writing a draft might be. She deliberately includes everything she can remember about the event, producing an unfocused draft with some editing errors. Both the unfocused
text and the errors in conventions will become teaching points in a few
days when students review her text.

After Ms. Alverez models, the students begin producing their texts
referring to their brainstorming webs and conferring with partners. Ms.
Alverez circulates to prod, encourage, and question students, noting
who needs to plan more or has no plan, who are beginning new events
not on their plans, and who actually are producing text. She interviews
those students still planning and the two who have changed their events.
She just observes the students producing texts—not wanting to interrupt their processes—but notices whether they pause, reread, refer to
plans, or stare into space.

Supporting Students' Reviewing

EVALUATING

When a critical number of students are ready to review their texts, the teacher asks students to evaluate her text (see Figure 6.2). First, the students react to the event. They want to know why Ms. Alverez didn't hear the bell; why she was scared to go in; what she was doing on the playground; what are saddle shoes. When recess tales began to spread, Ms. Alverez asks the students what the purpose of her piece is—to tell an entertaining story about an important event—and who the audience is—the students in our classroom.

Second, Ms. Alverez prompts the students' evaluation by asking a series of questions: What is the main event? Which details help describe that event? Are there confusing details or extra events that confused them when they read? Does it sound like me as a little, shy girl?

At the end of the discussion, the teacher summarizes their evaluation on a chart by turning their comments into specific characteristics that fit what writers need to communicate with readers.

- Purpose and audience—to entertain classmates.
- Focus on one real and important event (world knowledge).
- Use specific, elaborate details (world knowledge).

MRS GUY

Second grade was Mrs. Guy and my goal was to do well. However, my mother's goal was to make ti through without too much damage, if that was possible. As she was the only parent who voted against homework, Mom had her doubts.

Mrs. Guy was large and wide, a square shaped teacher. Her straight black hair reflected her squre body as it was divided into two sections with a part forehead to nape and redivided into four by the intersection of braids piled form ear to ear.

Square with sharp corners -- that was Mrs. Guy. Not round and comfortable like Gram.

One day, I guess I didn't hear the recess bell. Anyway, I looked around the playground for my friends and classmates. ONLY BIG KIDS! Uh-ohh! Mrs. Guy! Sharp, square, Mrs. Guy.

Through the shorts and noise of the playground I dashed and scampered up the stairs to the school door. Heaving open the door, the dim silent hall stretched out before me. Doors to classrooms were tightly shut. Silence. As softly as hard soled saddle shoes allowed, I walked down the length of the hall to Mrs. Guy's room.

There, I stopped. . . . Did I wish school was over….that I could go home? Probably but to do well, I knew I had to go in that classroom. Everyone was IN….except me. How could I get in?

Turning the knob softly, I pulled oopen the door, as Mrs. Guy glanced up from Story Hour. On tiptoe, I shrank down the row to my seat and slipped out of my coat as I sat down. Mrs. Guy continued readig; the kids looked and then continued listening; I sank into my desk and the story, leaning on one arm.

Survival. Escaping back into the unnoticed.

Comment: Are these details important?

Comment: Do you see what she looked like?

Comment: Why didn't you hear the bell? What were you doing at recess? Didn't the teacher miss you?

Comment: Is this the main event?

Comment: What details are in this paragraph? Do the details describe?

FIGURE 6.2. "Mrs. Guy."

- Cut extra or confusing events or details (world knowledge).
- Decide how to sequence the event—begin at the beginning or an exciting part (discourse knowledge).
- Use "I" or tell from your point of view (discourse knowledge and sociocultural membership).
- Describe when and where (time and space).
- Sound like yourself—voice (sociocultural membership).

She asks the students to evaluate their partner's drafts for both what is working and for what needs revising by thinking about these characteristics. She often passes out sticky notes, on which students jot key ideas generated in these peer conferences. As she circulates, she prods and encourages students to produce texts, to evaluate their texts, and to move into revision.

Lucy meets with her neighbor, Beth, to evaluate her text using the characteristics listed on the chart. Lucy first states that she chose to write about Charly because her dog was really special and she wanted to entertain her classmates with her story of him. Lucy and Beth quietly read her story and then evaluate it (see Figure 6.3).

REVISING AND EDITING

Once again Ms. Alverez models revision by having students compare her previous draft with her revised text (see Figure 6.4). Immediately, the students notice the title change and that Ms. Alverez cut out some events. They could picture standing alone in that hall and could hear the hard saddle shoes. They like the new word, *taptoe*, because it fits hard shoes. They also notice Ms. Alverez did not use full sentences ("Only Big Kids," "Silence"), speculate why she did that, and wonder if it is allowed (sentence structure). Finally, Ms. Alverez asks them to point out words (like *clambered* and *taptoe*) that appeal to their senses (word choice).

After their discussion of her memoir, Ms. Alverez asks them to revise by concentrating on describing one main event, by cutting events or details not important to the main event, and by choosing words that appeal to their senses and that sound like themselves.

Lucy and Beth decide to cut the part about the burned house, but Lucy wants to keep the background information. They also cut the first mention of moans and keep it only in the epilogue. They work hard on editing, especially the spelling errors. They rely on the classroom word wall and their online dictionaries to check the spelling of several words. Lucy recognizes she doesn't have paragraphs but she decides to make a book. What would be paragraphs will become pages in the book. Lucy also revises the title from "Charly" to "The Way She Smiled" because that's how she remembers Charly (see Figure 6.5).

Charly

I mournfully waved good bye to the car like I was never going to see it again. It wasn't the car I was upset about, it was the dog inside it. The thought of death and bitterness was the only thing on my mind. Charly, I looked up to, with out her I would be tworn in two. The only benefit is that I woudn't have to walk her. Otherwise, my life plot would be effected. Fortunatly God made friends to cheer me up. Even death couldn't break love I knew. The whole reason why she was going to the vet is that Charly had a tooth problem. All I know is that if got into her blood stream and traveled to her heart she would die for sure. So now she was stuck in this toothpulling mess. Mom and I knew that she would be strong enough to survive the anaasteisia but I still was worried about the fact she could die. Let me give you some backround on this poor little dog. Margaret picked Charly up one day at the pound. She took Charly home and fed her a feast of meet and other foods. Most of their meals were feasts. One sad day, Margaret died. Mr. Cahil, my uncle, took her in around November. As a late Christmas gift, charly was a new member of the family. Nearly three years had passed since then. In that time Charly's old house burned down. I wonder what they are they are doing to her. I imagine Charly looking at the fluid tubes and fainting. Her tasting the anestesia it looked like she was choking. The operation was nasty. Ten bloody teeth were on the table. I am sure Charly rested until her heroes came to fetch her. My stomach jumped up and down when the vet said charly could be nautious. Charly was land after a hurricane. Bandages over her legs and blood covered her mouth. Her hair was going in different directions like fallen down trees. Charly's soul was deep down in her legs and was buried in fear and pain. I hope that a sea full of tears was not behind my eyes. Mom scooped up Charly and walked out the door. I had to carry special dog Chicken flavored toothpaste. I know that sounds crazy but it is true. Charly is like an imagrant coming to America after a rough trip. Every stop, bump, and crosswalk Charly seemed to slip. I am wondering how the vets took her teeth out without taking all of them. Here we go again. Another stop means another slip. Charly limped into the kitchen as if she had broke her legs. She collapsed on her bed. I took the blankets from the living room and toppled them on Charly. In some way she smiled. "Thank you!" She seemed to say. That was nothing compared to the moans and shieks that woke me.

Epilogue

Charly, unfortunetly did not feel better. She moaned and shrieked that night. Her teeth were better but she was not herself again. She died January 18, 2006.

Comment: this is a story about Charly, my dog, and how I felt about him .

Comment: Wow! What a neat opening! You really showed how worried you were.

Comment: Who is Margaret?

Comment: Do you really need this background information? What does the old burned house have to do with the story?

Comment: I like how you compared Charly to the land after a hurricane.

Comment: Sea full of tears really shows how you felt.

Comment: I like how you compare Charly to an immigrant. What's that called? Oh yeah, a metaphor.

Comment: Do you want to tell about the moans here? You tell about them in the epilogue. I think it fits better there.

Comment: I am sorry Charly died. You must miss her.

FIGURE 6.3. "Charly."

Ms. Alverez observes what the partners are revising and editing. Some, like Lucy and Beth, are concentrating on the focus and details in their memoirs. While most have written about a focused, important event, she encourages seven students to revise their details by including Snapshots (Lane, 1992)—physical details that authors might see if they had taken photographs of the scenes they are describing. She also reminds three students of the mini-lesson she did on *Show, Don't Tell* (see Chapter 9). Because two sets of partners are only editing (not revising), she rereads their pieces with them and asks questions about the events encouraging them to make content changes.

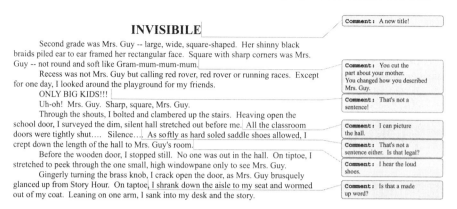

FIGURE 6.4. "Invisible."

While Lucy is a competent fourth-grade writer, not all memoir writers are. Now let's turn to a developmental continuum for personal narratives and memoirs that describes writing growth for diverse writers.

Personal Narratives and Memoirs in the Classroom: Developmental Continuum

Building on the developmental continuum in Chapter 4, we now present a specific developmental continuum for personal narratives and memoirs (Figure 6.6). Remember that students may not consistently exhibit novice, developing, or experienced descriptors. Students could be experienced in relating their personal experiences (world knowledge) and developing in using their personal voices (sociocultural membership).

Reading down the first column, *Monitoring the Process*, through planning, producing, and reviewing, you recognize the progression of novice, developing, and experienced writers as they become increasingly more metacognitively aware of their writing processes. As writers develop their ability to monitor their personal narratives, they think about events important to their lives, and with teacher support, reflect on the significance of the events as they plan, produce text, and review their work.

As you survey the *World Knowledge* column, you will notice how the writers' awareness of the purpose is evident in the world knowledge they plan, produce, and review. Novice writers produce unfocused texts with gaps in information. Developing writers focus on a main event but need support in adding and cutting details. Throughout the processes, expe-

The Way She Smiled

I mournfully waved good bye to the car like I was never was going to see it again. It wasn't the car I was upset about, it was the dog inside it. The thought of death and bitterness was the only thing on my mind. Charly I looked up to, with out her my life would be torn into two. The only benefit was I wouldn't have to walk her. Otherwise, my life plot would be effected.

FIGURE 6.5. "The Way She Smiled."

rienced writers focus on the importance of their events, considering the usefulness of details to their texts.

Looking down the *Discourse Knowledge* column, you will notice how awareness of the purpose of memoirs is exhibited in writers' knowledge about the genre. Novice writers' understanding of discourse may be reflected in the bed-to-bed structure (Graves, 1983) they use, in which each subevent in the experience from the initial event to the very last event, is given equal emphasis. As developing writers progress, they learn to focus on main events. They may organize their texts sequentially and try to make their descriptions interesting. As they continue to

(text resumes on page 111)

	Monitoring the Process	World Knowledge	Discourse Knowledge	Time and Space	Sociocultural Membership
Planning	**N:** Knows to tell about real-life experiences. Does not think about audience. Does not plan. Reads mentor texts if assigned. **D:** Knows purpose to tell about real-life experience. Has a vague awareness of audience. Needs teacher support to plan. May think about assigned mentor texts read. **E:** Monitors plans for purpose—to show reader an important experience. Keeps audience in back of his or her mind. Knows the benefits of plans. Recalls mentor texts and may skim again.	**N:** Chooses large event from life (e.g., summer trip). **D:** Uses brainstorming to select main event (e.g., moose in Yellowstone's mud pots event of summer trip). May brainstorm details. **E:** Brainstorms to find an important event from life. Plans details and subevents to support important event.	**N:** Thinks of large event as unbroken unit. May leave gaps between events. **D:** Knows to emphasize one main event. May plan details or events to support main event. **E:** Knows to emphasize one important event. Plans what sequence to use in retelling of event (e.g., start in the middle). May reflect on the significance of the event.	**N:** Assumes setting of events known. **D:** Is aware audience did not experience event. May plan setting. **E:** Includes where and when event occurred in plans.	**N:** Is unaware of own personal voice. **D:** Does not think about personal voice. **E:** Is aware needs to use own personal voice.

Producing Text	N: Thinks about what to write next. May write haltingly always with same tool. D: May or may not refer back to plan. May write fluently with different tools. May monitor writing for appeal to peers. E: Refers back to plan consistently. Considers if need to change plans. Writes fluently. Monitors draft for appeal to reader.	N: Writes what first comes to mind. D: Writes all remembers about the main event but details are incomplete. E: Selects relevant details from plan to develop main event.	N: Writes a bed-to-bed story. Does not focus on one main event. D: Focuses on one main event. Follows sequence of event but may have gaps. Writes interesting words as thinks of them. E: Elaborates on important event. May alter sequence of event for reader interest. Tries to show (not tell) using descriptive words.	N: May tell age and location (I was 6 years old. This summer . . .). D: Writes details of the setting in beginning. E: Weaves in setting details.	N: Concentrates only on own experience. May or may not sound like himself or herself. D: Considers what interesting to self. Writes in oral language voice. E: Considers what's important and interesting to reader. Tries to show own personality in voice.

(continued)

FIGURE 6.6. Personal narratives and memoirs in the classroom: Developmental continuum.

	Monitoring the Process	World Knowledge	Discourse Knowledge	Time and Space	Sociocultural Membership
Reviewing	**N:** Knows purpose to tell about own life. Does not understand the need to reread, evaluate, or revise for purpose and audience. Thinks first draft is final draft.	**N:** Does not recognize gaps or unnecessary details.	**N:** Does not evaluate or revise to focus on main event. Keeps series of equal subevents. May make small changes in words and conventions (spelling, punctuation, grammar).	**N:** Does not reread to evaluate or revise setting.	**N:** Assumes reader has had similar experiences. Uses own voice.
	D: Knows purpose to tell about a main event in life. May reread focusing primarily on conventions. Needs support to evaluate for purpose and audience. Monitors for peer's interest. May refer to mentor texts if reminded. Knows first draft needs reviewing.	**D:** Needs support for both adding elaborative details and cutting details that clutter.	**D:** Needs support to evaluate and revise focus on main event. May tell how felt during event. Uses support to include descriptive words. May make changes to conventions.	**D:** Needs support to evaluate and revise for interesting setting details.	**D:** Needs support to consider reader's viewpoint. Keeps own voice.
	E: Thinks about purpose to tell about an important event in life. Rereads to evaluate draft for focus on important event. Assesses revisions needed for reader. May reflect with teacher support on the emotional truth or significance of event. Refers to mentor texts for craft, as needed.	**E:** Evaluates how details contribute or detract from describing event and its importance. Revises by adding and cutting information to convey message.	**E:** Evaluates and revises the focus and sequence of events. Revises to show the significance of event, with teacher support. Revises words to show (not tell) event and feelings, with teacher support. Edits conventions as needed.	**E:** Seeks advice to evaluate on whether setting details clutter or enhance focus. Revises setting as needed.	**E:** Tries to evaluate how draft shows his or her viewpoint, yet also accounts for reader's potential differences, with teacher support. Evaluates and revises own voice to show personality, with teacher support.

FIGURE 6.6. *(continued)*

learn, they hone the focus, may change the sequence, try to show (not tell) events and feelings, and reflect on the significance of the event.

In the *Time and Space* column, you'll notice the similarity to the developmental continuum in Chapter 4. Gradually, writers include details about the setting for their experiences. Experienced writers may gracefully interweave setting information but also know to evaluate whether contextual details clutter or enhance the foci of their texts.

Considering *Sociocultural Membership* for personal narratives and memoirs, you know the voice in the piece should sound like the writer's and present the writer's view of the experience. In early stages of development, writers may either use their oral language or sound flat and not like themselves. As they progress, they plan, produce text, and revise so their personality is evident, especially in their use of dialogue. They also write to show their viewpoints and feelings instead of telling ("I mournfully waved" in "Charly" vs. "I was sad").

Again, we encourage you to think about how you might use the specific continuum in your classroom. First, you might decide that the continuum helps you anticipate what behaviors your students might exhibit when writing the genres, especially if you have not taught a genre before. Second, you might decide to use the continuum, like Mr. Frank, to obtain a class profile to plan future instruction in that genre. And third, you may decide to use the continuum to help you investigate one student's process when that student writes either on one or several genres.

We encourage you to begin the year with personal narratives; you will learn about the students who inhabit your classroom and so will they. Now, we turn to our second genre—fictional and imagined events. We describe that genre and its general characteristics first.

FICTION AND IMAGINED EVENTS GENRE

Fiction is very difficult to write well. Yet, when well written, we are drawn to fiction's universal human themes—comic and tragic, although few of us ever attempt writing it. Probably because parents, teachers, and librarians read more fiction than nonfiction to them (Duke, 2000), young children distinguish stories from informational books and can tell characteristics of stories, such as once upon a time, fake or made up, and lived happily ever after (Smolkin & Donovan, 2004).

You know that the genre of fictional and imagined events contains many members. In Table 6.2, we have listed a sampling of the genres. Some students may have read widely in a particular genre and know favorite authors of that genre. A few may have sampled the variety of genres. Research on girls' and boys' reading preferences is inconclusive:

TABLE 6.2. Sampling of Fiction and Imagined Events Genre

- Realistic story
- Fantasy
- Adventure, mystery, quest stories
- Picture-book story
- Graphic novels, comic strips, cartoons
- Science fiction
- Historical fiction, stories, interviews, role plays, character sketches
- Plays, radio scripts
- Myths, folktales, tall tales, fables, fairytales

no difference in preferences (Strum, 2003), boys prefer informational and girls realistic fiction (Coles & Hall, 2002), girls prefer realistic fiction and boys fantasy (Boraks, Hoffman, & Bauer, 1997).

In contrast, researchers investigating students' writing topics have found gender preferences (Fleming, 1995; Graves, 1975; Newkirk, 2002, 2004; Peterson, 2000, 2006). Girls write about immediate experiences, do not include violence or action, have both powerful and powerless girl characters, and may include boy characters. On the other hand, boys write about events beyond their experiences (aliens, inventions), include violence and action (Anderson, 2003), have powerful boy characters, and do not include girls. Now, you know gender statements are broad generalizations and you will find individuals who do not conform. As a teacher, you will want to discover your students' preferences so that you can introduce them to other genres or build upon their knowledge of a particular genre when they write. We have listed only a sampling of the many fiction and imagined events books that could serve as mentor texts in Appendix 6.1 of this chapter.

You recognize the common characteristics of fiction stories and may know the term, *story grammar* (Stein & Glenn, 1979), used to refer to those characteristics:

- Setting.
- Characters—main character(s), opposing character(s), minor character(s).
- Problem, goal, or quest.
- Series of events—often three events.
  - Action among characters as main character attempts to resolve problem or achieve goal but is thwarted by opposing character(s).
  - Dialogue among characters.
- Outcome or resolution—problem solved, outcome achieved, home returned to safely.

Many young students include characteristics of the story grammar in their oral and written stories because they have been read to as young children (Rentel & King, 1983). However, students from diverse backgrounds may bring different story grammars. For example, Arapaho students may not end their stories because they will be continued the next night—a serial pattern (Delpit, 1995). When students read mentor texts and write fiction, we investigate and discuss the characteristics with students.

Fiction writing does not need to be the typical story outlined in the story grammar; other options can be offered to students. For example, in every culture, myths explain the origin of the world and natural phenomena (see Virginia Hamilton's [1988] *In the Beginning: Creation Stories from Around the World*). While the Greek and Roman myths may be familiar to many teachers, Native Americans have creation myths, trickster tales, and how-and-why tales, for example. Students could compare myths and tales across several cultures or the same tale retold in many cultures, for example, the Cinderella story (see e.g., Ai-Ling Louie's [1982] *Yeh-Shen, A Cinderella Tale from China,* and John Steptoe's [1987] *Mufaro's Beautiful Daughters: An African Tale*). Students could write their own sociocultural versions of tales, like Stone's (2005) students did by changing the Cinderella setting (a prom), characters (DJ as the prince, angel as godmother, limo for a pumpkin), and dialogue (their oral language) or like Weih's (2005) students, who produce hybrid Native American tales weaving their own cultural experiences into the genre's characteristics.

Another option is telling the tale from the perspective of another character in the story. An engaging tale told from a different character's perspective is Jon Scieszka's (1989) *The True Story of the 3 Little Pigs as Told by A. Wolf.* Or students could take the perspective of an ordinary citizen or fictional character participating in historical or scientific events. Robert Lawson (1939) creates a fictional mouse who tells how he was crucial to Ben Franklin's inventions in *Ben and Me: A New and Astonishing Life of Benjamin Franklin as Written by His Good Mouse Amos.*

Audiences for students' fiction writing can range from the familiar to the unknown. Students enjoy writing stories for each other, often using their friends' names for characters. Writing and illustrating picture books for younger students is another common, familiar audience for students. Once again, we encourage you to search for unknown audiences for your students. Local town newspapers may occasionally have a featured section for student writing. If your town newspaper doesn't feature student writing, you might suggest it to the editor. Many magazines accept fiction by students. In addition to the previously cited magazines, *Merlyn's Pen* and *Skylark* are among the magazines that publish fiction by students (Rubenstein, 1998). And then think about creating a website, adding to your school's website, or visiting existing sites on the Internet. For example, the website fanfiction (*www.fanfiction.net*) is an archive of new stories or sequels based upon the characters and plots of books (such as Harry Potter sequels), video games, or movies. Fans post their new fictions, ask for help in revising, and accept constructive reviews by others (Black, 2005, 2008).

Authors will tell you that reading mentor texts is important to their writing. Students are no different; they will write what they are reading, viewing, or playing, borrowing characters, events, and language from the mentor texts for their writing (Bearse, 1992; Cairney, 1990). However, fiction books are not the only mentor texts for our students; the popular culture holds sway over their ideas—movies, TV programs, and video games, for example. Students, who are reluctant to read the books from our libraries, may be actively reading other genres, such as magazines (Smith & Wilhelm, 2002; Worthy, 1998). For the classroom scenario, we chose one of the popular culture genres—graphic novels. You might want to peruse your local bookstore to see the shelves of graphic novels, especially manga. To begin the classroom scenario, we first describe graphic novels and then present teaching graphic novels to a small group of students.

Classroom Scenario: Imagined Events in Graphic Novels

Since graphic novels are new to many teachers, we describe the genre before we describe the classroom scenario.

Introduction to the Graphic Novel Genre

Graphic novels and comics are categorized as "sequential art": text and art in panels differing only in length (Brenner, 2006). Based in the Japanese culture, *manga* (Japanese for "amusing drawings") has been translated into English but retains Japanese characteristics, such as back-to-front and right-to-left directions and variations in fonts and panel size. American versions of manga usually have front-to-back and left-to-right directionality. Graphic novels and comics are becoming increasingly popular: 2,685 published in 2006 for an estimated sale of $333 million (*Publisher's Weekly*, 2007).

Graphic novels are written for different audiences (for different ages, for boys or for girls, for different sociocultures). Defined more by format than genre, superhero fiction and fantasy genres dominate, although graphic novels are also in the nonfiction, memoir, and historical fiction genres (Brenner, 2006). You may have heard about Art

Speigelman's (1997) *Maus: A Survivor's Tale* that depicts his father's experiences in the Holocaust and his own coming to terms with those experiences. Maybe you have seen *The 9/11 Report: A Graphic Adaptation* by Sid Jacobson and Ernie Colón (2006) that is a riveting, readable version of the Commission's report.

The interplay between the drawings and the text involves the reader differently than straight prose does. Manga stories may have nonlinear plots or subplots, characters that transform in gender and species, and martial arts, swordplay, or physical fights. (Schwartz & Rubinstein-Avila, 2006). Since manga are written for a specific gender and particular ages, attention to the book's recommendations is needed to avoid age-inappropriate content (Brenner, 2006). For example, Japanese manga for adolescents contains violence and nudity but not sexual activity. Teachers need to consider their students' age and experiences with violence before introducing graphic novels about imagined events into their classrooms. Comic books or nonfiction graphic novels may be more appropriate for some classrooms.

Preparing to Teach

Ms. Adelizzi notices that a small group of her sixth graders are huddled around a book during downtime in class. The boys have been passing graphic novels around, starting a new one as soon as the last one was read. Curious, Ms. Adelizzi asks the boys to bring in the graphic novels they're reading. After school, she visits her local librarian and bookstore owner to learn about graphic novels. At home, she Googled "graphic novels" to find additional information.

Supporting Students' Exploring Ideas

When the boys bring in several graphic novels, Ms. Adelizzi calls them together to discuss what they like about the books. The boys quickly point to the drawings depicting characters in action. She worries about the violent fighting but the boys respond that it's a story—not the news. They also point out the character's quest and the supernatural powers. As they read, Ms. Adelizzi notices that their eyes dart from the drawings to the written dialogue and that they spend more viewing time on the drawings than the text. She also notices that when they turn a page, they survey the whole page, then proceed to the drawings in the panels, and lastly read the text. She concludes the boys have adopted different reading strategies for these books. When Ms. Adelizzi offers the boys the opportunity to write their own graphic novels, they excitedly accept.

Supporting Students' Planning

As a first step, she asks the boys to draw their main character and to think about who is an enemy and what the problem or goal might be. She leaves the boys to their drawings and their discussions of possible characters.

The next day, Ms. Adelizzi asks the boys to recall the story grammar outline they have used when reading stories: setting, characters, problem or goal, events or conflicts, resolution. Using a worksheet, each boy plans his main character, enemy, and problem. They do not outline events that might occur; instead, they finish their character drawings.

Supporting Students' Producing Text

Convening the group on a subsequent day, Ms. Adelizzi brings out a large, blank monthly desk calendar and gives each boy a sheet. They discuss the uniformity of the squares and whether they will change the sizes, putting four together to form a larger box or two together for a vertical box. However, when the boys start drawing, they stay within the calendar's box size.

As they draw, their settings and plot events emerge. Like graphic novels, text is a minor feature occurring primarily in dialogue between characters. Every so often, each boy shares his emerging story with the others, demonstrating he knows his purpose and audience: to entertain his classmates.

Ms. Adelizzi observes that the boys' plans had no events and that they are formulating the events as they draw—a what-next strategy. She wonders if she should ask them to return to planning but decides to discuss characters and events when they evaluate their drafts. She considers this project to be an inquiry through which she will learn what she needs to teach when the class writes fiction.

Supporting Students' Reviewing

EVALUATING

Looking over the boys' shoulders, Ms. Adelizzi asks each boy to tell his story because without their oral versions she is unsure who the characters are. Going first, Bobby recounts that after the hero's plane is shot down by Tikkis, a fight ensues and a many-headed monster joins the battle. Ms. Adelizzi asks why they were fighting and Bobby replies they are enemies. When Ms. Adelizzi also asks why the monster is in the story, Bobby says he is in the fight. Ms. Adelizzi recognizes that Bobby has drawn a typical fight story that stops with "Episode 1 To Be Continued" (see Figure 6.7).

FIGURE 6.7. Fight scenes from Bobby's graphic novel.

Next, Andy states that in his story, Santa's evil twin has captured the hero, Rob, who is now escaping. When asked why Rob was captured, Andy states Santa's twin is evil. Andy's story ends with Rob's escape and return to the North Pole in time to help Good Santa deliver presents. Ms. Adelizzi notices that Andy has more elaborate drawings than Bobby. Furthermore, Andy's plot contains an ending, although the central problem is unclear (see Figure 6.8).

Thinking about both Bobby's and Andy's stories, Ms. Adelizzi recognizes that neither hero had any real motive. She also notes that she

FIGURE 6.8. Excerpts from Andy's graphic novel.

did not ask the boys to think about motive—a topic for future mini-lessons.

In contrast to Bobby's and Andy's characters, Yan drew a manga character in a warrior's outfit, although he gave his character an American name—Brian. Telling his story, Yan relates, "Brian discovers his parents are kidnapped. He is told to put on a necklace that is an ancestor who talks in his head. The ancestor tells Brian he must kill the Trion to free his parents, who are the guardians of the sacred. Brian learns that Trion wants the sacred because if you have the sacred, you have unlimited power."

The boys are fascinated by Yan's story. Ms. Adelizzi asks the boys to identify the characteristics of manga: the drawing style, the necklace turning into an ancestor, the evil enemy, the sword fighting. When Ms. Adelizzi asked why Brian and Trion were fighting, the boys knew the fight was not just to free the parents but also to keep the sacred or power in the hands of good. However, Ms. Adelizzi notices that although the Trion is killed, Yan wrote a formulaic ending in which his character woke up from a dream (a *deus ex machina* ending, meaning "the gods intervene") rather than a true resolution to the plot. She wonders if he felt rushed because the other boys had finished earlier than he (see Figure 6.9). She also wonders whether the boys have a repertoire of conclusion strategies to call upon. She decides that next week she'll have students investigate how authors resolve their plots in the fiction they are reading.

Ms. Adelizzi noted that Yan's graphic novel incorporated the dimensions of our communication model:

- He created a believable fantasy world (world knowledge).
- He portrayed characters, problem, events, and ending, as well as manga characteristics (discourse knowledge).
- He drew the two settings (time and space).
- He drew a manga character and symbols and adopted the voice of the warrior (sociocultural membership).

REVISING AND EDITING

None of the boys were interested in revising their first story. While Bobby chose not to revise his Episode 1, his Episode 2 had a clearer setting and a problem emanating from the characters. Andy passed and went back to reading manga. Yan edited spelling, added details to the drawings in a few panels, started reading another manga book, and thought about a new story. Since Ms. Adelizzi approached the graphic novel writing as an inquiry on her part, she did not require the boys to revise their graphic stories. She learned that the boys needed to read more graphic novels

(continued)

FIGURE 6.9. Excerpts from Yan's manga, "The Problem": Manga elements, fight, and ending.

FIGURE 6.9. *(continued)*

and needed more discussion about the characteristics in those mentor texts. She also noted she needs to teach about character motive. She is already thinking about how she'll do this and has decided to collect stories from the local newspaper. Articles about local events and sports stories might provide some fodder for interesting discussions about why people act the way they do. Although the motives might not be evident, Ms. Adelizzi and her students can talk about possible motives. Finally, she needs to plan mini-lessons on how to end fiction (Murphy, 2003).

Since we figure the boys were also playing video games, we might suggest using those characters with their distinct powers and those alternative plot twists to gain levels as a basis for their drawing and writing (Ranker, 2006). We think students could create new fan fiction by creating graphic novels based on video games. Both video games and graphic novels represent visual literacy that students are engaged in out of school and that can be incorporated into in-school literacy.

As we present the developmental continuum for fiction and imaginary events next, remember the range of stories that Bobby, Andy, and Yan produced.

Fictional and Imaginary Events in the Classroom: Developmental Continuum

Some students really enjoy reading the various genres of fiction, but rarely do they recognize how difficult writing good fiction is. Bobby just enjoyed creating one fight scene after another. Andy recognized that his Santa story did not match the quality of the fiction he was reading. Only Yan included some characteristics of manga probably because he has read more manga than the other boys in the group. As you survey the developmental continuum (Figure 6.10), keep the three boys in mind. How would you place them on the continuum?

You will find the *Monitoring the Process* column for fiction to be similar to the one for personal narrative/memoir. Although all writers know the purpose is to tell a story they've invented in their minds, they increasingly monitor how they plan, produce texts, and revise while thinking about their readers.

Writers of fiction create worlds that, whether realistic or imaginary, readers buy into and find believable. They use their world knowledge to describe settings, characters, and events that readers willingly immerse themselves into (think Harry Potter). Surveying the *World Knowledge* column, you can see that writers progressively create detailed events and worlds. They may borrow characters or events from stories or media (Bearse, 1992; Cairney, 1990) and become increasingly inventive.

(text resumes on page 126)

	Monitoring the Process	World Knowledge	Discourse Knowledge	Time and Space	Sociocultural Membership
Planning	**N:** Knows purpose is to tell a story. Does not plan.	**N:** Chooses a fictional event or character.	**N:** Knows to write a story. Leaves out parts.	**N:** Ignores setting.	**N:** Is unaware of voice.
	D: Knows purpose to entertain. May think of peers as audience. Needs teacher support to plan. May think of fictional character or events seen or read.	**D:** Recognizes creating fictional events. Needs help to plan details and information.	**D:** May plan with graphic organizer, if assigned. May not plan episodes or resolution.	**D:** May plan for setting, with teacher support.	**D:** Does not think about voice or point of view.
	E: Knows purpose to imaginatively engage audience. Knows the benefits of plans. Monitors plans to think of entertaining events for readers. Thinks of mentor texts.	**E:** Plans details and information that creates a fictional world.	**E:** Uses story grammar. May not plan all events or ending. Creates a problem for characters. May think about motive.	**E:** Plans a detailed setting.	**E:** Thinks about voice and point of view that fits characters.

(continued)

FIGURE 6.10. Fiction and imaginary events in the classroom: Developmental continuum.

	Monitoring the Process	World Knowledge	Discourse Knowledge	Time and Space	Sociocultural Membership
Producing Text	**N:** Has no plan to follow. May monitor for conventions. May write haltingly always using the same tool. **D:** May or may not use plans. Thinks about each plot event in isolation. Pauses to think what comes next. May write fluently with different tools. **E:** Refers back to plan and may change plans. Writes fluently but pauses to reread and monitor progress. May think about mentor texts. Monitors draft for reader's interest and genre features.	**N:** Writes whatever comes to mind. **D:** May use plan for events. Invents plot events as writes. Needs support to add elaborative details and information. **E:** Refers to plans for events. Includes relevant elaborative details and information.	**N:** Thinks of events as writes. May use friends' names for characters. Uses everyday words. **D:** Does not connect events in plot. May write a problem. Uses formulaic ending (awakes from a dream). May use descriptive words if thinks of them. **E:** Connects events in plot. Has central problem. May have a motive for characters. Writes a resolution. Tries to use vivid words.	**N:** Ignores setting in story. **D:** Tells reader the setting. May use formula (e.g., "Once upon a time"). **E:** Incorporates setting appropriate for genre.	**N:** Writes without thinking about voice. **D:** Uses own voice. **E:** Uses own voice or voices of friends. May adopt a voice from media or mentor text.

Reviewing				
N: Knows purpose is to tell an imaginary story. Does not reread to evaluate and revise story for reader. Considers story done after first draft. **D:** Knows purpose is to tell an exciting story peers will like. Tries to monitor for purpose and readers' interest. Rereads for conventions. Recognizes has written a draft. May think of mentor texts. **E:** Thinks about purpose to create a believable fiction story. Rereads, evaluates, and revises to improve draft(s). May refer to plans or revert to planning. Considers revisions based on purpose and audience needs. Thinks about and may refer to mentor texts for craft ideas.	**N:** Does not recognize lack of detail or gaps between events. **D:** Needs support to evaluate events and whether details enhance or clutter. Revises with support. **E:** Evaluates whether details fit the world created. Revises for consistency in details about world.	**N:** Keeps unconnected episodes for plot. Does not have a resolution; story stops. May change a word or a convention. **D:** Needs support to evaluate transitions between events. Keeps formulaic ending. Uses support to revise to include descriptive words. May change some words or conventions. **E:** Evaluates and revises transitions between events, problem, and resolution. Revises for own inventions to genre. Uses teacher support to consider motives. Revises for descriptive words and conventions.	**N:** Does not revise to add a setting. **D:** Needs support to revise for interesting setting. **E:** Evaluates and revises setting to fit world created.	**N:** Does not evaluate voice. **D:** Tries to revise by adding voices of friends to characters. **E:** Evaluates whether characters' voices believable, with teacher support. Attempts revisions to characters' voices, with teacher support.

FIGURE 6.10. *(continued)*

Looking at novice writers in the *Discourse Knowledge* column, you see that they write events in the plot as they think of them, using a what-next strategy (Bereiter & Scardamalia, 1987) and just stop writing without any resolution (Donovan, 2001). Developing writers use a chronological sequence for plot events (writing *then* or *the next day*) but they don't connect the events causally (Donovan, 2001; Langer, 1986) and have formulaic endings, such as waking from a dream (also called *deus ex machina*). Only experienced writers create a problem or quest, connect events causally, and consider motives (Donovan, 2001). They seek to write fitting resolutions and may invent unusual characters or plots.

You notice that *Time and Space* translates into setting for fiction and so is similar to personal narratives. Writers move from a formulaic opening like "On a space ship in the outer galaxy" to settings that are incorporated into their texts (Langer, 1986).

In the *Sociocultural Membership* column, you realize that writers develop their voices in fiction similarly to personal narrative voices. From using just their own voices, writers begin to incorporate additional or other voices appropriate for the worlds they're designing, such as the voices of friends or the voices found in stories or media.

Many students enjoy writing fictional or imaginary stories. However, we recognize how difficult the task is to create believable worlds, plausible characters, and causally connected plot events. We applaud the attempts students make in fictional writing, even when they lack essential characteristics, like motive. We encourage students to try many fictional genres, such as fables and tall tales, as well as other genres, like poetry—our next genre.

POETRY GENRE

Why do many teachers shy away from poetry? Introduced to the language play of poems and nursery rhymes, young children orally play with words. But when they enter school, if students think poems must rhyme, then their poems become trite—the "roses are red" variety. Many teachers are reluctant to read and write poems; maybe they think poems must rhyme. When students listen to and read poems, they discover poetry has many genres that may or may not rhyme, such as free verse, haiku, and limericks. They also find poems on a multitude of topics—baseball, rain, pets—including the silly and the serious. They discover that poetry expresses the essence of an object, idea, or feeling condensed into a concise form.

In Table 6.3 we list two categories in the poetry genre: poets' poems and school poems. We define poets' poems as genres of poems that

TABLE 6.3. Sampling of Poetry Genres

Poets' poems

    Free verse
    Concrete poems
    Haiku
    Limericks
    Poems in two voices
    Narrative poems
    Songs, raps

School poems

    Acrostics
    Recipe poems
    Diamante[a]
    Cinquain
    Color poems, noise poems, "I wish" poems[b]
    "I used to … but now" poems

[a]Seven-line diamante invented by Tiedt (1969).
[b]Koch (1970/2000, 1973/1990).

are commonly available in published anthologies. School poems were invented for students to write and usually have a formulaic structure. In our work with students, students have written both types; however, you will not find mentor texts for school poems. So, we favor poets' poems.

Poets choose words for the images they invoke and the sounds they make when read aloud. Poets create visual pictures in readers' minds, not only through simile and metaphor, but also through the specificity of the images their words summon. Poets think carefully about the sound of each word and the rhythm of a line—how the words hit the ear and roll off the tongue. Thinking of sound and rhythm, poets also consider where the lines break or where to place each word. Poets string words along a line or break up words into chunks to alter the pace or to emphasize an image. Poets often rewrite poems breaking the lines differently in each revision until they achieve the pace and emphasis they want.

When reading and writing poetry, teachers and students can explore how word choice creates the message for readers:

- Visual images words invoke.
- Sounds words make.
- Feelings words imply.
- Rhythm words have.
- Places words occupy on the line.

In addition to word choice, students can investigate the structure of poems. For some poems, such as the limerick, the structure follows a specific rhythm and rhyme for its lines. For free verse, the poet carefully decides to break the line to achieve a rhythm. In the case of concrete poems, poets place the words on the page to depict the shape of the subject or the meaning of the idea.

And finally, when students read a variety of poems, they can search for poetic devices:

- Simile—an explicit comparison between two things using *like* or *as.*
- Metaphor—an implied comparison stating one thing *is* another thing.
- Alliteration—the repetition of the same initial sound.
- Onomatopoeia—the meaning of the word is its sound.
- Rhyme—the same sound at the ending syllable.
- Repetition—the same word(s) or phrase(s) are repeated.

Although English language arts is the usual content area for poetry, in other content areas students can express their knowledge in poetry. Songs or raps can relate scientific or historical topics, such as the protest and war songs from several eras. Content-area teachers may be more comfortable with the structure of school poems than poets' poems. For example, acrostic is a common form used to express the characteristics of a concept or recipe poems can outline an experiment or observation. However, we encourage content-area teachers and their students to experiment with poets' poems, too.

In every poetry inquiry, students and teachers begin by reading many poems. Flooding the classroom with poetry books and poetry collections, including audio collections, students read, read, read and listen, listen, listen—for poems are meant to be read aloud. Then, they share the poems they like by reading to partners, neighbors, and the class or creating podcasts for others to enjoy. You may have heard of former Poet Laureate Robert Pinsky's Poetry Project that collected the favorite poems submitted by children and adults. The project has produced three anthologies of poems (the latest is *An Invitation to Poetry* [2004] in both book and DVD forms) and has archived poems at *www.favoritepoem.org.* A class collection of poems worth sharing would constitute an enjoyable inquiry into poetry.

Students can share the poems they collect and write with various audiences. Obviously, younger students, especially kindergarteners and first graders who enjoy word play, are attentive audiences. Senior citizens would like to be invited to a poetry slam at school or at their senior center and they have time to give the students! Students can create podcasts and, with permission, create a poetry slam for TeacherTube. Some town newspapers print students' poetry. Finally, all of the previously cited magazines, plus *The Louisville Review, The Sow's Ear Poetry Review,* and *Whole Notes,* accept poetry submissions by students (Rubenstein, 1998). Unknown audiences do exist; we just need to communicate with them.

Now we turn to teaching poetry in a content-area classroom.

Classroom Scenario: Poems for Two Voices

The fifth-grade teacher, Ms. Stone, incorporates a variety of texts into the students' study of American history. Over the course of the year, the students will read and write several genres to communicate their learning of history. In the scenario, the fifth-grade social studies class is learning about explorers and will communicate their learning in poems.

Preparing to Teach

Ms. Stone recognizes that she was taught the European point of view about explorers—discovering new lands—and not the point of view of the native peoples who had been living on the land for centuries. Therefore, she includes the two perspectives in her students' study of explorers. In addition to the social studies textbook, Ms. Stone collects informational and fiction books from the school library and websites to visit. To reinforce the two perspectives, Ms. Stone plans to have the students write poems in two voices, using Paul Fleischman's *A Joyful Noise: Poems for Two Voices* (1988) as a mentor text.

Supporting Students' Exploring

The students discuss the reasons European explorers came: gold, glory, God. Ms. Stone reads *Encounter* by Jane Yolen (1992) aloud to the students first just to hear the story of the Native American boy seeing Columbus's ships arriving. During the reading, the students ask questions, such as "What is the symbol on page one?"; "What does the dream mean?"; and "Why doesn't the boy want to meet the new people?" After the reading, the students discuss the story and write their reactions and questions on sticky notes that they place on a class chart.

On the second day, when Ms. Stone rereads the book, she asks the students to pay close attention to the words that tell the reader about the two perspectives: the Taino boy's and the explorers'. Every few pages, the students offer words and phrases that Ms. Stone writes on a chart: "Taino boy's words" (*their skin is moon to my sun*) and "Our words" or "Explorers' words" (*pale skin, white skin, skin lighter than mine*).

On the third day, Ms. Stone shows Paul Fleischman's *A Joyful Noise: Poems for Two Voices* (1988). The class notices how the lines in the two columns are printed. Ms. Stone points out that sometimes both insects talk simultaneously (words are on the same line in both columns), while at other times only one does (a line in only one column). Students also remark that sometimes they say the same words and other times they say different words. Dividing the class into two voices, they read several poems aloud.

Supporting Students' Planning

After exploring the differing perspectives of Columbus and the Taino boy and exploring the structure of two-voice poems, Ms. Stone thinks the students are ready to combine their explorations. She asks the students to think about the Taino boy and the explorers: "What does each one think when they see each other? What would they say to each other when they meet? And what does each do?" In pairs, the students plan their poems on *Think, Say, Do* charts writing the Taino boy's perspective in one column and the explorers' in the other (see Figure 6.11).

Taino boy	Christopher Columbus
Think • These strangers aren't human • Are they parrots? • About strangers	• The island is his • He can get gold • I have to get at least what I'm here for • The gold I found is perfect • Indians are savages • Weve finally arrived on an island
Say • "Do not welcome them" • Do not call them friends • "We must see if theyre true men"	• "Evil" laugh → not happy • Sneaky laugh
Do • Trade and give • Give them a feast • Talk to zemis	• Give gifts • Steal, (take) • Serpant smile • Puts in a flag • Lets the taino boy touch the stick • Sailed a long way

FIGURE 6.11. Think, say, do chart.

Supporting Students' Producing Texts

During the next social studies period, Ms. Stone asks the poetry pairs to draft a poem to share with the fourth graders. The class decides that fourth graders would know Columbus's (world knowledge) and the explorers' perspective but may not have information about the Taino's point of view (sociocultural membership). Pointing to the class chart comparing the Taino boy's words from *Encounter* (Yolen, 1992) to their own words, Ms. Stone encourages them to choose words that fit each perspective.

Marline and Tszyu begin to write their poem referring to their planning chart and the class chart of words (see Figure 6.12). Ms. Stone notes that Marline and Tszyu have produced several lines. Other students are also producing poems. Two pairs of boys have written about fights between the explorers and the Taino boy in their poems; typical, Ms. Stone thinks and chuckles, shaking her head.

FIGURE 6.12. Draft poem in two voices.

Supporting Students' Reviewing: Evaluating, Revising, and Editing

Ms. Stone reminds the students that a poem in two voices is an organizational structure (discourse knowledge) that poets use to reveal each person's perspective (sociocultural membership): Have they included statements that show their differences? She asks the students to review their word choices: Did they use Taino words and explorer words? Finally, she asks them to check their line breaks (discourse knowledge): Do they have some words on the same line in both columns? Do they have some words on one line in the Taino's column and on another line in the explorer's column?

As Ms. Stone circulates, she stops by Marline and Tszyu, who ask, "Can we read you our poem?" (see Figure 6.13). After reading, the girls ask, "Did you notice it rhymes?" Ms. Stone chuckles and asks them to think about revising their line breaks. "Do you want the words describing their eyes and speaking on the same line in each column?"; "And do you want the lines about gold and smoking on the same line, too?"; "Don't forget to edit for spelling."

Although Ms. Stone never mentioned rhyming, the girls were proud they could rhyme. No one else in the class rhymed. The class

Taino Boy	Christopher Columbus
Canoes are coming	Look I see land
What are those creatures?	Now I see sand
"Do not welcome them!" I call	We'll put in the flag standing tall
His eves are blue and grey like the shifting sea, he barked like a dog	Who pinched me?
They hid their bodies in many colors	I want to make many dollars
His skin was moon to my sun	We want the gold then we're done, you tought us how to smoke
And all you did was cough and choke	
You evil dictator we don't want you here	What if I let you tough my spere?
It bit my palm and the blood cried out	We're are going to find gold I have no doubt
Your heart is very, very cold	We want to have all of your gold
He had a surpent smile	If you don't five us gold, we'll stay awhile
If we don't five them gold will they fight	We shall attack tonight
Their large machines make lots of noise	Concuring this land will bring us joy

FIGURE 6.13. Revised poem in two voices.

produced a range of two-voice poems (discourse knowledge). All poems contrasted Taino words from Yolen's book and their own or explorer's words (sociocultural membership). The primary difference among the poems was the number of contrasts included (world knowledge). One pair composed a three-way conversation among the Taino boy, Christopher Columbus, and the Chief—an interesting discourse invention.

Poetry in the Classroom: Developmental Continuum

Reading mentor texts is helpful when learning to write every genre: Wide reading of poetry helps students explore how poems work. Searching for specific words that convey visual and sound images is what keeps poets revising and revising their poems. As students' vocabularies increase, their poems will gain in their precision. In Figure 6.14, we describe the development of that precision.

Students' views and experiences with poetry affect how they create poetry. The broader the reading of poetry, the more tacit and explicit information they bring to writing poetry. Clearly more experienced readers of poetry bring more information to monitoring their own process of creating poetry. Interestingly, when students have not had a great deal of exposure to a wide variety of poetry formats, they tend to focus on rhyme (McMackin, Allan, & Topham, in progress). They may think that the purpose of poetry is to express ideas through rhyme. In contrast, as students grow as poets, they know poetry's purpose is to create an artful message, monitor visual and sound images, and think about the poet's craft in mentor poems.

Surveying the *World Knowledge* column, you see the subject of the poem changes from a familiar topic, to a variety of possible topics, to a message that may be descriptive, emotional, or literal. Writers increasingly search for and incorporate precise words, recognizing the pivotal role language plays in poetry.

You know that *Discourse Knowledge* is dependent upon the variety of poetry writers have read. Novice writers prefer school poems that have simple structures to follow. Developing writers may use the pattern of a mentor poem and may revise for word choice and rhyme. They need to be taught poetic devices, such as, onomatopoeia. Experienced writers choose the structure of their poems as well as evaluate and revise word choices, poetic devices, and line breaks.

The *Time and Space* dimension in poetry considers the visual and sound images that the writer wants to invoke in the reader. You can predict the progression from concrete or trite images, to trying to convey visual images, to inventing original sensory images.

(text resumes on page 137)

	Monitoring the Process	World Knowledge	Discourse Knowledge	Time and Space	Sociocultural Membership
Planning	**N:** Is unaware of purpose for poetry. Does not plan. May not read poetry voluntarily. **D:** Needs teacher support to plan. May read poems voluntarily. Reads assigned poems. Thinks purpose is to describe for reader. **E:** Knows purpose is to create art with language for reader. Knows the benefits of plans. Monitors plans to fit poem. Reads poems for the poet's craft.	**N:** May choose familiar topic. **D:** May choose from a variety of familiar topics. May plan for details. **E:** Knows poems can have many different messages. Considers several messages in plans. Brainstorms details for chosen message.	**N:** Thinks of formulaic poem (e.g., acrostic). **D:** Aware of different forms of poetry. May brainstorms words. **E:** Selects specific poetic form. Plans sensory images. Brainstorms words.	**N:** Does not consider sensory detail. **D:** May plan for sensory detail with teacher support. **E:** Plans for sensory detail.	**N:** Is unaware of voice. **D:** Doesn't think of voice in poetry. **E:** May think about voice and point of view for poem.

Producing Text					
N: Focuses on rhyme. May write own poem reluctantly. May check if following school poem pattern. Writes always with same tool. **D:** May refer to plan. Pauses frequently to think of word choices. May write fluently with different tools. May refer to mentor poems. **E:** Refers back to plan and changes as needed. Pauses to think and reread draft for message. Writes fluently. May think of craft in mentor poems.	**N:** May copy a poem. Writes what recalls about topic. **D:** Knows to use specific words. Needs support to elaborate on ideas. **E:** Tries to select precise words for topic. Represents ideas creatively.	**N:** Follows school poem pattern. Inserts some of his or her own words. May write in sentences. Focuses on rhyming words. **D:** Uses mentor poem as a pattern. Inserts own words. May select words from plans. May rhyme. Needs instruction in poetic devices. **E:** Selects words from plan but replaces with more precise words when appropriate. Only rhymes when fits poem (e.g., limerick). Considers line breaks. Uses some poetic devices.	**N:** Describes topic concretely. May use trite image (e.g., red sun). **D:** Tries to convey original visual images. **E:** Invents own images using all senses.	**N:** Concentrates on description. **D:** Focuses on visual images. **E:** Tries to consider message wants to invoke.

FIGURE 6.14. Poetry in the classroom: Developmental continuum.

(continued)

	Monitoring the Process	World Knowledge	Discourse Knowledge	Time and Space	Sociocultural Membership
Reviewing	**N:** Knows purpose is to write a poem—not a story. May reread for rhyme. Considers first draft of poem finished. **D:** Thinks purpose is to create a poem that rhymes. Rereads for rhyme. Monitors draft for word choice. May reread a mentor poem. **E:** Thinks about purpose to create an artful message in poetic form. Monitors word choice, poetic devices, and line breaks. Tries to monitor for sound and rhythm. Thinks about and may reread mentor texts for craft.	**N:** Does not evaluate message. **D:** Evaluates the message with teacher support. Tries to revise message. **E:** Evaluates and revises the preciseness and creativity of the message.	**N:** May revise to force lines to rhyme. May change a word or conventions. **D:** Uses support to evaluate word choice. May revise word choice and rhyme. Needs support to evaluate and revise poetic devices. **E:** Evaluates and revises word choice for precision, imagery, sound, and uniqueness. Evaluates and revises line breaks for meaning and sound. Consults a thesaurus. Reads poem aloud and seeks teacher help on rhythm of poem.	**N:** Does not evaluate literal description or trite images. **D:** Tries to revise visual images. **E:** Evaluates and revises images to incorporate appropriate senses.	**N:** Does not think about readers' reactions. Is unaware of voice. **D:** May attempt to evaluate for readers' reactions or feelings with teacher support. Uses own voice. **E:** Seeks teacher support to evaluate and revise for readers' reactions or feelings. Attempts to match voice to message.

FIGURE 6.14. (continued)

For the *Sociocultural Membership* dimension, we focus again on voice and point of view. As you see, many writers do not consider their voices or points of view when writing poetry. As students progress, they gradually begin to invoke feelings or points of view in their poems and attempt to revise voice to match their messages.

Students who have read many poems often enjoy writing poems. Some novice or reluctant writers prefer the short length of poems to the longer memoirs, stories, or reports. We encourage you to discover the fun of writing poems with your students, if you have not already done so.

CHAPTER SUMMARY

Most students enjoy the genres of *writing to entertain*—personal experiences, fictional and imaginary events, and poetry. With families and friends they have had opportunities to tell stories about their experiences, to playfully use language (invent nicknames), and to recount movie plots. Most students have read fiction, although their experiences with personal experiences genres and poetry genres will vary widely. Although these are genres students encounter, they are some of the most difficult to write.

The classroom scenarios for each genre highlight good instructional practices. First, the teachers' instructional practices include the cognitive processes of planning, producing, and reviewing texts. For each specific genre (personal narrative and memoir, graphic novels, two-voice poems), teachers prepare their instruction by gathering mentor texts and planning activities. With their students, they explore ideas for their drafts and investigate characteristics of the genre. Teachers provide planning strategies, such as a lifeline or story grammar. They instruct, encourage, and question while students plan and produce texts. Returning to the characteristics of the specific genre, teachers and students evaluate, revise, and edit their pieces. Second, the dimensions of our communication model are addressed during the writing and reviewing of the students' drafts. Embedded in the classroom scenarios is the recognition of the distances between writers and their audiences in world knowledge, discourse knowledge, time and space, and sociocultural memberships.

Building on the developmental continuum in Chapter 4, we again emphasize instruction by describing a specific developmental continuum for each genre. Surveying the progressive development of novice, developing, and experienced writers helps teachers understand how students monitor and incorporate their world knowledge, discourse knowledge, time and space, and sociocultural memberships when they plan, produce, and review their texts. Using their understandings of students, teachers can plan instruction that supports students' writing to entertain known and unknown audiences.

Writing to entertain offers a variety of genres. Reading mentor texts and writing for different audiences will produce many discussions among your students. Instead of a curriculum sequence, we anticipate that you'll look for situations to arise for writing to entertain audiences (Purcell-Gates, Duke, & Martineau, 2007). Similarly, we expect you will find situations in which writing to inform audiences occur, our next chapter.

APPLICATION BOX

Think about situations in which your students could write to entertain. Brainstorm purpose, audience, and genre that you and your students would like to try out. Use the outline of the classroom scenarios and the suggested mentor texts in Appendix 6.1 of this chapter to plan your instruction. Have you explored ideas for the genre in your journal so that you can write with your students? What do you learn about writing from writing your draft? What do you learn about your students' products and processes? What would you revise the next time you teach the genre?

Resources for Writing to Entertain

Mentor Texts for the Personal Experiences Genre

Codell, E. R. (2004). *Sing a song of tuna fish: A memoir of my fifth-grade year.* New York: Hyperion.

Beginning with the occasion on which she egged a car with her mother, teacher turned writer Esmé Raji Cooper recounts memories from 1979, her year in fifth grade. Each chapter begins with the phrase, "Let me tell you something about...." Notice how Cooper focuses on one important event per chapter and discuss why the event was significant to her. Grades 5–8.

Dahl, R. (1986). *Boy: Tales of childhood.* New York: Putnam.

The author of *Matilda* and *James and the Giant Peach* recounts stories of his early life and incidents from his boarding school days. Themes from his many novels—including a general disdain for most grown-ups—can be seen in the very personal and touching personal narrative. Grades 5–8.

dePaola, T. (1999). *26 Fairmont Avenue.* New York: Putnam's.

The title launches a series of books Tomie dePaola has authored featuring the events of his childhood. Students will enjoy discussing why each topic is a significant memory to the author. Grades 3–6.

Greenfield, E., & Little, L. J. (1979). *Childtimes: A three-generation memoir.* New York: Crowell.

African American poet Eloise Greenfield has compiled family stories or childhood memories of grandmother, mother, and daughter that span the 1880s to the 1950s. Notice how the authors set the contexts for the memories by including "landscape" sections that describe the historical events of the time. Study the structure of the text that includes three main sections, one for each person, and short-titled segments of text featuring important memories. Grades 5–8.

Siegel, S. C. (2006). *To dance: A memoir.* New York: Atheneum.

In the graphic novel, Siena Cherson Siegel describes her passion for dance and her career as a young ballerina. Discuss the visual images and the role that they play in narrating her story. Also, notice how the author explains ballet through text and graphics for her audiences unfamiliar with ballet. Have your students compare her graphic personal narrative with a more traditional form. Grades 3–8.

Spinelli, J. (1998). *Knots in my yo-yo string.* New York: Knopf.

The Italian American Newbery medalist presents a humorous account of his childhood and youth in Norristown, Pennsylvania, in the 1950s. Investigate how the small everyday events of his childhood became seeds for his later writings. Grades 5–8.

Mentor Texts for the Fiction and Imagined Events Genre

Contemporary Realistic Fiction

Clements, A. (2005). *Lunch money.* New York: Simon & Schuster.

Students will easily sympathize with entrepreneurial sixth-grader Greg Kenton, who sets out to make his fortune by selling a self-authored comic to his classmates. Point out and discuss the conflict in the plot—commercialism in the schools—and how Greg is changed by the experience. Grades 3–6.

Patron, S. (2006). *The higher power of Lucky.* New York: Atheneum.

Since her mother died, Lucky has constantly worried that Brigitte, her guardian, will tire of small-town desert life and return to France. To forestall the inevitable, Lucky runs away, right into a dust storm. Use the Newbery winning title to discuss plot structure—the events take place over four days, but much backstory is needed to frame the events. Notice too, the tight plot structure—even seemingly insignificant events turn out to play a role in the storyline. Grades 3–8.

Perkins, L. R. (2005). *Criss cross.* New York: Greenwillow.

While all Newbery award winners could be mentor texts, *Criss Cross*, which describes a summer and spring in the intersecting lives of four teens living in a small town, has particularly interesting writing. Engage your students in a discussion of how Perkins develops the main characters and their perspectives; notice the small connections between events that link the characters; and admire Perkins's use of figurative language and her descriptive passages. Grades 5–8.

Historical Fiction

Curtis, C. P. (2007). *Elijah of Buxton.* New York: Scholastic.

Elijah Freeman, age 11, was the first black child to be born free in a community of escaped slaves established in Canada in 1849. Embarking on a life-changing journey, Elijah chases a no-good preacher who stole the money that Elijah's neighbor saved to purchase his family out of slavery. Elijah's voice is distinctive and well worthy of close study to see how the Newbery award–winning author develops his characters. Grades 3–6.

Paterson, K. (2006). *Bread and roses, too.* New York: Clarion.

Set in Lawrence, Massachusetts, during the 1912 textile mills labor strike known as the "Bread-and-Roses strike," two young teens, Rosa and Jake, survive difficult living conditions. Since Paterson alternates between their points of view in chapters, your students can compare the two characters' perspectives. Grades 5–8.

Peck, R. (2004). *The teacher's funeral: A comedy in three parts.* New York: Dial.

Fifteen-year-old Russell hopes to quit school after the death of his schoolmarm in 1904 rural Indiana. But those dreams are dashed when his older sister Lizzie volunteers to be the teacher in the one-room schoolhouse. If you and your students can stop laughing long enough, examine the details that make the time period come alive. Grades 3–8.

Fantasy

Collins, S. (2003). *Gregor the overlander.* New York: Scholastic.

Eleven-year-old Gregor and his baby sister Boots fall down an air duct to find themselves in an underground world deep below New York City inhabited by pale-skinned humans who are at war with giant rats. Reluctantly, Gregor accepts the role of hero, fulfilling an ancient prophecy. Notice how Collins incorporates cliffhanger chapter endings; examine how she creates a fantastical world; and discuss how Gregor is changed by his journey. Grades 3–6.

Funke, C. (2004). *Dragon rider.* New York: Scholastic.

Even the staunchest disbeliever in magical creatures will have lingering doubts after reading how a young dragon, a brownie, and an orphan boy journey to find the dragon's home-place at the Rim of Heaven. Help your students to notice how the detail Funke provides about the behaviors of magical creatures makes the readers believe they exist. Grades 3–6.

Myth/Traditional Literature

Hennessy, B. G. (2006). *The boy who cried wolf.* New York: Simon & Schuster.

The humorous and cleverly illustrated retelling of Aesop's classic fable closely matches the original version, but does not include an explicit statement of the moral at the end. Compare Hennessy's retelling with other versions of the tale and examine the structure of the fable. Grades 3–6.

O'Brien, A. S. (2006). *The legend of Hong Kil Dong, the Robin Hood of Korea.* Cambridge, MA: Charlesbridge.

In graphic format, O'Brien presents Hong Kil Dong, a hero figure of Korean folklore. Use the graphic version of the traditional tale to discuss the quest motif in traditional literature. Examine how the dialogue in the graphic novel expresses the class structure and value system of the time period and location. Grades 3–8.

Osborne, W., & Osborne M. P. (2000). *Kate and the beanstalk.* New York: Atheneum.

The retelling of the traditional tale *Jack and the Beanstalk* features a plucky heroine who outwits the giant, avenges her father's death, and restores her family's fortune. Use the book as a model for students' own retellings of traditional tales examining which characteristics of the story remain the same and which have been changed. Grades 3–8.

Graphic Novels

Holm, J. L., & Holm, M. (2005). *Babymouse: Queen of the world.* New York: Random House.

Babymouse longs for glamour, excitement, and adventure, but life is the same day after day until she is invited to Felicia Furrypaws's slumber party. She soon learns that hanging out with the popular crowd isn't all it's cracked up to be. Notice how the illustrations indicate shifts between reality and Babymouse's fantasies. Grades 3–5.

Trondheim, L., & Parme, F. (2007). *Tiny tyrant.* New York: First Second.

Very used to getting his own way, the young king of Portocristo bullies a range of characters including his unfortunate bodyguard, his cook, a paleontologist, and Santa Claus. Students will have fun discussing the clever ending of each short story. Grades 3–6.

Varon, S. (2007). *Robot dreams.* New York: First Second.

A lonely dog sends away for a kit and builds a robot. The two become friends quickly but disaster strikes when the robot seizes up after swimming at the beach. The wordless graphic novel offers students a model of how an artist uses frames, perspective, and sequencing to tell a story. Grades 3–8.

Mentor Texts for the Poetry Genre

Florian, D. (2007). *Comets, stars, the moon, and Mars: Space poems and paintings.* New York: Harcourt.

Encourage your students to identify the factual information in the collection of poems about the planets and outer space. Also examine the different rhyme schemes of the poems. Grades 3–8.

Janeczko, P. B. (Ed.). (2005). *A kick in the head: An everyday guide to poetic forms.* Cambridge, MA: Candlewick Press.

The poems have been carefully selected to exemplify 29 different poetic forms from the familiar to the eclectic. Notes on the forms are included. Discuss how the structure of each poem is well matched to its content. Grades 3–8.

Myers, W. D. (2006). *Jazz.* New York: Holiday House.

The collection of poems written by Walter Dean Myers and illustrated by his son, Christopher Myers, is a tribute to the sounds, rhythms, instruments, and diverse styles of jazz music. Notice how the rhythm of each poem matches the form of jazz that it celebrates. Grades 4–8.

Soto, G. (2006). *A fire in my hands.* New York: Harcourt.

Everyday life in the San Joaquin, California, valley is the subject of the poems. The author's notes describing the inspiration for each poem will inspire your students to write about small, but meaningful, moments in their own lives. Grades 5–8.

Chapter 7

Writing to Inform

As adults, we write more to inform than to entertain. We write student reports, school newsletters, grant proposals, and consumer complaint letters to known and unknown audiences. In each case, we carefully consider our specific purpose—to inform about progress, to report classroom events, to petition for money, to argue for a car repair. We also carefully consider our audience—parents, school community, funding agents, car dealers—and estimate how well our world knowledge, discourse knowledge, distance in time and space, and sociocultural membership match our audience's.

In this chapter, the purpose is to inform in situations where audiences actually need information (Purcell-Gates, Duke, & Martineau, 2007). Mirroring Chapter 6, we discuss three genres: (1) to persuade, (2) to explain, and (3) to give directions. When thinking about situations, you will want to exploit the content-area curricula and issues in the community or nation. What are contemporary issues that have roots in your science, social studies, and health curricula? Or, how can you connect your school curricula to contemporary events and issues? We seek to have school curricula be useful in students' lives rather than be inert facts to be memorized.

We will emphasize audiences beyond the school—in the community or nation—who need to be informed. Writing for less familiar audiences will challenge students to think about what world knowledge, discourse knowledge, time and space, and sociocultural membership(s) they share with readers. Estimating how readers differ is what all writers grapple with when they write to inform.

As in Chapter 6, for each genre we:

- Introduce the genre and list examples.
- Provide characteristics.

143

- Present a classroom scenario.
- Describe a developmental continuum.

At the end of the chapter in Appendix 7.1, we provide resources for mentor texts for all three genres.

We urge you and your students to seek situations and audiences for these genres so that students practice writing them. When students are familiar with a variety of different genres, they will be able to choose the appropriate genre called for by the particular situation. If you are keeping a journal, have you included situations or topics on which you could inform others in your list of territories? Do you have entries that you could turn into a persuasive letter to the editor, an informative article for the newspaper, or directions about a teaching activity for your colleagues? Now, we explore the persuasive genre.

TO PERSUADE GENRE

If you have ever listened to a young child ask for a new toy or ice cream cone, you know the persuasive genre is used early in life. However, the young child argues primarily from the position of entitlement ("I want a new toy") rather than from a reasoned, logical position ("My old PlayStation is slow; the new one is faster and has better graphics"). In fact, even adults often try to persuade from an opinionated position rather than from a factual position.

Although students have oral experience persuading family, teachers, and friends, they encounter few, if any, written examples of logical arguments. Yet, many state tests require students to write a persuasive essay. While we recognize students need to practice for high-stakes writing (Chapter 10), we prefer to find realistic situations in students' lives about which they can argue a position.

When students are discussing an issue or situation of burning interest to them, then we advocate teaching the persuasive genre. We need to listen to their playground, hallway, and cafeteria discussions to find those out-of-school issues that concern students. Often, articles in the local community newspaper can alert us to issues that connect with our students or the curricula. For example, for years a town discussed whether to continue in the consolidated school district or to build their own high school. Students never formally presented their arguments to the school committee, but we know they had them and would have argued their positions, if given the forum to do so.

We encourage you and your students to explore the genres listed in Table 7.1 (see Appendix 7.1 at the end of this chapter for mentor texts). Many teachers have students write about the books they've read.

TABLE 7.1. Sampling of Persuasive Genres

- Requests
- Complaint letters
- Letters to the editor
- Editorials, op-ed columns
- Political cartoons
- Posters, campaign posters
- Bumper stickers
- Ads
- Reviews of books, music, art, performances
- Protest songs, raps
- Debates
- Speeches
- Essays

But, think about whether those assignments are book reports (written to show one has read the book) or reviews (written to persuade peers to read or not read the book by citing its strengths and weakness). One bookstore of a national chain collects students' book reviews in a notebook that patrons can peruse for suggestions. Mentor texts for book reviews can be easily found in magazines for students, for example, *Merlyn's Pen* or *Stone Soup.*

These genres have common characteristics, even though they have different forms:

- Statement of problem, issue, or concern.
- Position of writer.
- Facts known or evidence supporting position.
- Counter position(s).
- Facts or reasons to refute counter position(s).
- Action to be taken by reader or opinion to be changed.

Although we include the feature of refuting counterarguments, students, on their own, rarely include counterarguments (Crowhurst, 1990; Ferretti et al., 2000; Nippold et al., 2005). In oral arguments, the opposing views are supplied by the listener, not the petitioner. Refuting another's argument requires the writer to have considerable knowledge about the issue and to take another's perspective—often a difficult task even for adults. Therefore, as you will see in the classroom scenario, although we give students a planning strategy that includes a section for opposing positions, students have difficulty thinking of counterarguments.

When students write to persuade, they must think about the audience they are addressing. Depending upon the issue, students may write to a familiar audience (principal or parents) or to unknown audiences.

The unknown audiences could be the citizens and officials in town, their congressional representatives, or the president of the United States. When students read hobby or special-interest magazines, they may react to a particular article and write a letter to the editor either agreeing or disagreeing with the author of the article. Perhaps they want to express their reactions to a consumer report in *Consumer Reports for Kids* or a report on an athlete in *Sports Illustrated Kids*. Finally, *Creative Kids, Merlyn's Pen, Stone Soup*, and *The Writers Slate* accept students' essays, reviews, and editorials (Rubenstein, 1998).

Now, we turn to a persuasive writing in a classroom.

Classroom Scenario: To Persuade

Although we encourage letters to the editor about a local issue of concern to students, students may choose to write letters about a global issue (global warming) or a personal concern (more recess). Whatever the issue students choose, we encourage them to write to a real audience—someone whose opinion they want to change or someone who can take action on the issue.

Preparing to Teach

Reading the town paper, Ms. Smith notices that two issues are causing a stir in town: the conversion of a business building into a mall and teens hanging out at a playground. She starts looking for letters to the editor, books, and persuasive essays on the Internet that might serve as mentor texts for persuasive writing. She also thinks about the colonial history they are studying—patriots' versus loyalists' positions on the tea tax. Before the students write their own persuasive letters, she plans several activities so that students will learn how to persuade.

Supporting Students' Exploring Ideas

First, for homework, Ms. Smith assigns the students to find a persuasive piece from the newspaper—an ad, movie review, or letter to the editor. In addition, they are to identify who was doing the persuading, what he or she wanted the reader to do, and whether the arguments were convincing. In class, they share and discuss their examples.

Second, in social studies, the class outlines the patriots' versus the loyalists' positions on the tea tax, such as the following excerpt:

Patriot	Loyalist
• Work hard—want to keep money	• Tax is only 3 pence
• Little taxes add up	• Anyone can afford that

When the students debate the tax, they realize how the arguments went back and forth—one statement made in reaction to the other's statement.

Third, Ms. Smith reads *Don't Let the Pigeon Stay Up Late* by Mo Willems (2006). After enjoying the pigeon's silly reasons for staying up late, the students chart the pigeon's arguments and the owner's counterarguments. For example, the pigeon argues he'll watch educational TV and the owner replies the pigeon never watches educational TV.

Fourth, the students role-play arguing for their own computers at home. In one scenario, the students argue with silly arguments, like the pigeon. In a second scenario, the students put forth reasonable arguments, for example, the family has too many users for one computer.

Finally, the class analyzes a student's essay that Ms. Smith found on the Internet. They locate the author's position in the first paragraph, the reasons supporting her position in the second paragraph, her arguments against opposing positions in the third paragraph, and finally the restatement of her position in the last paragraph. Rereading the essay, the students name the characteristics, which Ms. Smith writes on a class chart.

Armed with knowledge about how to persuade from the five activities, Ms. Smith asks the students to think about an issue or concern they feel needs a remedy. She reminds them of the local issues—the mall and the playground—and suggests they look in the local paper for issues of interest to them. The students return to their mixed-ability tables to brainstorm ideas together.

Supporting Students' Planning

The next day, the students share the issues they are thinking about—a proposed mall, parking in town, global warming, disease in Africa—and personal concerns—recess, food in the cafeteria. Although Ms. Smith wants the students to take a stand on a local issue, she know the students need to be invested to formulate arguments; so she wisely does not force students to write about local issues. Using a graphic organizer (discourse knowledge) Ms. Smith gives them, the fifth graders plan the facts, pros, and cons to include in their letters.

As you can see in Figure 7.1, Jeff includes factual information and arguments for and against his position of unlimited time for parking in town. When he looked in the newspaper for issues, Jeff found an article and letters about the new parking rule, read some of the positions taken by citizens, and discussed it with his parents. He is well prepared to plan his arguments.

Ms. Smith notices, however, that facts and counterarguments (world knowledge) are difficult for many students. First, some students

Letter to the Editor

ISSUE Parking Spaces

The Facts I Know

You can only park 2 hours a day in Reading Center.	To own a spot, you are put in a lottery first.
It is $240 a year for a parking space that is first come first serve.	It cost $30 a month for your own spot.

My Position on the Issue is:

Not long enough time

Different Viewpoints

For My Position	Against My Position
Not promoting shopping	2 hours is enough to do your shopping
Not affordable for part time employes.	That's there problem
It not clear enough to the town.	We said it on the town channel, that's enough.
We can't go into town twice without getting a ticket	You only need 1 trip into town.

Request for Action:

Unlimited

FIGURE 7.1. Persuasion graphic organizer: Parking.

do not have the factual information needed to support their position. For example, a student knows that organizations are helping to rebuild homes in New Orleans, but that's all she knows. Equally uninformed, another student states she learned about AIDs in Africa from an *American Idol* program. In contrast, one student resourcefully uses the Internet to find global warming information. Two students, who live in the neighborhood affected by the proposed mall, had heard their parents' factual arguments and use their facts like Jeff did. Ms. Smith makes a mental note to spend more time gathering factual information for issues next year.

Second, thinking of counterarguments is difficult for some students (world knowledge and sociocultural membership). Ms. Smith recognizes that taking another's perspective is hard for fifth graders to do. Yet, as she confers with the students, she tries to help them think about an opposing reason or position. Counterarguments range from the questionable ("put animals in cages to save them " vs. "animals need to be free"), to reasonable based on one's experiences for longer recess ("need exercise" vs. "have work to do in school") to arguments from facts about global warming ("turn your computer off at night [because] the average households contribute an average 41,500 pounds of gases" vs. "it takes too long to turn on"). Recognizing the range of ability among her students, Ms. Smith determines whom to push for counterarguments and whom to work toward just presenting a reasonable position.

Supporting Students' Producing Text

Three days later, Ms. Smith gathers the class together on the rug for a check-in: Whose plans were complete? With their plans in hand, Jeff and seven other students leave the rug to begin drafting their letters (see Figure 7.2). Three need more planning time because they switched their topics or need help with sections. The rest are unsure how to begin to organize their letters; so using the book about the pigeon wanting to stay up late, Ms. Smith outlines the parts to a letter and the students fill in the pigeon's arguments:

1. State position—need later bedtime.
2. Explain your arguments—more time for homework.
3. Discuss other points of view—do homework earlier.
4. Conclusion.

Then, referring to the outline of the pigeon's arguments Ms. Smith confers with the students, in pairs or individually, until each student is clear about how to state a position and how to explain arguments. Eventually

Title: Parking Spaces

I think that our town council is stupid to think that people only need 2 hours a day in R_____ Center? You can only make one trip into town. You can't switch spots. That's wrong!

Could you two hours in town center? Say you're a part time employe? Say you work at a wage of $20 every two hours. That$20 all goes to paying the parking ticket. And to get a parking spot you are put into a lottery and If you get picked you have to pay $240 a year for a spot that might not even be open! It's a first come first serve spot. And to get a spont that only you and your work car use you are put into a lottery and then it costs $30 a month for a terrible spot. And say a cop sees you in your spot and go do something else maybe pick up your kids or do library or something else and go back into town and the cop sees you again. Zip! Good-bye $20 more dollars. And it wasn't told to the town enough so tons of people got tickets. Do you think that that that would be fair to the town.

FIGURE 7.2. Excerpts from rough draft on parking spaces.

everyone is writing and talking, while Ms. Smith circulates conferring with students.

Supporting Students' Reviewing

EVALUATING AND REVISING

After a week of drafting, Ms. Smith reviews a persuasive writing chart (discourse knowledge) with the class:

1. Introduction: Describe your issue—What is not happening and what needs to happen (time and space—existence of issue or problem).
2. Explain your point of view—Support with facts to convince your reader you are right (world knowledge).
3. Discuss other points of view—Prove they are wrong (world knowledge and sociocultural membership—perspectives).
4. Conclusion—Leave readers with a strong thought that will have them side with you or take action on the problem (sociocultural membership—voice).

Students evaluate their drafts and help each other. Most students stated the issues clearly enough. However, as their plans illustrated, factual support and counterarguments often needed work. So as Ms. Smith conferred with students, she differentiates who needs to concentrate on explaining fully their supporting facts and who needs to work on countering opposing positions.

Ms. Smith grins at Jeff's steaming draft on parking and wonders to herself: Did someone in the family get a ticket? They discuss his three arguments: part-time workers, returning to town again, and notice about the rule change. After his conference with Ms. Smith, Jeff rewrites his second and third paragraphs in order to elaborate on his three arguments (see Figure 7.3). Jeff begins with an introductory statement ("many problems") and indicates his first and third argument ("First what if you're a part-time employee?"), although he does not indicate explicitly the second ("And guess what, you can't go to do something else ..."). He begins counterarguments but leaves the section incomplete and does not write a conclusion.

MORE REVISING AND EDITING

During a week of revising, the students elaborate and clarify the details supporting their arguments and consider whether their audiences would be convinced. Finally, the students edit their persuasive writing and write a final copy. Jeff completes his counterarguments and writes a conclusion (Figure 7.4). Throughout his drafts to his final copy, Jeff retains his indignant fifth-grade voice, talking directly to the reader and using words such as *Wrong* and *No!*

Although the classroom teacher did not have the students send the letters to appropriate known and unknown audiences, as we would have done, we did notice several interesting events in the scenario. First, we found the range of topics interesting even though we know students have many opinions about issues. Second, we assume some parents helped students with their facts and arguments especially on local issues and find that appropriate for fifth grade. Third, we agree with Ms. Smith that providing facts and thinking of counter positions is difficult for fifth graders. Fourth, we think Ms. Smith provided substantial preparation about the persuasive genre before the students wrote. Without the graphic organizer and teacher support, we think many students would not have been cognizant that facts, pros, and cons were needed in their arguments. And finally, Ms. Smith stated that next time, because the genre was so difficult for fifth grade, she would model and explain her processes by writing a persuasive letter, focusing especially on finding facts, supporting arguments, and counterarguments; we concur. Yet, surveying the class's persuasive pieces, we found novice persuaders, developing persuaders, and even one or two experienced persuaders (who may have had some outside help) that we describe in the next section.

(text resumes on page 156)

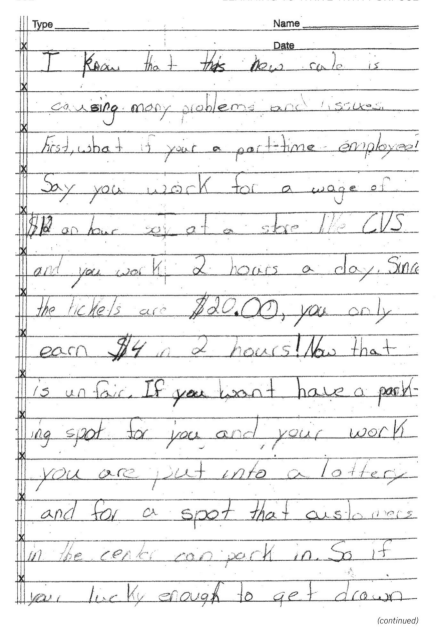

Type_____   Name_____
                                    Date_____

I know that this new rule is causing many problems and issues. First, what if your a part-time employee? Say you work for a wage of $12 an hour say at a store like CVS and you work 2 hours a day. Since the tickets are $20.00, you only earn $4 in 2 hours! Now that is unfair. If you want have a parking spot for you and your work you are put into a lottery and for a spot that customers in the center can park in. So if your lucky enough to get drawn

(continued)

FIGURE 7.3. Revised paragraphs on parking.

Type _____ Name _____

Date _____

it is $240 a year. And for a spot that only you and work can park in is $30 a month. For a terrible spot that is on the out skirts of town. And guess what, you can't go to do some thing else after you've been in town and go back into the center and the cop see's you agian ZIP! There goes $20. And third, the news of the new rule barely got out to the town. So guess what? Loads and loads of peop.

(continued)

FIGURE 7.3. *(continued)*

Type _____   Name

                                                   Date

got tickets when the rule was
enforced. There wern't even any
signs to mark the new
rule. The only said it on
the town channel. So, do
you still think that it's
fair to those who have to quit
there jobs? Or what about those
people who had to pay the tickets
they had no idea about? You
decide.

        There are probably wrong
about what you think about this issue.
First, you would think that is probably

FIGURE 7.3. *(continued)*

There are probably 1 or 2 things that you are wrong about this issue. First, you would think that this is probably letting more people into the town, right? Wrong. It preventing the big time shopers from spending trec money. And do you think that saying it on the town channel is enough. Some people don't even watch that channel. Plus, there were no signs to tell anyone about the rule. You still think it's fair? You think people want to be rushed in Reading center.

So, do you still think it's fair that Reading citizens have to be rushed doing there business in the center? No! Do you think part-time employees should be spending there pay checks on parking tickets? No! You think it's fair that the town didn't know about it. No! If we don't do anything about it the town will keep getting money. So protest and release this tyranny!

FIGURE 7.4. Excerpts from final copy on parking.

Persuasion in the Classroom: Developmental Continuum

As we stated in the beginning of the persuasive genre, most students have little experience with written persuasion (Crowhurst, 1990; Green & Sutton, 2003). Therefore, we expect to find more novice and developing writers in our diverse classrooms, although we did meet a few experienced writers in the fifth-grade classroom, most likely due to support from their teacher or parents. Students who are experienced writers in the personal narrative genre could be novice or developing writers in the less familiar persuasive genre.

Glancing down the *Monitoring the Process* column in Figure 7.5, you recognize the pattern is similar to the same columns in Chapter 6. From their oral experiences, all writers know the purpose is to persuade an audience. With instruction, writers think about how to address their readers and how to review their texts for convincing arguments.

Surveying the *World Knowledge* column, you can see in the descriptions that all writers select a concern or issue they are invested in but differ in the type of information they use to support their position. Personal experiences and personal opinions are often put forth as reasons. Most writers need support to research facts and evaluate their facts (De La Paz, 2005).

Because the persuasive genre in its written discourse is unfamiliar for many students, you can expect that writers vary widely in their *Discourse Knowledge*. Relying on their oral arguments, novice writers write a story about their experiences and may plead rather than argue (Clark & Delia, 1976; Crowhurst, 1990; Felton & Kuhn, 2001). Developing writers use teacher support to plan, state their opinions or position, and write reasons (De La Paz, 2005; Green & Sutton, 2003; Yeh, 1998). Also, they may restate their opinions (Crowhurst, 1990) or restate the problems for their conclusions (Nystrand & Graff, 2001) instead of suggesting actions to be taken. They need teacher support to evaluate their reasons, tie their reasons together, and change their command language to persuasive language (Yeh, 1998). Only experienced writers present their arguments and counterarguments (Ferretti et al., 2000; Nippold et al., 2005).

Surveying the *Time and Space* column, you realize writers increasingly recognize whether readers, at a later time and in a different locale, have knowledge that the concerns or issues exist and how much background information readers need.

As you can surmise, who the audience is affects the voice and points of view in the *Sociocultural Membership* column. A known audience and mutual concern calls for a more personal voice and point of view than an

(text resumes on page 160)

	Monitoring the Process	World Knowledge	Discourse Knowledge	Time and Space	Sociocultural Membership
Planning	**N:** Knows purpose is to persuade. Writes for a known audience. Does not plan.	**N:** Chooses personal concern to address.	**N:** Knows purpose is to argue but pleads or tells a story.	**N:** Assumes the concern is known.	**N:** Thinks only of own perspective.
	D: Knows purpose to convince. Thinks about known audience. Needs teacher support to plan. Needs teacher to assign mentor texts.	**D:** May choose personal concern or a popular national issue to address. Lists own experiences for facts. May list ideas from adults or media. Needs to research facts.	**D:** Knows to argue for own position. Plans opinion and a reason or two for position with teacher support.	**D:** Does not plan background information.	**D:** Needs teacher support to recognize another perspective.
	E: Knows purpose is to convince known and unknown audiences of his or her position. Monitors detailed plans for argument. Thinks about assigned mentor texts for genre features.	**E:** Chooses a local, national, or global issue. Researches and records facts in plans.	**E:** Plans position and reasons for position. Lists counter arguments. Notes position or action to be taken on issue.	**E:** Provides background information and explains why issue exists.	**E:** Plans for different perspectives.

(continued)

FIGURE 7.5. Persuasive letters in the classroom: Developmental continuum.

	Monitoring the Process	World Knowledge	Discourse Knowledge	Time and Space	Sociocultural Membership
Producing Text	**N:** Focuses on conventions. Writes haltingly, always using same tool. May keep purpose and known audience in back of mind. **D:** May refer to plan. Monitors what listed as reasons. May write fluently with different tools. May keep purpose and audience in back of mind. **E:** Refers back to plans consistently and may return to planning. Monitors whether argument is convincing and logical. Writes fluently with pauses to think. May refer to mentor texts. Keeps purpose and audience in mind.	**N:** Uses own experiences as facts. **D:** Writes opinions. Writes own experiences. May include some relevant facts. **E:** Writes position on issue. Writes researched facts related to issue. May express a citizen's concern on issue.	**N:** Tells a story about own experiences. May plead or use self-referential words (e.g., I need) to state position or action. **D:** States opinion, position, or problem. May write report of facts. May write reasons but does not tie reasons together or to position. Restates opinion, plea, or problem. May use command vocabulary (you should). **E:** States position clearly. Presents support logically. Counters opposing positions with facts. States position or action to be taken. Searches for convincing vocabulary.	**N:** May state concern vaguely. **D:** Uses teacher support to give background about existence of concern or issue. **E:** Includes background about existence of issue.	**N:** Thinks reader has the same opinions. Uses a pleading voice. **D:** Reasons from own perspective. Uses a believable personal voice. **E:** Tries to address different perspectives. Tries to have factual, yet convincing, voice.

Reviewing	**N:** Knows purpose is to persuade. Thinks about known audience. Does not reread, evaluate, or revise for purpose or audience. Thinks first draft is final draft. **D:** Knows purpose is to persuade an audience to own opinion. Tries to monitor to see if draft is convincing. Knows first draft needs reviewing. May think of mentor texts, if texts are available in class. **E:** Thinks about the purpose: to convince reader to a position or to act. Tries to monitor logic of reasons and refutations and seeks teacher's advice. Considers if needs to research facts or points of view. May reread mentor texts.	**N:** Does not evaluate and revise to add facts. Assumes own experiences are convincing. **D:** Needs support to evaluate facts. Revises to include sufficient facts, with teacher support. **E:** Evaluates pertinence of facts for position. Revises by elaborating on facts to support position. Uses teacher support to research countering facts.	**N:** Thinks a story of own experiences justifies position. May make small changes to words or conventions. **D:** Needs support to evaluate opinion, position, or problem. Needs support to evaluate and revise facts and reasons. Evaluates and revises persuasive words with support. Makes some changes to conventions. **E:** Evaluates reasons and refutations of opposition. Evaluates logic of draft, with teacher support. Revises argument. Evaluates and revises words for persuasiveness. Edits for conventions.	**N:** Is unaware of the need to alert reader of existence of concern. **D:** Needs support to evaluate and revise background about existence of concern or issue. **E:** Evaluates if background sufficient to convince reader issue exists. May seek support to revise.	**N:** Thinks reader should "Do what I say." **D:** Tells reader what should do or opinion should have. Needs support to consider reader with different perspective. Keeps personal voice. **E:** Tries to revise for different perspectives and counter arguments on issue. Revises for objective and convincing voice.

FIGURE 7.5. (*continued*)

unknown audience and a global issue where different viewpoints occur. Writers increasingly become aware of different perspectives (Clark & Delia, 1976). However, few students include different perspectives in counterarguments (Ferretti et al., 2000; Yeh, 1998) unless they receive instruction (De La Paz, 2005).

Although many of the persuasive genres can be challenging for students, practice in formulating a logical, convincing argument is useful across the content areas. For example, although explaining history, historians build arguments for their interpretation of the facts. Similarly, although scientists explain phenomena, they use evidence to support their conclusions. Mathematicians provide justifications for their proofs and processes. Therefore, when students practice forming arguments about concerns and issues, they can learn (and invent) ways to convince unknown audiences. When they have teacher support and instruction, then students can tackle the genre and become active citizens or consumers as well as future mathematicians, scientists, and historians.

Now, we consider the second genre in writing to inform—the to explain genre—which includes the common school report among other genres.

TO EXPLAIN GENRE

Young children are interested in explaining what they know, remembering facts in encyclopedic fashion (Chapman, 1995; Newkirk, 1987, 1989). We sustain their interest in information by incorporating the many genres of writing to explain (see Table 7.2). In addition to the familiar news reports, biographies, and informational books, you will also find less familiar genres like narrative nonfiction (an increasingly popular hybrid text), historical "you are there" scenes and eyewitness reports (personal accounts of events), and photographies (information explained primarily through photographs coined by author Russell Freedman). We have listed a sampling of mentor texts in Appendix 7.1 at the end of this chapter.

You will also notice in Table 7.2 we have listed the "school report" as a specific genre that occurs in the situation of schooling and is driven by content-area curricula. We encounter two types of school reports in classrooms. First, we see reports that are collections of facts in which the students pedantically write all they have learned about a social studies topic; the Erie Canal, for example. Second, and our preference, we see inquiry reports in which students ask investigative—not literal or factual—questions. For example, how did the Erie Canal affect the

TABLE 7.2. Sampling of To Explain Genres

- Fact sheets, telegrams, news sound bites
- Resumés, applications, cover letters
- School reports
- News reports, feature articles, sports reports
- Biographical sketches, profiles, biographies, interviews, oral histories, obituaries
- Documentaries, photographies
- Informational books, narrative nonfiction, nonfiction picture books
- Science reports, observational reports, experiment reports
- Social studies reports, historical "you are there" scenes, historical journals or diaries
- Eyewitness reports, survey reports, reporter-at-large
- Sketches of places, travel articles or letters
- Brochures

economy of the United States? Or, how did the Erie Canal and the Ohio River comparatively affect the economy of the United States? We prefer inquiry reports because students are more likely to synthesize information and draw original conclusions.

For the explaining genres, writers research information to answer their inquiry questions or to satisfy their curiosity. Students can explore different resources for information. For example, with Internet access to the Library of Congress's American Memory (*memory.loc.gov/ammem*), students can compose photographies of the Dust Bowl or read slaves narratives collected during the Depression to surmise what living in those eras was like. Using archives of NASA (*marsprogram.jpl.nasa.gov*), students can view pictures and read information about the terrain and speculate about the evidence for or against past existence of life on Mars.

Having gathered their information and drawn their conclusions, writers' purposes change from collecting data to reporting to audiences. Although it contains a variety of genres, they do share the following common characteristics:

- Accurate facts or evidence.
- Organized facts with sections that are linked using, for example, a sequence of subtopics, a cause-and-effect chain of events, or a chronology of a lifetime.
- A conclusion, a thesis, or headline that synthesizes the evidence.

While you and your students explore how writers include the common characteristics in mentor texts, you can note also the particular characteristics of a specific genre. For example, eyewitness reports use

I, the personal pronoun; news reports have *lead paragraphs* (the five W's); sports reports often have *figurative language* in lead paragraphs and headlines. Or, by reading informational books and nonfiction picture books on one topic, such as Abraham Lincoln, students can find the individual twist each author has given to the subject. Exploring differences among mentor texts and genres will encourage your students to include both the common and the variable characteristics—maybe even their own inventions.

Audiences for the many genres of explaining information can be varied. To find audiences beyond the school, we recommend contacting local historical societies and local special-interest groups, such as the local Audubon group. For example, Johnston (2006) reports that his students produced a Newcomers' Guide for the newcomers' welcoming group, a realtor, and the guidance counselor to offer to new community members. Magazines and newsletters for students, such as *The New Girl Times, The Write News, The Writers' Slate*, and the online site *KidNews* (*www.kidnews.com*) accept informational articles by students (Rubenstein, 1998). As you will see in the classroom scenario that follows, the students presented their findings to a local science group, town and highway officials, and school board members and parents, as well as younger students.

Classroom Scenario: Science Report

In several chapters, we have referred to Ms. Arnold's students who presented their science results to different unknown audiences. Now, let's trace how Ms. Arnold and the eighth-grade class spent the year.

Preparing to Teach

Skimming the town paper, Ms. Arnold reads that a walker had found a bloated dead frog in the watershed near the school. Upon analysis, the frog's carcass was found to contain a large amount of salt. Wondering where the salt was coming from and whether the salt was contaminating the school's drinking water, Ms. Arnold knows she has a science project for her students to investigate throughout the year. She plans instruction in several areas: what a watershed is and its topography, how to conduct an investigation and test the water samples, how salt affects human body systems, and how the town's water is treated at the local water plant. Then, she lists four jobs students will need to learn: (1) physical characteristics—responsible for identifying the physical characteristics of the stream; (2) chemist—responsible for testing specific parameters of water quality; (3) pollutant concentration—responsible for measuring the concentration of pollutants; and (4) weather observers—responsible for tracking daily weather.

Supporting Students' Exploring Ideas: Data Gathering

Ms. Arnold reads the article about the frog to the students and shows them a topographical map of the area. After the students learn where the town gets its water and what a watershed is, they hypothesize the sources that could pollute the watershed behind the school—the state's highway salt shed, the gas station, the landfill, the golf course. With hypotheses to examine, students are assigned to a team and begin reading more information about watersheds and water treatment, for example. They also learn how to conduct the tests they would need to collect their data, such as measuring water flow.

In science journals, every Thursday afternoon, teams record their measurements at two sites in the watershed: (1) the Franklin Brook (FB) site near two intersecting highways, and (2) the Back of School Site (BOSS) that was away from highways (the control site) and record their reflections on their learning. Looking at Figure 7.6, you can see that the students collected data and measured the water samples. While they drew conclusions from their data (not polluted by fertilizers), they were also unsure about what other data meant. In addition, they learned about the equipment ("breaks easily"), themselves ("hot," "nervous"), and their peers ("messing around").

Later in the year, the students review all of the data they had collected and draw their conclusions (Figure 7.7). Look at the specificity of the data in April. Note also the excitement communicated by the capital letters they used when writing their conclusion: "OVERSALTING THE HIGHWAYS."

When the students' analysis produced a spike in salt during the winter and not in the fall or the spring, Ms. Arnold recognizes that the students have data that no town official, state highway official, or citizen has. The students need to communicate their data to protect their town's watershed. Therefore, Ms. Arnold and her co-teachers contact different audiences, and students begin planning their presentations.

Supporting Students' Planning

Each team chooses the audience it will report to: younger students, parents, school committee members, town and highway officials, and local environmental experts. To help the students pull out information from their science journals, Ms. Arnold outlines the sections of a science report (discourse knowledge):

1. Problem and hypothesis.
2. How conducted the investigation and what measured.
3. Results—measurements of salt content and graph.

(text resumes on page 165)

Part 1: 11/18
    We gathered much data (see previous page). Currently in FB watershed, the roads have been salted and an oily substance can be found in the brook. In the water the oily substance might be pollution which was caused by dumping. Other than that, the water's conditions appear stable. I think that the data we gathered this week shows that FB is not getting polluted by fertilizers and such, which in the levels of phosphates and nitrates are so minimal. I think that is very good, because I feel that people shouldn't be allowed to dump dangerous substances such as fertilizers into their drinking water source. This week, I've learned that we need to be careful of our equipment, because it brakes easily. Also, since our humidity doesn't seem accurate, we should take good care of our equipment, because the bad data might be attributed to broken equipment. I am curious about what some of our data means, because I don't know how to interpret a lot of our measurements.

Part 2:
    While we were outdoors, I learned that I don't do well in very warm situations. I wore my winter coat outside, and became extremely hot. This made me very uncomfortable. Outside, I saw rotting leaves on the ground. I heard my classmates' and twigs crunching beneath our feet. I tasted the crisp winter air in my mouth. I saw fir trees, the brook, and countless leaves on the ground. I felt very warm, and tired from walking while carrying a suitcase of equipment. I felt nervous while doing my experiment because I didn't want to do it incorrectly. I was nervous while walking across the bridge, because I didn't want to fall in the brook. Also, I felt frustrated with my peers, because they kept messing around.

        12/8   (Roads were salted 12/7)
Weather
air temp 40.5°F
barometric pressure: 70.1
humidity: 36%
rain gauge: 1 inch
cloud cover: overcast
light breeze
precipitation - non
Chemistry
p.h.= 6.0
turbidity: 0
nitirate: 0ppm
Dissolved Oxygen: 8.4
Chloride 232ppm
Alkalinity: 20
Physical Characteristics
• odor around water of decaying leaves
• strong flow
• no change I water level on bank
• color of water: brown and transparent
• lots of stumps and branches in the river

FIGURE 7.6. A sampling of early entries in science notebooks.

April 14
Observations
- There is not much salt at f____b____l____, so there is probably not a problem of natural salt
- Snow days—1/6, 1/7, 1/26
- FB2 site—spiked up levels of salt on the 14th of January, when it was snowing—reached levels of a little more than 8,000g of cl/min.
- FB1—highest levels were on 1/10, ˉ2,000g of cl./min.
- FB5—spiked WAY high on the 14th of January—reached either 15,000 or 25,000 (still a huge spike.)
- FB6 highest levels on February 1st—reached ˉ 6,119g of cl./min.—rest of levels ranged from ˉ1,500 to ˉ 5,100.
- FB5—lowest levels were on 11/12 (ˉ 1,800) other levels were pretty much constant with this. 1/4 reached ˉ4,450.
- WH site—on the 14th of January, it reached its second highest level of about ˉ12,000g of cl./min. but on 3/17 (a date that is only recorded by WH), there is a high of 15,000. It was pretty constat from < 2,000—7000 for other days.
- Most highs are in the winter
- FB6 gets a higher amount of salt, but unfortunately 1/14 was not recorded, so we don't know if it got higher on that HIGH SALT day.
- OVERSALTING THE HIGHWAYS
- If it were just the saltshed, we would never see an increase in salt after the WH site
- It's not just the saltshed.

FIGURE 7.7. April entry in science notebook.

4. Conclusion.
5. Recommendations for action.

She reminds the students that their purpose is to explain their investigation and their results to a specific audience. Because they had been investigating all year, the students have extensive data from their own exploration (world knowledge). Now, for their different unknown audiences, they need to select only the most important information from their journals and also add information, such as how they investigated, because their audiences had not been with them (time and space). Furthermore, they have to decide how to communicate the information so that their specific audience (younger students or officials) will understand their investigation (world knowledge and sociocultural membership).

Supporting Students' Producing Text

From their plans, students begin drafting their reports, concentrating on their purpose—to explain their investigation and their results. In addition, Ms. Arnold asks them to conclude with their thoughts about the experience and what they learned.

Since the different teams are reporting to different audiences, Ms. Arnold also expects them to be inventive in how they address their particular audience but she saves that for their reviewing process. Each team works to produce a written draft of their presentation but you know not all teams are busy! Students need varying degrees of encouragement.

Supporting Students' Reviewing: Evaluating, Revising, and Editing

Since the students are communicating to audiences outside of school, Ms. Arnold and the other teachers help the students carefully evaluate their texts. In Table 7.3, we have translated their criteria into the dimensions of our communication model and the elements you will meet in Chapter 8.

As you can see, the teachers emphasize reporting the science knowledge and methods that the students learned and the science report genre using the vocabulary of science. The students recognize that none of their audiences were present during the investigation and so they include descriptions of the watershed and how they collected data. And finally, the teachers want the students to present themselves as scientists. The students need to show that their conclusion is based on evidence—observations and measurements. Students are encouraged to adjust their objective tone to their audience—younger students or environmental experts.

Each team reviews its draft, revises, presents before a group of peers and a teacher, and revises again. Before a team presents to an audience, the presentation is approved by a teacher. As the students practice, evaluate, and revise their presentations, they carefully consider their specific audience. One team presents to a younger sibling to find out if its presentation could be understood. In Figure 7.8 on page 168, we share excerpts from a presentation to younger students; note the French fry reference. They also refer to the younger students' study of ecosystems and advise them to tell their parents.

Another team, presenting to local environmental experts, clarified their data in a PowerPoint chart and evaluated their presentation for a scientific voice (see Figure 7.9 on page 168). Their teammate, a struggling student, made a diorama of the watershed to accompany the PowerPoint presentation. Note the scientific voice and vocabulary when addressing knowledgeable adults.

Some teams scramble to revise in time to present. A few teams do not present because their presentations were evaluated to be not clear or

TABLE 7.3. Evaluating Ms. Arnold's Science Reports

	Text element	Science report
World knowledge	Topic development	• Purpose to explain the Franklin Brook investigation.
	Idea generation	• Clear statement of problem and hypothesis.
	Detail treatment	• Clear statement of how data was collected. • Clear statements of results. • Graph depicting results is clearly labeled. • Mathematical statements of data.
Discourse knowledge	Genre knowledge and organizational structure	• Science report to different audiences. • Problem/hypothesis. • Method of data gathering. • Results and graph. • Conclusion.
	Sentence construction	• Active verbs in sentences. • "We" acceptable pronoun, with referent. • Complete sentences.
	Word choice	• Science vocabulary. • Mathematical measurements for results. • Terms defined for young audience.
	Conventions	• Spelling and punctuation correct on PowerPoint presentation. • Spelling correct on graphs and posters.
Time and space	Contextual knowledge	• Description of brook area. • Description of how and when gathered data.
Sociocultural membership	Voice	• Conclusion based on evidence. • Objective, factual voice of a scientist. • Matches voice to audience—younger students versus experts.

complete enough for unknown audiences. However, most teams helped each other during the investigation and the presentations.

In their conclusions, the students expressed that they had learned how to investigate and learned new information. However, they were really impressed that *kids* could institute changes in their town. Due to the students' results, the state highway department instituted a low-salt policy for the area and the town appropriated money for continued study of the watershed. Students presenting to younger audiences encouraged them to take a stand and make changes in town—"kids can make a difference."

S: "Has anyone ever heard of chloride? (pause) Chloride measures the amount of salt in the water. Isn't that amazing? Who eats french fries? (pause) Who doesn't like too much salt on their french fries? I don't! Well, your water has a lot of salt in it and it is half way to the point where you can taste the salt."

K: (show salt comparison) "See, this is the proportion of salt in our tap water, compared to how much salt there should be. We are way over the limit!"

N: "Make sure to tell our parents to go to town meetings and learn more abut the town and its water. You all are invited to come to the meetings with your parents."

S: "Another way that you can help is to tell your parents not to use pesticides on your lawn. The pesticides run into the drains and affect our water. They do this by going into the ground, sitting there until it rains, and running off the lawn into the drain. The drain brings the pesticides to the water treatment plant. The water gets somewhat filtered, enters your faucets, and comes out as your tap water that you use everyday."

FIGURE 7.8. Excerpts from students' reports to younger students.

Present graph of chloride data
C: "This graph shows the chloride data we collected this year at the test site. We began testing the water on October 14, 2004. When we took the chloride test, the amount of salt in the water was 208 milligrams per liter. Salt levels stayed in this area through November and the first couple of days of December, rising a bit and then falling slightly. On December 7th, the highways were salted. As you will remember, our hypothesis was that the road salt used to melt ice was causing the high salt levels in F____B____. Therefore, this was a crucial time to collect data. When we went to test the water two days later on Thursday, December 9th, we found that after the salting, chloride levels had jumped to 232mg/L. However, on the 16th of December, the level of salt contamination dropped."

M: "In the early days of January, the chloride contamination again rose to a new high level of 273mg/L, and then dropped slightly. By mid-January, high amounts of salt appeared in our water, a record of 281mg/L. After a brief drop, the salt hit the same level again. However, by early February, the chloride levels had dropped to around their original points."

FIGURE 7.9. Excerpts from PowerPoint presentation to adults.

Inquiry Reports in the Classroom: Developmental Continuum

School reports are so prevalent in classrooms that we have selected inquiry reports to describe in a developmental continuum (see Figure 7.10). If we chose another genre, eyewitness reports, for example, we would need to change some descriptors, like the sociocultural voice from the objective voice to the first-person voice. In presenting an inquiry report continuum, we assume you will adapt it as needed to fit other genres.

(text resumes on page 172)

	Monitoring the Process	World Knowledge	Discourse Knowledge	Time and Space	Sociocultural Membership
Planning	N: Knows purpose is to tell facts. Does not consider reader. Does not monitor (evaluate) usefulness of resource to inquiry. Does not plan.	N: Has a topic. Needs support to find useful resource. Copies full sentences or has incomplete notes.	N: Knows reports have facts.	N: Assumes reader knows how and why inquiry is conducted.	N: Unaware of voice.
	D: Knows purpose to report facts to a reader or the teacher. Needs teacher support to plan and to monitor usefulness of resources. Needs teacher support to monitor completeness of notes. May think of mentor texts.	D: Asks a question, with teacher support. Needs support to find pertinent resources. Needs support to organize notes.	D: Knows reports contain subsections. Needs teacher support for specific organization. Mixes everyday vocabulary and content terms in plans.	D: Needs support to describe how and why inquiry is being conducted (i.e., science investigation or historical context).	D: Does not think about voice.
	E: Knows purpose is to explain information to an audience. Monitors usefulness of resources and completeness of notes and plans. Thinks of mentor texts for craft.	E: Formulates an inquiry question and subquestions. Collects data from various resources. Evaluates usefulness of resources. Paraphrases information. Organizes notes.	E: Knows several genres for reports. Uses specific organization in plans. Uses content terms in plans.	E: Describes how and why inquiry is being conducted (i.e., science investigation or historical context).	E: Anticipates the need to have an objective voice of discipline.

FIGURE 7.10. Inquiry reports in the classroom: Developmental continuum.

(continued)

Producing Text	Monitoring the Process	World Knowledge	Discourse Knowledge	Time and Space	Sociocultural Membership
	N: Concentrates on what is interesting to self. May write haltingly always with same tool.	N: Writes what remembers or what is most interesting.	N: States topic (e.g., My report is about . . .). Lists information using familiar words. May use chronological sequence. May sequence by most interesting sections. May sequence sections in any order.	N: May include sketchy description of interest in inquiry.	N: Uses own voice. Uses a conversational voice.
	D: May refer to notes in plans. Needs support to monitor information and organization. May write a section fluently. Keeps purpose to inform in back of mind.	D: Includes data in notes. Includes relevant information in each section but may not be complete.	D: May sequence sections but may not link them. Needs teacher support for organization and for graphs and charts. Mixes familiar vocabulary and content terms in text.	D: Includes minimal context information for inquiry: the how, when, and why.	D: Mixes conversational tone with objective tone. Tries to adopt the voice of discipline.
	E: Monitors to see if plans are working in text-so-far. Monitors information for clarity and completeness. May return to planning. Keeps purpose to inform a specific audience in mind.	E: Selects information from plans. Considers what was learned and what information is important to inquiry. Represents ideas fully and accurately.	E: Considers order and organization. Links subtopics. Includes graphs and charts with text as needed. Uses content terms.	E: Describes context of inquiry easily: the how, when, and why did the inquiry.	E: Adopts an objective voice. Works to use voice of discipline.

Reviewing					
N: Knows to report facts. Does not consider audience. Considers report done after first draft.	**N:** Does not evaluate whether information is relevant. Does not recognize need to have precise evidence or facts.	**N:** Does not evaluate or revise organization. May add drawings or copied pictures. Does not revise for content vocabulary but may change a word or convention.	**N:** Does not evaluate description of topic of report.	**N:** Is unaware how voice represents a discipline. Keeps own voice.
D: Knows purpose is to inform an audience of facts. Recognizes need to check data or facts. Needs help monitoring for accuracy, clarity, and organization. May think of mentor texts.	**D:** May evaluate information for relevancy. May elaborate on data and learning, if encouraged. Needs support to revise for completeness of information.	**D:** Uses support to evaluate and revise sequence of subtopics. Needs help with transitions between sections. Uses support to evaluate and revise illustrative material or charts. Needs teacher support to evaluate conclusion. May revise to include content terms. Edits for some conventions.	**D:** Needs support to evaluate and revise context of inquiry: the how, when, and why.	**D:** Needs teacher support to revise voice for objectivity of discipline.
E: Thinks about purpose: to inform a specific audience. Monitors for accuracy, clarity, and organization. Refers to mentor texts for craft.	**E:** Evaluates and revises for clarity, accuracy, and completeness of data.	**E:** Evaluates and revises sequence of and transition between sections. Evaluates and revises conclusion. Evaluates and revises illustrative material or charts if needed. Edits for content terms and conventions.	**E:** Evaluates and revises context of the inquiry: the how, when, and why.	**E:** Uses teacher support to evaluate and revise the voice of the discipline. Tries to use an objective, yet interesting, voice.

FIGURE 7.10. (*continued*)

Skim the now familiar descriptors in *Monitoring the Process* column. However, remind yourself that even young students know the purpose of reports is to inform and that stories are different from information texts (Donovan, 2001; Donovan & Smolkin, 2002). With the report genre, monitoring the usefulness of the sources, the completeness of notes, and the use of mentor texts gradually increase.

Reading down the *World Knowledge* column, you will notice the descriptions of the three writers increase in the completeness and pre- ciseness of their knowledge of resources and content. First, you know resources are crucial to inquiry. Novice writers latch on to the first resource they find about their topic without considering its usefulness (Coiro, 2003), whereas experienced writers consult and evaluate mul- tiple resources for their usefulness to the inquiry (Many et al., 1996). Second, you know students need to locate and extract important infor- mation from their resources. Novice writers do not evaluate the rele- vancy of their data (Coiro, 2003; Graham, Harris, & MacArthur, 2006) and may note facts just because the facts are interesting to them (Many et al., 1996). Only experienced writers combine information from dif- ferent sources (Coiro & Dobler, 2007; Many et al., 1996), like websites, interviews, and experimental data.

In the *Discourse Knowledge* column, you notice that writers move from their general knowledge that reports have information to spe- cific knowledge about the characteristics of reports. Not knowledge- able about the genre, novice writers rely on the genres and vocabulary that are familiar to them (Ball, 1992; Chapman, 1995). They may create hybrid texts, may list information, use a story or chronological sequence, or order their information by what is most interesting to them (Cham- bliss, Christenson, & Parker, 2003, Newkirk, 1987, 1989). Developing writers include the different sections or subtopics in the report but do not connect them together (Donovan, 2001; Donovan & Smolkin, 2002; Graham et al., 2006; Langer, 1986; Many et al., 1996; Spivey & King, 1989). Only experienced writers organize reports by connecting the sections or subtopics (Donovan, 2001; Langer, 1986), include measure- ments, graphs, or illustrative material, and incorporate content terms (Lemke, 2004).

Referring to the *Time and Space* column, you can see that all writ- ers know that the reader was not present. Interestingly, many students describe, at least partially, the how, when, and where of their science inquiries. In contrast, students need instruction to recognize and include the historical context in a report on an event or person (De La Paz, 2005).

For the *Sociocultural Membership* column, you probably agree that stu- dents need to expand their repertoires from their own conversational voice to the objective voice of disciplines (Lemke, 2004). Novice writers rely on their own voice from their home community (Ball, 1992), while developing writers mix a personal, conversational voice with an objective, factual voice of disciplines (Kamberlis, 1999). Even experienced writers will need teacher support to produce an objective, yet interesting, voice as they move toward becoming members of the discipline community (Lemke, 2004).

We hope you and your students will find situations to write many of these genres, not just the report, in different content areas in order to learn how to explain to different audiences. Now, we discuss the genre family of giving directions.

TO GIVE DIRECTIONS GENRE

In language arts textbooks, we frequently encounter the lesson that asks students to write how to make a peanut butter sandwich. We think you have situations right in your classroom in which students can instruct instead of using the trite sandwich lesson!

Think about classroom situations in which you could incorporate these genres. Physical education provides situations in which students could write directions for a specific play or strategy. Health curricula have opportunities to write manuals for better diets and advice letters about bullying. Math has myriad situations for comparing students' problem-solving strategies. Geography provides maps; science provides diagrams. You can mine every curricula area for opportunities to give directions.

These genres occur in everyday life, too. Students may be using mentor texts at home without really thinking about them. Students may be reading recipes, game directions, hobby instructions, maps, or advice columns, for example. In Table 7.4, we have brainstormed suggestions for the giving directions genres. See Appendix 7.1 at the end of this chapter for a sampling of mentor texts.

Now think about audiences for instructions. Younger students and peers are ready audiences. But, who in the community might benefit? Could the school committee benefit from a manual on better diets for the cafeteria? Could city officials benefit from a map for a bike path to school? Do potential parent coaches need a manual about coaching young children in T-ball?

Have you ever given directions for something you do on automatic pilot? Most writers know to put the steps in order but are amazed at the amount of detail needed for inexperienced audiences! You may have encountered recipes that leave out a detail or a step assuming that the cook is experienced (for example, many recipes state "Cream the eggs

TABLE 7.4. Sampling of Instructional Genres

- Recipes
- Game directions
- Directions for a sports move
- Directions for playing an instrument
- Directions for making an object or putting a toy together
- Directions for technology—cell phones, iPods, DVDs
- Manuals for survival or for computer programs
- Maps, diagrams
- Advice letters and columns, handyman columns
- Science experiments or observations
- Math problems, math problem-solving processes

and sugar" but do not list the steps: beat the eggs and then add the sugar very gradually while still beating the eggs.). Thus, depending on the specific genre, characteristics for directions include:

- Detailed steps to follow.
- Steps in sequential order.
- Signal words for sequence (i.e., first, next).
- Command or second-person sentences (i.e., you . . .).
- Labeled diagrams or illustrations.
- List of ingredients or equipment, if needed.
- Alternative steps or helpful hints, optional.

Crucial to all directions are specific details and sequential order, whereas other characteristics may be optional. Let's now observe a classroom scenario.

Classroom Scenario: Directions for Technological Devices

In the classroom scenario, the teacher asks her students to think about technology that their grandparents have difficulty using and so need directions.

Preparing to Teach

Deciding to incorporate writing directions into her language arts curriculum, Ms. Schmidt thinks her students are familiar with game directions and recipes but may not have written directions themselves. She decides to limit the topic to technology and to assign their grandparents as their audience.

Supporting Students' Exploring Ideas

Ms. Schmidt opens the project by asking the students to think of their grandparents—What types of technology did grandparents have difficulty using? Immediately, hands shoot up and a list is created—DVDs, e-mail, cell phones, MP3 players, digital cameras, CDs, and iTunes (world knowledge). Grinning, Ms. Schmidt comments she could use help using her cell phone.

Next, Ms. Schmidt asks the students to remember how they wrote their memoirs; they focused on one, most interesting event and not the entire day or the entire trip. Directions need to be focused, too. For example, how could the big topic of digital cameras be focused or narrowed to a smaller set of directions? The students suggest directions for how to take pictures of people and how to load pictures on the computer. For cell phones, they suggest how to make a call, how to set an alarm, and how to change ring tones. The students begin to choose a narrow topic for their directions.

Supporting Students' Planning

The next day, Ms. Schmidt gives the students *How-to Planning* sheets (discourse knowledge). The students choose their narrow topics and plan four or five steps (Figure 7.11).

Interrupting their planning, Ms. Schmidt asks them to think about whether a diagram would help a grandparent understand a step. For

How to ...

Step 1	Step 2
For a cell phone you have to press the off button and hold it down to turn it on.	When you want to call someone you have to dile the number of the person you want to talk to

Step 3	Step 4
To talk to that person when you are done diling you have to press a green button with a phone on it that says talk.	You press that button and then the phone will start ringing and then when they answer you can talk.
	Step 5
	When you are done talking you press the red button across from the green b. that says off.

FIGURE 7.11. An example of a how-to planning sheet.

example, would a drawing of a cell phone help the reader locate the correct button?

Supporting Students' Producing Text

The next week, the students write their drafts using their plans. Following Ms. Schmidt's suggestion, they write each step on a separate piece of paper. One or two students change topics but most write their drafts easily. Many students insert diagrams or drawings into their steps (see Figure 7.12).

Supporting Students' Reviewing: Evaluating and Revising

Once students have rough drafts, Ms. Schmidt and the students develop a list of text characteristics to evaluate their drafts (see Table 7.5).

Students return to their desks and begin to revise. To assist their revisions, Ms. Schmidt suggests they bring in their iPod or cell phone, if their parents say they can. Over the next three days, Ms. Schmidt circulates, giving feedback primarily on the details in their directions.

Do you need to set an alarm on your phone but you don't know how? Well I can teach you. First make sure your phone is on. To turn it on you either have an on button or hold down the red phone button.

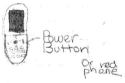

Next press the ok button or whatever button takes you to your options or menu. Now you click the side arrow keys until you get to the settings bar. Then press the down arrow key until you reach tools and press ok.

Last but not least you will see a list of tools and press the down arrows keys until you get to the alarm clock. Then press ok. Now you will set your time using all the arrow keys and press ok to set and save you alarm. To exit press the red phone button and you are finished.

FIGURE 7.12. Example of a draft for directions.

TABLE 7.5. Class's List of Direction Features

1. What are you giving directions for and to whom? (purpose and audience)
2. Are the steps in the correct order? (discourse knowledge)
3. Have you included enough details in each step for the reader to know what to do? (world knowledge)
4. Are transitional words used between steps? (time and space)
5. Is a diagram needed? (time and space)
6. Do the directions sound easy, fun, encouraging, and respectful? (sociocultural membership)

Note. Our terms are in parentheses.

Note the revisions Sue made to "How to Set an Alarm" (Figure 7.13). Sue added clarifying details for locations and functions within her three steps.

After revising and receiving feedback from Ms. Schmidt, the students produce a final edited set of directions. Everyone had definite steps but the preciseness of the details varied among the final drafts. Some students included labeled diagrams to show locations. They clearly learned that writing directions was exacting work—much harder than just showing a grandparent how to do it or doing it for them.

Although the class did not send the final drafts to their grandparents, we would have. We also would have used the familiar audience of grandparents to assist the students thinking about the unknown audience of seniors at an assisted-living residence. We think many seniors would welcome the students' help and the students would benefit from writing to unknown audiences. Now, we turn to a developmental continuum for directions.

Directions in the Classroom: Developmental Continuum

We have fun writing directions with students. They usually choose a topic in which they are "experts." However, the key is narrowing the topic to one small action—not how to play the trumpet but how to form your lips on the mouthpiece—an embouchure.

Can you predict our descriptions in the *Monitoring the Process* column in Figure 7.14? You know that students know the purpose of directions and bring their various experiences with directions to the writing situation. Increasingly, students monitor what readers need as they plan, produce, and review their directions.

In the *World Knowledge* column, you know students first need to choose a narrow topic rather than a huge one (like in personal narratives). Second, students increasingly discover how precise and explicit the details in their directions need to be.

1

How To Set an Alarm On Your Phone

Do you need to set an alarm on your phone but you don't know how? Well I can teach you. First, make sure your phone is on. To turn it on you either have an on button ~~or~~ you can hold down the red button with the ~~phone~~ phone on it. ~~button.~~

Power Button

Or red phone

Next, press the ok button in the center of all the arrows ~~or whatever button~~ to take you to your options or menu. ~~Now you~~ After click the side arrow keys until you get to the settings bar. ~~Then~~ Now press the down arrow key until you reach tools. ~~And~~ Press the ok button after that.

located at the top of the screen

OK Button

OK Button

Down Arrow Keys

Side Arrow Keys

Which ~~will~~ most likely be in the corner of your screen and say settings right on it.

Which will list lots of options like calls, messaging and get it now.

(continued)

FIGURE 7.13. Revised directions.

FIGURE 7.13. *(continued)*

In the *Discourse Knowledge* column, you know that while students know directions have steps, they often have gaps in their sequences. Both novice and developing writers may use sequential words (first, next) and may use insider jargon they have learned from their experiences, such as sports jargon—hat trick, walk-off homer, or take it to the hoop—and assume, perhaps incorrectly, that their readers understand. Experienced writers introduce the task, explain how the reader will benefit from the directions, and consider adding hints or alternative ways to perform the task.

In the *Time and Space* column, you recognize that students include varying degrees of explicitness for how, when, and where to perform actions. As they learn, students begin to recognize the need to label diagrams to show readers where buttons, for example, are located on

(text resumes on page 183)

Planning	Monitoring the Process	World Knowledge	Discourse Knowledge	Time and Space	Sociocultural Membership
	N: Knows purpose is to tell someone how to do a task. Does not plan.	N: Chooses a huge task (how to play basketball). Needs support to narrow topic. Has gaps in knowledge.	N: Knows directions contain steps. Has gaps in sequence of steps and details.	N: Assumes reader shares the same experiences with task.	N: Assumes reader is like self.
	D: Knows purpose is to tell reader how to perform a task. May think about known reader. Needs teacher support to plan.	D: Chooses a narrow task. (free throws) with help. Uses own knowledge or experience in plans.	D: Needs graphic organizer to sequence steps. May overlook steps in sequence and detail needed.	D: May know there is a need to tell how and when to perform steps but may be general rather than specific.	D: Realizes reader may be naïve but needs support to include specific language in plans.
	E: Knows purpose is to explicitly tell how to perform a task. Tries to predict reader knowledge. Monitors plans for explicitness and completeness.	E: Chooses a focused task. May interview or read to supplement own knowledge.	E: Organizes plans into sequential steps and details needed. Decides if or where diagrams would be useful.	E: Recognizes need to inform explicitly how and when to perform steps.	E: Recognizes need to use explicit language due to reader's naivety.

Producing Text	N: Writes general, imprecise steps.	N: States task. Skips steps. Uses general words or imprecise details. Uses insider jargon without explanation (e.g., take it to the hoop).	N: Assumes task and steps are clear.	N: Concentrates on own experiences. "Do it this way" voice.
N: Writes directions off top of head without plan. May write haltingly with same tool. Thinks about telling how but disregards reader.				
D: May follow plan. May write fluently with any tool. Pauses to think of how to do steps.	D: Writes steps based own experience. Has few details in steps.	D: May introduce task. Writes steps in sequence but may have gaps. Mixes imprecise and explicit wording. Uses insider jargon. May use command sentences and sequential terms (e.g., next). May draw a diagram, if teacher support.	D: Includes details telling how, when, where to do steps inconsistently.	D: Uses a conversational voice. Tries to adopt encouraging, knowledgeable voice.
E: Refers to plan. May revise plan. Monitors draft for sequence and explicitness. Monitors draft for purpose (to show how) and own predictions of reader's knowledge.	E: Uses plan to select steps and pertinent details.	E: Introduces task and explains how reader could benefit from directions. Sequences steps. Chooses explicit wording, explains terms, includes sequential terms. Uses directive sentences (e.g., commands or you). Includes diagram, if useful.	E: Includes details to show how, when, and where to do steps. May tell why a step is important. Labels diagrams, if used.	E: Adopts a helpful, knowledgeable, advisory voice. Uses encouraging voice, especially in introduction and closing.

FIGURE 7.14. Directions in the classroom: Developmental continuum.

(continued)

	Monitoring the Process	World Knowledge	Discourse Knowledge	Time and Space	Sociocultural Membership
Reviewing	**N:** Knows purpose is to tell how to do a task. Does not think about reader. Considers only own way of completing task. Thinks first draft is final draft. **D:** Knows purpose is to tell how to do a task. Needs support to think about reader. Needs support to reread and to monitor for sequence and explicitness in draft. Knows first draft needs reviewing. **E:** Thinks about purpose: to explain how to do a task and potential reader. Monitors sequence and details for clarity and accuracy. Monitors word choice for helpful voice. Monitors revisions for purpose and predictions of reader's ability to follow the directions. May refer to mentor texts.	**N:** Does not recognize task chosen is huge. Does not evaluate for missing steps or incomplete information. **D:** Needs support to evaluate for explicit details within steps. **E:** Evaluates and revises for explicit and precise details in steps.	**N:** Does not evaluate and revise to add steps or to change sequence of steps. Needs support to add sequence words and details in steps. May change a word or conventions. **D:** May evaluate and revise introduction. Needs support to evaluate and revise sequence in steps and preciseness of wording. May recognize and revise insider jargon if support. May evaluate and revise diagram, with support. May revise conventions. **E:** Evaluates and revises sequence in steps, preciseness of wording, and usefulness of labeled diagram. Revises explanations of insider jargon for clarity as needed. May add hints or alternative actions. Edits for conventions.	**N:** Assumes anyone can follow directions. **D:** Needs support to evaluate details that tell how, when, and where to do the steps. **E:** Evaluates and revises introduction for benefits in following directions. Evaluates and revises details to tell how, when, and where to do the steps.	**N:** Does not evaluate for voice. **D:** Keeps conversational voice. May revise to add an encouraging voice. **E:** Seeks feedback to evaluate and revise for a helpful, advisory, encouraging voice.

FIGURE 7.14. *(continued)*

devices. They revise their introductions to clarify the context or the benefits gained by following the directions.

Skimming the *Sociocultural Membership* column, you know to look for voice and point-of-view differences. Novice writers who have less experience thinking about sociocultural communities and their impact on writing assume readers are like themselves and adopt a directive voice: "Here's how to do it." With instruction and opportunities to consider voice and points of view, writers recognize that the reader may be inexperienced and adopt an encouraging voice: "Do you need to set an alarm on your phone but don't know how? I can teach you." Using a helpful, advisory voice in their directions, they recognize readers may have different perspectives, such as fear or uncertainty regarding technology.

Giving directions for an activity you do well can be challenging. Until you write for a naïve reader, you probably do not recognize how many steps you automatically perform and the details you automatically pay attention to. When students write directions, we expect missing information—details and steps. Treated lightly and with humor, missing information can be fun when students perform each other's directions. We recommend students perform each other's directions before sending them to an unknown audience.

CHAPTER SUMMARY

"Writing to Inform" is a companion chapter to "Writing to Entertain." Therefore, the emphasis is once again on good instructional practices when students write these genres: to persuade, to explain, and to give directions. Writing to inform needs effective instructional practices because students are less familiar with the many written genres of writing to inform than with the genres of writing to entertain. They may know informational books are different than fiction books; they may have read or certainly been given oral directions; and they may have argued orally with relatives, friends, or teachers. What they have not done, most likely, is written in the genres and so not carefully considered their specific characteristics, purposes, and audiences.

We share classroom scenarios to illustrate how three teachers prepare to teach to persuade, to explain, and to give directions. In each respective scenario, the teacher has students either explore issues of concern, collect and analyze data, or choose a technological device. Then, the teachers have students explore the target genre and discuss the common characteristics of the genre. Throughout planning, producing, and reviewing texts, the teachers support the students by reviewing the genre characteristics and encouraging them to consider the specific audience with whom they plan to communicate. Embedded within their considerations of their respective audiences are the dimensions of our communication model.

We include a developmental continuum for each genre, specifically designed with the characteristics of the genre in mind. Each research-based continuum identifies characteristics of novice, developing, and experienced writers for the targeted genre. As with the continua in Chapters 4, 5, and 6, the continua in this chapter can be used to supply the teacher with information about the strengths and needs of the entire class, a small subset of students, or individual students.

Students need opportunities in the write to inform genres and the write to entertain genres so that they learn to select the most appropriate genre for the communicative situations they encounter. Having practiced and tried out different genres, they may invent a hybrid genre because the situation warrants it.

In these two genre chapters we have presented specific characteristics for the genres. If we looked closely at how writers compose texts within these genres (and others), we'd notice that they pay attention to common elements such as topic development and the treatment of details. In the next chapter, "Reading to Evaluate," we take up those common elements used to evaluate all texts.

APPLICATION BOX

Choose one of the genres—to persuade, to explain, to give directions—to teach in your classroom. What situation in your classroom, school, or community lends itself to one of these purposes? What different audiences could students communicate with?

Think about the students in your classroom. How familiar are they with the genre you've chosen? What instruction will they need to write effectively? Will you follow the instructional outline of the teachers cited in this chapter or will you need to alter the instruction to better suit your students? Sometimes students need to spend considerable time planning before attempting to produce texts. Thinking about your students, survey the developmental continuum for the genre so that you have an idea what to expect.

Using Appendix 7.1 of this chapter, collect mentor texts and also consult with a friendly librarian. If you have explored these genres in journal entries or have listed topics in your territories, choose a topic to write with your students. Students like to see how a teacher plans, produces, and reviews a draft and they learn teachers aren't perfect writers either.

Resources for Writing to Inform

Mentor Texts to Persuade

Gore, A. (2007). *An inconvenient truth: The crisis of global warming.* New York: Viking Juvenile.

Al Gore has adapted his adult book on the global warming crisis for a younger audience. The text employs a range of persuasive argument techniques including logic, emotional appeal, refuting counterarguments, and powerful images. Grades 5–8.

Odyssey: Adventures in Science (*www.odysseymagazine.com*)

Occasionally, this magazine includes articles that outline the pros and cons for an issue. In February 2008, "Biofuels: Fuel for the Future or Foolishness," Pfeiffer outlines both sides and ends with a position. In April 2008, the issue of animal rights is argued is two essays: (1) "Point—Apes Need Rights" and (2) "Counterpoint—But Research on Apes Helps Cure Human Diseases." Have students find the evidence the authors cited for their positions on biofuels and animal rights. Grades 4–8.

Orloff, K. K. (2004). *I wanna iguana.* New York: Putnam.

In a series of letters, a young boy persuades his mother to let him adopt an iguana as a pet. The boy employs a range of arguments built on logic, emotion, and even blackmail. Use this book with students of all ages to evaluate the boy's attempts to convince his mother. Grades 3–8.

Scieszka, J. (1989). *The true story of the three little pigs.* New York: Viking.

Alexander T. Wolf gives his side of the story in this fractured fairytale. Claiming that wolves get a bad rap because their diets consist of "cute little animals," he cites the cold and rude behavior of the pigs as evidence for his case. Ask your students to discuss how well the wolf pleads his case. Grades 3–6.

Stone Soup (*www.stonesoup.com/books*)

Stone Soup magazine has compiled many reviews of books written by students. Have your students evaluate the reviews to determine whether strengths, weaknesses, and recommendations are included in the reviews. Then, your students can submit their reviews. Grades 4–8.

Van Allsburg, C. (1990). *Just a dream.* Boston: Houghton Mifflin.

A callous and careless young boy is convinced that he should play a role in preserving his environment when, in a series of dream images, he is shown a glimpse of the consequences of pollution and congestion. Discuss the power of images as instruments of persuasion. Grades 3–8.

Mentor Texts to Explain

Abadzis, N. (2007). *Laika.* New York: First Second.

This complex graphic novel blends fact and fiction to tell the story of Laika, the dog that was launched into orbit on Sputnik II in 1957. The novel features the stories of Laika, the rocket engineer, and the lab technician who cared for the dog. Discuss how the images and text present the complicated political and ethical issues involved in the research conducted by the author. Grades 6–8.

Jenkins, S. (1998). *Hottest, coldest, highest, deepest.* Boston: Houghton Mifflin.

The text presents superlative geographical features through paper-collage images and brief text. Notice how the author makes a one-sentence statement about an extreme geographical area in larger fonts and includes related information about other areas in smaller type. Use the text as a model of an alternative structure for an explanatory text. Grades 3–8.

Montgomery, S. (2006). *Quest for the tree kangaroo.* Boston: Houghton Mifflin.

This photo essay describes a scientific expedition to study the tree kangaroo population of Papua New Guinea. Examine how Sy Montgomery describes the setting of her research; she uses vivid descriptive imagery to help the reader envision the lushness of the Cloud Forest. Grades 3–6.

Simon, S. (2006). *Horses.* New York: HarperCollins.

Seymour Simon is known for his spectacular photography and engaging informational texts. In *Horses*, he presents an overview of human relationship with horses, breeding practices, and horse care. Discuss the organization and how Simon engages the reader's interest. Then compare *Horses* to other books by Simon. Grades 3–6.

Siy, A., & Kunkel, D. (2005). *Mosquito bite.* Cambridge, MA: Charlesbridge.

Your skin will crawl as you and your students read this informational text about mosquitoes and their life cycles. Notice how the authors embed factual information about the mosquito within a hypothetical scenario in which a young boy experiences a mosquito bite. Notice, too, how much information is presented through images and diagrams. Grades 3–6.

Thimmesh, C. (2006). *Team Moon: How 400,000 people landed Apollo 11 on the moon.* Boston: Houghton Mifflin.

In *Team Moon*, Catherine Thimmesh presents stories of the people "behind the scenes" who supported the launch of Apollo 11, from the seamstresses who sewed the astronauts' boots to the Radi Telescope operators who made sure the images were broadcast around the world. The text is notable for its intriguing structure; she weaves stories about the people who made it all happen into a sequential description of the voyage. Also note the author's creative use of language. Grades 5–8.

Mentor Texts to Give Directions

Ancona G. (1994). *The piñata maker/El piñatero.* New York: Harcourt.

This bilingual photo essay characterizes the creative process of a piñata maker. The steps for making piñatas are embedded in a narrative presentation of the artist's work. Discuss the alternative structure for giving directions. Grades 3–8.

Borgenicht, D., & Epstein, R. (2007). *The worst-case scenario survival handbook: Junior edition*. San Francisco: Chronicle Books.

A spin-off from the adult series for a younger audience, *The Worst-Case Scenario Survival Handbook* includes directions on how to weather a variety of challenging situations, including a bad report card, a nosy sibling, and a bicycle accident. Have your students evaluate the effectiveness of the instructions and study the ways that the instructions are written. Grades 3–8.

Irvine, J. (1992). *How to make super pop-ups*. New York: Morrow.

In this activity book, students will learn how to create their own pop-up books. Evaluate the clarity of the step-by-step directions and accompanying line drawings. Grades 3–8.

Kids Discover (*www.kidsdiscover.com*)

Each issue of this magazine focuses on a specific topic or theme and includes an activity section. For example, in April 2008, on conservation, the activity section was on "Reusable Ideas", such as directions for turning egg cartons into seed pots or jewelry boxes. Grades 3–6.

Lupton, E., & Lupton, J. (2007). *D.I.Y. kids*. New York: Princeton Architectural Press.

This activity book encourages students to do the work of designers by creating graphics, toys, home décor, and furniture. The text is notable for its characteristics: interviews with designers, directions for a variety of projects clearly illustrated with photographs, and a rating system that indicates the help, time, mess, and cost associated with each project. Grades 3–8.

Scholastic Art (*www.scholastic.com/products/classmags/art.htm*)

Each issue of this magazine focuses on a specific art theme or technique. In the "Scholastic Art Workshop" section, the concepts of the articles are applied to art projects. Materials, steps, and pictures with explanations are given. For example, in March 2008, the issue was on Mexican muralists and the workshop was "Telling Your Visual Stories." Examine the clarity of the directions and pictures, and try out their effectiveness. Grades 3–6.

Sports Illustrated Kids (*www.sikids.com*)

Each issue of this magazine contains a column, "Tips from the Pros," in which steps for a sports move are outlined, often with hints, too. In April 2008, Ronnie Creager, a pro skateboarder, instructed how to land a kick flip. In March 2008, San Antonio Spurs basketball guard Brent Barry gave directions for three-point shooting. Have students follow the directions to evaluate the clarity. Grade 3–8.

Chapter 8

Reading to Evaluate Writing

In Chapter 5, we introduced writers' journals and invited you to keep a journal (or journals) along with your students. After reading Chapters 6 and 7, the genre chapters, perhaps you began to transform some of your journal entries into extended texts, such as stories, poems, raps, letters, podcast scripts, or PowerPoint reports for known and unfamiliar audiences. If you have a draft, you have probably been rereading it and thinking about whether it is good. Maybe you have even looked back at Chapter 6 or 7 to find where the genre characteristics were discussed and students' writing evaluated in the classroom scenario to see how you have been doing.

In this chapter, we consider how we evaluate writing—the first component of reviewing. Perhaps in the past, you have had teachers who have evaluated your writing by focusing just on conventions; they may have used a red pen to identify misplaced punctuation marks and grammatical flaws. We know, however, that there is much more to good writing than punctuation and grammar. When evaluating writing, many teachers now look not only at the conventions of writing but also at the concepts that are expressed in the written text. Although states and the literature on evaluation label and group the elements differently, everyone includes common elements that contribute to good writing, for example, idea development, organization, voice, word choice, sentence fluency, and conventions (Spandel, 2004). Writers use these elements or traits for all purposes, audiences, and genres. Since these elements are universal, we incorporate them into our evaluation of writing, framing them so they align with the four dimensions of our communication model.

When teachers teach the elements of writing explicitly and define good writing, students tend to produce higher quality texts than when teachers do not directly incorporate the elements into the writing curriculum (Jarmer, Kozol, Nelson, & Salsberry, 2000). Writers should be familiar with these elements and know how to evaluate texts using them.

In this chapter, we:

- Emphasize the message or content of communication.
- Present an Evaluation Guide to examine writing products.
- Look at the writer and then go beyond what we can learn from the Evaluation Guide.
- Outline a process for evaluating writing.

We return to reviewing in Chapter 9 to look at the other two components of reviewing: revising and editing.

EMPHASIZING THE MESSAGE OF WRITTEN COMMUNICATION

When trying to judge the quality of a piece of writing, first and foremost, we keep in mind that we write to communicate our thinking. Of primary importance, especially in earlier drafts, are the writer's ideas and how the ideas are organized and expressed. Elements of writing that focus on meaning are often referred to as content-level features (Bratcher, 1994; Olson & Raffeld, 1987; Patthey-Chavex, Matsummura, & Valdés, 2004). When we evaluate content, we tend to think about what is being said. For example, we consider whether details need to be added or deleted, whether thoughts need to be restructured, and whether the language used is clear and appropriate. In short, we focus on the message.

Most often, we do not need to worry about individual word choices, how sentences are structured, spelling, capitalization, usage, or punctuation—surface-level features—until the writer's intended message—the content—is clear. Occasionally, changes at the surface level are necessary to enhance meaning. When the misspelling of a key word makes it impossible for a reader to understand the text, for example, the writer should stop and correct the spelling in an early draft. For instance, if a student is recording moon observations and writes *konsilasuns* instead of *constellations*, readers may find their understanding disrupted unless the spelling is corrected. Usually, however, the communication of ideas should precede judgments about surface features when evaluating writing. Therefore, we present content or world knowledge first in the Evaluation Guide, as you will see in the next section.

LOOKING AT WRITING PRODUCTS: THE EVALUATION GUIDE

In this chapter, we introduce the Evaluation Guide—an instrument that connects the elements of writing to the four dimensions of our communication model (see Figures 8.1, 8.3, 8.4, and 8.5). The Evaluation Guide focuses on content-level and surface-level elements, just as most research-based forms of evaluation do. In addition, the guide helps us account for the impact that distance between writer and reader has on the quality of writing.

In the Evaluation Guide, we demystify the elements of writing. Notice that across the top of each figure, we identify a target dimension—world knowledge—for example, in Figure 8.1. In the first column, we identify the major text elements that contribute to the target dimension. For instance, in the world knowledge section of the guide you will find topic development, idea generation, and detail treatment. Moving onto the center column, you will notice specific characteristics. In this part of the guide, we "unpack" each element and identify the qualities that make each one unique. Finally, in the right-hand column, we provide concrete questions that correspond to each element. Keeping the questions in mind will help you evaluate your students' work and help students evaluate each other's work. Let's take a closer look at how we can evaluate each dimension, beginning with world knowledge.

World Knowledge

When evaluating world knowledge, we are really considering whether the writer's knowledge has come through in what has been written and if the knowledge has been conveyed in a way that meets the reader's needs. As you can see in the first column of Figure 8.1, we think about the three elements of world knowledge: topic development, idea generation, and detail treatment.

Looking at the center column of our Evaluation Guide for world knowledge, you will notice that for topic development, which is the overarching text element, we want to see if the paper contains a topic that is clear, focused, narrow enough, yet also broad enough, to serve the writer's purpose and audience. Next, we move from topic development to the middle level of specificity: idea generation. We determine if the main events or points are emphasized. Finally, we move to the most pre-

Text Elements	Characteristics of Text Elements	Evaluating Text Elements— Does the text include ...

Topic development	• The major purpose for writing the text is evident and clear.
	• A topic that is focused.
	   o A story has a clear problem.
	   o An informational text has a central theme, question, or problem.
		• A purpose, topic, and theme that is readily apparent?
		• A topic that is narrow enough to serve the writer's purpose yet broad enough to entertain or to inform?
		• A topic that is focused?

Idea generation	• Main points or events are emphasized.
	   o When writing to entertain, writers generate ideas to plot out major events.
	   o When writing to inform, they describe key points.
		• Main ideas and main events that are pertinent to the theme, topic, purpose, and reader? (Extraneous main ideas or main events are not included.)
		• Main ideas and main events that are elaborated when necessary to provide information or to enhance the piece?
		• Main ideas and main events, as well as major subtopics, that reflect a solid understanding of the topic?

Detail treatment	• Details are specific and accurate. • Details should be directly connected to the topic.	• Details that reveal information or add to the beauty of the piece? • Details that enhance the piece and help develop the main ideas or main events? (Rather than details that repeat the same information or ideas in different ways.) • Details that are specific, relevant, and concrete? • Details that are significant and carefully selected? (Not every possible detail.)

FIGURE 8.1. The Evaluation Guide: World knowledge.

cise level of world knowledge: detail treatment. We determine how accurate and specific the details are that support the ideas in the piece. We check to see if the details connect directly to the main ideas, which in turn support the topic.

An awareness of differences in the amount and type of world knowledge writers and readers share enables writers to make decisions about their topic—the big messages they want to convey. They determine which ideas they will choose to include and how much emphasis each will get, as well as how much supporting detail to provide.

Now, let's take a look at a report written by Kristin, a fifth grader, to see how we would evaluate it using the elements of world knowledge.

For the past several weeks, Kristin and her classmates have been writing research reports on topics that align with their science curriculum. She has worked through several drafts to produce her report (see Figure 8.2).

We can see that the title, "Heredity," and first few sentences let the reader know the broad topic of the report. Although Kristin has researched this topic, whether she really understands the key ideas in her report (e.g., dominant and recessive genes) is not clear. She does not develop the ideas fully (e.g., what chromosomes are and what role they play in heredity).

Often, the ideas or details are ambiguous ("That's why me, Karla, and Nathaniel have both X and Y genes"). Furthermore, she adds irrelevant details when she introduces information from the TV show she watched. She is making valid connections to her own life, but the information does little to enhance the piece or to demonstrate her knowledge of the concepts about which she is reporting. As a result, we do not get a clear sense of Kristin's understanding of the topic. We return to Kristin's report when we present each dimension. Now, we explain how to evaluate discourse knowledge.

Heredity
By Kristin XXXX

Who do you look like? The answer to this question might come from heredity. Heredity is when we get our traits from our parents. We get them through genes. Plants and animals also have genes. The genes determine our hair color, curly or straight hair, freckles, blood type, skin color, eye color, height, weight, and lots of other information about how we look and how our bodys function. [Comment: Kristin's heading and first few sentences introduce the topic of her report.]

An article on the Internet said that we have 46 genes. We have 23 genes from our mothers and 23 genes from our fathers. We get one gene from each parent. The genes are on chromosomes. Chromosomes are like threads, they are inside cells. Some genes are dominant. If your mother has a dominant gene and your father has a recessive gene, you will have your mother's trait. Dominant genes are written with a capital letter. No matter what, some genes will dominate. For example, if you can roll your tongue, have double jointed thumbs, have dimples. Sometimes parents who both have black hair can have a child who has red hair. This is because some genes are dominant and some are recessive. My mother has freckles but my father doesn't. I look like my mother but Nathaniel and Karla look like my father. [Comment: Kristin understands that her report should contain information from different resources. She uses the Internet, her experiences, and general knowledge.] [Comment: Kristin uses a comma when a period is necessary.] [Comment: These sentences, and others like them, make us wonder how much world knowledge Kristin has and how effectively she is able to take on membership in a scientific community.]

Genes also determine if you are a boy or a girl. You are a boy if you get an X chromosome from your mother and a Y from your father. If you are a boy, you get XY and if you are a girl, you get XX. Genes are necessary for people. That's why me, Karla and Nathaniel have both X and Y genes. [Comment: Kristin does not take into consideration a distant reader who would not know who Nathaniel and Karla are (time and space).] [Comment: This sentence is ambiguous.]

DNA is a combination of genes and chromosomes. It stands for deoxyribonucleic acid. Genes live inside these DNA molecules. There have been cases where police officers use DNA to convict criminals. They take samples from a person's body or hair that has fallen off and send it to a lab. The lab does tests on the sample and can determine if the person is guilty or innocent. I saw a show on TV where a man was in prison for a crime he didn't commit. He was there for eight years, the DNA proved he was not the person who killed the man. [Comment: Kristin uses some scientific vocabulary (discourse knowledge and evidence of sociocultural membership).] [Comment: Irrelevant details.]

In conclusion, it is important for us to know about heredity. Genes, chromosomes and DNA are like blueprints for our bodys. They determine what we look like and what our bodys can and can't do. We get these traits from our parents. Heredity allows this to happen.

FIGURE 8.2. Kristin's heredity report.

Discourse Knowledge

As was the case with world knowledge, we examine the writer's discourse knowledge (see Figure 8.3) on any given piece of writing by focusing first on the broader elements of the dimension and then proceeding to look at narrower elements. In this case, we progress from genre knowledge, to organizational structures, to sentence construction, to word choice, and finally, to conventions.

We look first at genre knowledge. Does the chosen genre serve the writer's purpose and the intended reader's needs? Has the writer included features that characterize the chosen genre or a blending of genres? (You know to look back to Chapters 6 and 7 for discussions of genre characteristics.) Next, we consider how the piece is organized and how seamlessly the writer moves the reader through the piece. We think about leads, transitions, conclusions, the sequencing of ideas, the relationship between and among ideas, and paragraph breaks.

Once we consider how the piece is organized, we take a closer look at the sentence construction. Are the sentences crafted so they help the writer communicate both simple and complex ideas? Do the sentences vary in construction so they emphasize key ideas, add variety to the composition, and enhance the flow of the writing?

Moving from the sentence-level element to the word-level element, we consider the writer's word choice. We look to see if words and phrases are used effectively to engage and/or inform the reader, whether the writer includes strong, accurate, precise nouns and verbs, and whether the writer includes the specialized vocabulary of a particular discourse and sociocultural community. For example, we might ask if the words in a letter to a member of Congress would convince the representative to vote for a bill.

Finally, we look to see how the writer's use of conventions impacts the message being communicated. Has the writer employed grammar (subject/verb agreement, possessives, complete sentences, or effective fragments), word usage (commonly confused words such as *its* and *it's*), and mechanics (punctuation and spelling) that enable the reader to accurately comprehend the writer's intended message?

If we go back to Kristin's science report (see Figure 8.2), we see that she is using a nonfiction genre (report writing) to communicate her ideas. Kristin understands that reports provide information from multiple sources: Internet, science texts, and her background knowledge. Kristin's report is organized in a text structure of main ideas and details that serve her purpose. Her lead, although not overly engaging, does introduce the reader to her key idea. Kristin breaks her report into paragraphs, with each paragraph focusing on one topic. She transitions from one paragraph to another without losing her reader, using the

Text Elements	Characteristics of Text Elements	Evaluating Text Elements— Does the text include ...
Genre knowledge	• Genre is chosen to fit purpose and audience. ○ Some texts entertain while others inform. • Genre-specific characteristics that signal the chosen genre—for example: ○ In stories, realistic characters and rising action. ○ In informational texts, a convincing argument. ○ See Chapters 6 and 7 for specific characteristics.	• A genre that achieves the writer's purpose and the reader's needs? (The writer might experiment with genres, blending characteristics from more than one to achieve purpose and audience needs.) • Accepted features of the chosen genre(s)? • Appropriate vocabulary and style for the genre?
Organizational structure	• An effective organizational pattern. ○ In stories, story grammar. ○ In informational texts, such as cause/effect, compare/ contrast. • The piece is structured around a beginning, middle, end, or introduction, body, and conclusion.	• An engaging lead or introduction? • Smooth transitions? • An effective conclusion or satisfying resolution? • An organization of ideas or events that is logical and appropriate for the genre? • Clear relationships between and among ideas or events? • Paragraph breaks—indentations— that logically chunk related ideas?
Sentence construction	• Sentences that vary in length and structure to serve the writer's purpose and engage the reader.	• Sentences that vary in length to change the pace or emphasis of the writing? • Sentences that vary in structure (e.g., simple, complex, compound)? • Sentences that are uncluttered (Eliminates "I think ..." "I will tell you about ...")? • Dialogue, if used, that sounds natural and serves a specific purpose (e.g., to move the story line along, to reveal information)? • Fragments, if used, that are effective?

(continued)

FIGURE 8.3. The Evaluation Guide: Discourse knowledge.

Text Elements	Characteristics of Text Elements	Evaluating Text Elements— Does the text include ...

Word choice	• Words that are carefully chosen to fit genre, purpose, and audience. For example:
	  ◦ Using concrete, descriptive words when writing stories.
	  ◦ Using scientific terms when writing a science report.
		• Language that serves the purpose, reader, and genre?
		• Language that goes beyond over-used words and expressions?
		• Verbs and nouns that are strong and precise?
		• Words that have an appealing sound?
		• Specialized vocabulary, if appropriate, that is characteristic of a particular sociocultural community?
		• Specialized vocabulary, if appropriate, that is defined/explained in the text?

Conventions	• Grammar = complete sentences, fragments—when used deliberately, subject/verb agreement, and possessives. • Mechanics = punctuation and spelling.	• End punctuation? • Internal punctuation? • Evidence that words with inflectional endings were spelled correctly? • Evidence that the writer used the structure of the word (or related base word) to spell? • Complete sentences? • Fragments only when they are used deliberately for effect? • Agreement of subject and predicate? • Correct use of apostrophe "s"?

FIGURE 8.3. *(continued)*

word *also* in the third paragraph to make a transition from the preceding paragraph, as well as the word *genes* in the third sentence from the end of the second paragraph and again in the first sentence of the third paragraph to create a seamless transition. Kristin concludes the report with a short summary, which brings closure to her report.

When we look at Kristin's sentence construction, however, we see that many of the sentences in Kristin's report are short, choppy, simple, declarative sentences (see the first paragraph). If she used more complex sentence constructions, Kristin could link related ideas and concepts together for better comprehension by her readers. When evaluating Kristin's word choice, we note that she attempts to use some scientific vocabulary (genes, chromosomes, dominant, recessive, deoxyribonucleic acid, molecules), but we do not have a clear sense that she understands what they mean or how the terms are semantically related to each other.

In a few places Kristin did not follow standard conventions of writing. For example, she used a comma to connect two independent clauses

196 LEARNING TO WRITE WITH PURPOSE

in the second paragraph when she should have used a period to separate them. She also had a few misspelled words, such as *bodys*, but in general there are no major problems with conventions. Next, let's look at the time and space dimension.

Time and Space

When we talk about time and space (see Figure 8.4), we are really talking about contextual knowledge. We want to ensure that writers situate ideas or information in a context that enables readers to grasp their messages.

To investigate time and space, we want to see if Kristin included enough information and the right kind of information to provide adequate background knowledge for her intended reader(s). Many times novice and developing writers assume—sometimes incorrectly—that their readers will understand what they are trying to communicate even when they have not provided an adequate context. For example, did you notice in Kristin's report that she writes about Karla and Nathaniel without specifying who they are? Her teacher knows Kristin's family so she does not have to speculate about who these people are, as a distant reader would need to do. Even though Kristin is writing for her teacher, a known reader, she should supply background information, or context, nonetheless. Now, let's consider the sociocultural membership dimension of our communication model.

Text Elements	Characteristics of Text Elements	Evaluating Text Elements— Does the text include ...

Contextual knowledge	• Awareness on the part of the writer that the piece may be read by an unknown reader in a different time and/or in the writer's absence.	• Language that signals when and where events occur to the degree that is necessary for the reader to comprehend the text?
		• Factual or circumstantial information that creates a shared knowledge between writer and reader?
		  ○ Does the *amount* of information provide adequate background information for the reader?
		  ○ Does the *type* of information provide a comprehensible context?
		• Nouns and pronouns that are specific enough for the reader to interpret?

FIGURE 8.4. The Evaluation Guide: Time and space.

Sociocultural Membership

When we speak of sociocultural membership (see Figure 8.5), we are referring to the writer's voice. Many times in the literature *voice* is defined as the "writer's presence in a piece of writing" (Romano, 2004, p. 21). We expand this definition to include the beliefs, values, customs, and language use of the writer that point to membership in a sociocultural community (Gee, 1996, 2004). In addition, voice includes the writer's recognition that members of different communities may communicate in different ways; therefore, *voice*, as we define it, also encompasses a writer's attempt to try on other people's way of communicating (e.g., the voices of people in different disciplines).

Now let's evaluate whether Kristin was able to take on the voice that reflects her membership in a sociocultural community of fifth-grade scientists. To evaluate voice, we need to focus on the language Kristin used to express her ideas and the values and beliefs that are revealed through her writing.

Text Elements	Characteristics of Text Elements	Evaluating Text Elements— Does the text include ...
Voice (beliefs and language use of a sociocultural community)	• Awareness that texts are created for readers who represent diverse communities. 　○ Sometimes writers and readers are members of a community that shares similar social and cultural experiences. 　○ Sometimes writers and readers are members of different social/cultural communities that may not or do not share similar experiences. • Differences in sociocultural membership are recognized and taken into account by the writer. • Language and structure helps identify the writer as a member of a recognizable sociocultural community.	• A unique and genuine style of language that supports the writer's purpose? • Language that indicates membership in a sociocultural community? • Language usage that reflects the ideas, beliefs, values, and customs of a sociocultural community? • Language that recognizes potential differences in sociocultural membership between the writer and reader (e.g., writer explains why family traditions are important in his or her culture). • Willingness to try on different ways of using words and sentences for purpose and audience? • Language that is natural and shows the writer's personality, when appropriate? • A theme, position, or message that remains consistent throughout the piece? • A consistent perspective (first person, second person, third person, observer, or participant)?

FIGURE 8.5. The Evaluation Guide: Sociocultural membership.

Kristin is attempting to use the language of a scientist, with some success. The conversational voice she uses to connect her personal information (such as family resemblances she writes about or a recently viewed television show) with her research moves her report away from the specific language and objective voice of research reports. In addition, in several places Kristin introduces concepts (such as heredity), but she does not fully explain them like a scientist would. We are left wondering exactly how much Kristin knows about heredity. For example, she writes, "Dominant genes are written with a capital letter" but she never clearly explains what dominant genes are, or their function.

We imagine that Kristin reminds you of students in your class or students you have had. Our analysis of her paper indicates that Kristin, like most writers, has many strengths and some weaker areas. Kristin's strengths include:

- Her developing world knowledge about heredity.
- Her genre understanding that reports can be written using a descriptive text structure to convey information about a topic.
- Her use of paragraphs to separate main ideas and transitions to move smoothly from one idea to the next.

Kristin will continue to work on:

- Developing her world knowledge of heredity.
- Learning and using content-specific vocabulary.
- Combining short sentences into longer ones that can show relationships among ideas.
- Providing a context for her writing.
- Writing in a consistent scientist's voice that is appropriate for her purpose and audience.

In the next section, we evaluate her paper from a different perspective in order to gather even more information about Kristin and her writing.

LOOKING AT WRITERS:
GOING BEYOND THE EVALUATION GUIDE

In order to evaluate writing comprehensively, we need to know what elements a writer is or is not using effectively in a particular piece of writing. We can do this by looking at each individual dimension of our communication model. We could take a piece of writing and evaluate it using Figures 8.1, 8.3, 8.4, and 8.5, as we just did, evaluating each of the ten elements separately. By evaluating a paper with the 10 elements, we could cull information about what was written, but we should not stop with the product. Here's why. When we consider the product alone, we cannot understand *why* the product looks the way it does unless we understand also how the writer's world knowledge, discourse knowledge, awareness of time and space, and understanding of sociocultural memberships influenced the writing.

When we evaluated the writing earlier in this chapter, we found that Kristin's paper did not demonstrate a solid understanding of the science topic of heredity; the product did not show sufficient evidence of world knowledge. Many of us would probably assume that Kristin should gather additional information before she considers revising her report. We might send her back to review notes in her science notebook and find additional resources to read. These recommendations might help Kristin produce a more effective second draft. Or perhaps not. We know that Kristin's paper did not demonstrate a sufficient level of development and understanding, but we do not know *why* Kristin's paper demonstrated a lack of world knowledge. Without knowing *why*, it is nearly impossible to provide accurate, informative feedback that will help Kristin become a more accomplished writer.

So, let's see if we can determine possible reasons for Kristin's apparent lack of world knowledge.

- Was it because Kristin had not yet acquired a depth of related science knowledge (world knowledge)? (We might assume lack of knowledge was the root cause for Kristin's underdeveloped paper, but the following questions might surface other causes.)
- Or was it because she did not fully understand what types of information belonged in a research report (discourse knowledge)?
- Or was it because she assumed her reader would be her teacher, someone who shared the same time and space with her and therefore wouldn't need as detailed a report as a distant reader might require (time and space)?
- Or was it because Kristin was hesitant to try to approximate the language and voice of scientists? Or could it be that she did not understand how to take on the voice of a scientist (sociocultural membership)?

Each question commands a different type of response.

- If Kristin did not convey an understanding of heredity because she lacked scientific knowledge, we might advise her to review her science journal and handouts with a classmate before she revises (world knowledge).

• If Kristin's problems occurred because she did not know how much information reports require or how to use specific content vocabulary correctly, we might provide her with a graphic organizer from Kidspirations to show key words and their relationships and then she could work on the definitions (discourse knowledge).

• If she misunderstood her audience, a conversation about her intended readers and their needs might be in order (time and space).

• If Kristin's difficulties stemmed from a hesitancy to adopt the language and voice of a scientist, perhaps we would give Kristin some science research reports to read as mentor texts (sociocultural membership).

The analysis of Kristin's report illustrates both the limitations of using an element-based form of evaluation to examine the product alone and the advantages derived from combining an element-based form with a comprehensive look at what the writer knows about the dimensions of our communication model. We used our Evaluation Guide to help us focus on key elements of Kristin's report. Then we stood back to consider what knowledge and understandings of writing Kristin brought to this text. Kristin's teacher noticed repeatedly throughout the life science unit on cells and heredity that Kristin struggled to understand the key content-related vocabulary, which undoubtedly impacted her ability to express her world knowledge. Therefore, before Kristin revises her report, her teacher will meet with her to review key terms and provide Kristin with a graphic organizer that will visually show relationships between the key terms.

Let's take a look at one more example. Let's say that Dakarai wrote a science report that lacked a clear organizational structure.

• Did he not know enough about his topic to generate a specific research question that would help structure his report? If so, Dakarai might need more prior knowledge before he could generate an inquiry question on which to focus his report (world knowledge).

• Did he not understand how reports are organized? If so, perhaps having an outline that highlighted the components of a science report would be helpful (discourse knowledge).

• Did he forget that the reader would not know to whom *we* referred unless he first identified *we*. If so, we would review with Dakarai the need to provide a context for his distant readers (time and space).

• Was Dakarai's report disorganized because he did not know that researchers often report scientific findings in a sequential organizational pattern? If so, Dakarai would need to hear and read examples of texts that follow a commonly accepted research report structure (sociocultural membership).

To evaluate writing fully, we need to consider the product and the writer's world knowledge, discourse knowledge, understanding of time and space, and recognition of sociocultural memberships.

Finally, we would be remiss if we did not consider the impact the *process* itself plays in what and how students write. Throughout this chapter we have been looking at the *products* students craft; yet, in some cases when investigating how we can help writers grow and produce higher quality texts, we need to back up even further and investigate the *processes* they are using to create the product. Did the student plan? Was the planning effective? Did the student use the plan that was created? Was the student able to take ideas from the plan and then generate a text? Did the student continually monitor the writing along the way? For additional information on evaluating the cognitive writer's *processes*, please refer back to the Inquiry Guide in Chapter 2 and the Developmental Continuum in Chapter 4.

Before we conclude this section, we pause to explain why we have decided to use guides and developmental continua rather than rubrics in this book. You might recall in Chapter 4 we noted that the formatting of our developmental continuum resembled a rubric, but since the continuum did not focus on a specific instructional outcome, we did not consider it a rubric. Proponents of rubrics advise that rubrics are more effective when designed to meet specific needs of the children who will use them (Schirmer & Bailey, 2000), created with input from students (Spandel, 2006; Yoshina & Harada, 2007), and used to measure specific criteria. For example, Hillocks and his graduate students (2007) created three rubrics to measure specific elements of narrative writing for students in grades 6 through 8: episodic elaboration, specificity, and style.

Although the four raters in Hillocks' study (2007) sustained relatively high levels of inter-rater reliability, other researchers acknowledge that raters can find it challenging to remain objective when scoring writing, even when using rubrics (Shermis, Burstein, & Leacock, 2006). You may have read articles that question the value of rubrics (see, e.g., Kohn, 2006) and articles that applaud rubrics (see, e.g., Spandel, 2006). We recognize both the benefits and potential limitations of rubrics and propose, with our Developmental Continuum and Evaluation Guide, alternative means of data collection to evaluate writers and writing.

A PROCESS FOR EVALUATING WRITING

We're sure you will agree that having a manageable, systematic process for evaluating drafts makes this task much easier than it would be otherwise. Consequently, we designed the following sequence of steps to guide you through this evaluation process:

First, think about the student whose paper you will be evaluating and what you already know about the writer. What types of writing experiences has the student had? Does he or she enjoy writing and see him- or herself as a writer? What do you know about this writer that will help you understand the information you collect while evaluating the current draft?

Second, read the writing to grasp a sense of the entire piece, while holding in mind the elements of writing. What's your general impression of the draft? Has the writer achieved the purpose for writing and met the intended reader's needs?

Third, identify elements in the text that illustrate a couple of strengths the student brings to this particular paper. What strengths will you draw attention to when you give feedback? What strengths will you want the student to build upon in future drafts?

Fourth, determine an element or two that would help the writer become a better writer and significantly improve the quality of the paper. Often, we are tempted to point out all the weaknesses, but we limit our feedback to a significant element or two on which to focus. Did you remember to look first at content and then at surface elements? What element, that if improved, will help the writer in the future?

Fifth, think about the writer's understanding of world knowledge, discourse knowledge, recognition of time and space, and understanding of sociocultural memberships. How did these understandings influence the writing?

Finally, consider the writing process this student used for this piece of writing. How did the student's planning, producing, and reviewing processes influence the quality of the text?

Earlier in the chapter, we evaluated Kristin's paper by thoroughly evaluating every element in order to explain the elements to you. In the reality of a classroom, we realize that you will rarely, if ever, thoroughly evaluate every element. Instead, we recommend that you use the steps above to learn more about individual students by focusing on one or two strengths, and one or two improvements.

CHAPTER SUMMARY

When reviewing their texts, writers first need to evaluate what is and is not working before they can successfully revise. To evaluate, we organize common text elements into our Evaluation Guide according to the dimension of our communication model. Within the guide, we break down each dimension into smaller elements. The elements for world knowledge are topic development, idea generation, and detail treatment. For discourse knowledge, they are genre knowledge, organizational structure, sentence construction, word choice, and conventions. The text element for time and space is contextual knowledge and for sociocultural membership is voice. The guide enables us to know what elements a writer is or is not using effectively in a particular piece of writing.

But we do not stop there. In order to provide feedback that will enable a writer to improve the quality of his or her work, we need to consider *why* he or she composed the text the way he or she did. In other words, we need to determine how the writer's world knowledge, discourse knowledge, understanding of time and space, and awareness of sociocultural memberships influenced his or her writing. Hence, to evaluate writing fully, we consider first the student and what he or she brings to the task. Then, we consider the student's cognitive processes (planning, producing, and reviewing texts) and the elements of writing within the four dimensions of our communication model.

Evaluating writing can be challenging, but having an Evaluation Guide can help teachers judge what contributes to the quality of writing before determining what needs to be done to improve a particular text. Evaluation (knowing what to revise) is the first component of reviewing. In the next chapter, we take a look at the final two components of reviewing: revising and editing.

APPLICATION BOX

Select a writing sample from one of your students and evaluate the piece. Consider both the elements of writing from Figure 8.1, 8.3, 8.4, and 8.5 and the dimensions of our communication model. What is your general sense or overview of the quality of the piece? What are the strengths of the piece? What are one or two elements that would improve the piece? You might want to interview the student to learn why he or she made certain decisions or how he or she wrote the piece—processes. What feedback would you give the student about his or her processes and product? How would the feedback help the writer and not just the piece of writing (Calkins, 1994)?

Chapter 9

Knowing How to Revise and Edit

We often think about writers and the cognitive writing process when we use the word *revision*, but in reality, we make revisions in all aspects of our lives (Angelillo, 2002). How many times, for example, have you taken a lunch count and had to revise it when someone announces, "I forgot. I'm buying lunch today"? Or think about when you set up your classroom and four weeks later you rearrange the desks to make a different configuration. Our students revise in art when they reshape their clay projects or add more details to their drawings; they revise in math when they realize that a calculation does not make sense and they reexamine how they determined the answer; and they revise in science when they make adjustments to their initial hypotheses.

Talking to students about revisions they make in school and in their daily lives outside the classroom may help them see that revision is a universal process—not something that belongs just to the domain of writing and not something that only poor writers do. In fact, in previous chapters of this book we have seen students engage in revision. For example, in Chapter 6 we saw Lucy revise the title of her memoir about Charly, her dog, and think about cutting background details. Writers, such as Lucy, revise for several reasons: to rectify any mismatches between the text they carry in their heads with the words they have on paper (Fitzgerald, 1988; Holliway, 2004), to clarify their own thinking (Fitzgerald, 1988), and to make the writing more precise and interesting (Dix, 2006). Revision can be a means of "reconceptualizing or rethinking" our ideas (Fitzgerald, 1988, p. 124).

When writers revise, they emend their plans, reshape the focus of their piece, add or delete ideas, correct inaccuracies (world knowledge); reorder information, restructure sentences, fine-tune word choices (discourse knowledge); modify contextual information (time and space); as well as adjust their voice (sociocultural membership). Sometimes we can see when writers engage in these revision processes, but other times the processes are completed inside the writer's head and, therefore, are unobservable (Dix, 2006).

In this chapter, we pick up where we left off in Chapter 8, "Reading to Evaluate Writing," where we described the elements of writing and explored how to evaluate texts. We probably all agree that writers need to evaluate what to revise before they can make effective decisions about how to revise. Yet, even when students can evaluate *what* to revise, many still have a great deal of trouble determining *how* to revise.

In this chapter, we:

- Define *revising* and *editing.*
- Examine challenges many writers face when preparing to revise and edit.
- Provide a repertoire of effective actions for revising and editing.

DEFINING REVISING AND EDITING

Before we explore different aspects of revision, we want to make sure we share a common definition for this term. Fitzgerald and Markham (1987) define *revision* as

> making any changes at any point in the writing process. It is a cognitive problem-solving process in that it involves detection of mismatches between intended and instantiated texts, decisions about how to make desired changes, and making the desired changes. Changes might or might not affect the meaning of the text, and they might be major or minor. Also, changes might be made in the writer's mind before text is written on paper, while text is written, and/or after the text is written. (p. 4)

As you can see, this definition characterizes revision as a problem-solving process. Sometimes when we revise, the text's meaning is preserved—for example, when we substitute the word *thrifty* for *frugal.* Although these words have shades of differences in meaning, both represent the same central concept; thus, the essence of what was being communicated would not change.

More often than not, however, the meaning is changed in one of two ways when we revise:

1. Concepts in the text are changed slightly when we make word- and sentence-level additions, substitutions, deletions, and consolidations (Faigley & Witte, 1981). For example, we might start with a basic sentence and add more relevant information to it.

- The original sentence might read: *Wind and rain can cause small pieces of rocks (sediments) to erode, be carried away, and deposited in other locations.*
- The revised sentence might read: *Wind and rain can cause small pieces of rocks (sediments) to erode, be carried away, and deposited in other locations. Over millions of years, the weight of the deposits causes the bottom layers to cement together, producing new sedimentary rock.*

2. Concepts are changed significantly—so much so that the essence of the original text is appreciably altered (Faigley & Witte, 1981). Writers who construct this type of meaning-changing revision might refocus a piece:

- Instead of drafting a persuasive essay on school reform—a broad topic, the writer might revise the essay to limit its scope to just the role of high-stakes testing and its effect on teaching practices.
- While revising a narrative story, a writer might change the setting of a story, which in turn would have a significant impact on the overall storyline.

You probably noticed the title of this chapter includes both revising and editing. Although some educators use these two words interchangeably, we view them as distinctly different. When we talk about *revising*, we talk about improving the quality of the message: Are the ideas communicated clearly and completely? Does the text accurately represent the writer's intended message? Has the writer achieved his or her purpose and met the needs of his or her audience? When we talk about *editing*, we talk about making changes to conventions: Are the words spelled correctly? Are grammar, punctuation, and capitalization rules applied appropriately? Has the writer carefully proofread, using conventions that are suitable for his or her purpose and audience?

When discussing revising and editing, we keep in mind a subtle, but very important distinction: helping writers versus helping the writing (Anderson, 2000; Calkins, 1994). When we help writers, we provide support and instruction they can use to improve the current text *and* we help them add to a growing bank of actions or strategies they can use in future texts. On the other hand, when we help the writing, we *fix up* the current text without providing writers with new knowledge or strategies they can transfer to future texts.

Before we look at some specific strategies or actions, let's consider the important role writers play as critical readers of the texts they are producing.

CHALLENGES MANY WRITERS FACE WHEN PREPARING TO REVISE AND EDIT

Before deciding how to revise, writers must consider what they have already written, what they are trying to say (what's in their head), and how their intended readers will interpret what has been written (Holliway, 2004; Nystrand, 1986). Once they evaluate *what* to revise (Chapter 8), writers consider how they can make their texts clearer for their intended readers.

Novice writers tend to revise individual words or read and revise sentence by sentence (McCutchen, Francis, & Kerr, 1997). In addition, they often rely on a "don't look back, just keep writing" strategy perhaps because young children have limited experiences with "linguistic knowledge, topic knowledge, reading their own texts, and understanding their readers' perspectives" (Holliway, 2004, p. 339). In other words, they have limited experience with the dimensions of our communication model.

Experienced writers, on the other hand, tend to analyze and problem solve (Holliway, 2004), while keeping in mind their purpose, what they have already written, what they intend to communicate, and their readers' needs. Experienced writers keep in mind an entire piece when they are revising (McCutchen et al., 1997).

In general, elementary grade children do not identify as many problems while reading texts as older students, largely because younger children are less likely than older students to recognize discrepancies and gaps while reading (Beal, 1990). Many students *correct* inconsistencies or fill in missing words in their texts while reading so the information in the text fits together logically; therefore, they find few problems to identify, analyze, problem solve, and revise (Beal, 1990; Harper, 1997). Yet, students need to be able to read critically, to identify and analyze texts (McCutchen et al., 1997), and to select from an array of effective action plans in order to make meaning-changing revisions to their writing (Harper, 1997).

Let's return to Sam, the experienced sixth-grade writer we first met in Chapter 2 when he was working on a memoir about stunt kites for a magazine contest. As we observed Sam's processes, we noticed that he thought about revising on at least two occasions. First, he discussed his draft with Matt, who suggested that Sam include a drawing and more detail about stunt kites for an audience who may not be familiar with the sport. Second, in response to his teacher's question, Sam reread his draft and decided to focus on his dad and cut out some irrelevant information, such as the details about his mom. His teacher's question helped him move from a personal narrative—a story about an event in one's life—to a memoir, a story in which the author reflects on the significance of the event.

Clearly, Sam was reading his draft critically as he moved fluently within the cognitive writing processes. Never far from Sam's thoughts were his intended readers. Well aware that they and he probably did not share the same level of knowledge about stunt kites or similar experiences with them, Sam thoughtfully revised his writing so his readers would understand what he was trying to convey. Yet, many novice and developing writers rarely engage in revision (Beal, 1990). Summarizing the research, Fitzgerald (1988) identified the following five reasons why children, in general, do not revise. We have referenced our communication model and/or the writer's cognitive processes at the end of each reason.

1. Students might lack the knowledge they need to plan and reach goals or they may have difficulty accessing the knowledge (world knowledge and planning).
2. Many children find it challenging to generate ideas and, at the same time, translate their ideas into words and sentences (producing text).
3. Effective writers step back and evaluate their work from the perspective of their anticipated readers. Children's egocentrism may limit their ability to take another perspective (monitoring).
4. Children may be able to identify a problem but not know exactly where or how the text should be revised (world knowledge, discourse knowledge, time and space, sociocultural membership, monitoring).
5. Young writers may not know how to revise so the piece sounds the way they want it to sound (sociocultural membership).

In addition to these five reasons, other scholars have provided alternative explanations for students' reluctance to revise. Some students view revision as a task they should do at the end of writing to make sure the piece makes sense, or they confuse revision with editing and want the paper to look right—spelling, punctuation, and capitalization (Angelillo, 2002; Dix, 2006). Other students revise during planning and see no need to make meaning-changing revisions once the text is produced (Dix, 2006). Furthermore, students may find it more challenging to revise for meaning when their topic knowledge is limited (McCutchen et al., 1997) or when they are working in nonfiction genres (Dix, 2006). Finally, when students do not have an authentic purpose for writing, an audience other than the teacher, or a vested interest in their texts, they may see little reason to revise (Angelillo, 2002).

Once students evaluate what to revise, they will need a repertoire of strategies or actions they can use to make revisions and edits. In the next section of this chapter, we introduce concrete strategies or actions that students can use to improve the quality of their texts.

A REPERTOIRE OF EFFECTIVE ACTIONS FOR REVISING AND EDITING

Those of us who work with upper elementary and middle school students know that their writing, especially early drafts, can be underdeveloped, disorganized, and lacking in voice. Unfortunately, many students rely on one or two (often ineffective) revision strategies or actions regardless of their purpose, their audience, or the genre of their text. We all know students, for instance, who revise by tossing in additional adjectives, or who replace common words with words they pick from a thesaurus. Once places in texts have been evaluated, writers need to know how to transform the text to meet both writer's and readers' needs.

Through direct instruction, upper elementary and middle school students can learn how to detect mismatches between what they write and what they want to say and how to make changes that will positively impact their writing (Fitzgerald, 1988; Hillocks, 2007; Spandel, 2004). Students need an assortment of actions they can easily call upon to make purposeful decisions about their writing (Harper, 1997) and to rework their texts (Harper, 1997; Heard, 2002; Hillocks, 2007; Lane, 1992; Spandel, 2004).

For the rest of this chapter, we share actions that are structured around the four dimensions of our communication model and the related text elements outlined in the tables in Chapter 8. We have given each action a name, so we have a common language to use when talking with students about revision and editing. Also, in Appendix 9.1 at the end of this chapter, you will find a list of mentor texts that can serve as examples for the actions. Let's begin with world knowledge.

Revision Actions for World Knowledge: Topic Development, Idea Generation, and Detail Treatment

Time to Roam

Developing a topic takes knowledge of the topic, time, and often several attempts at reshaping ideas. Before students settle on a research topic or a question that will guide their research, have them take time to read widely to build world knowledge about their topics. Spend time having them discuss, develop, refine, and reshape their topics or questions, if necessary. You might want to introduce graphic organizers for different text structures to help students organize their ideas before writing and during revision. In Chapter 5 we talked about keeping a writer's journal, a wonderful place for students to explore ideas and shape them into substantive topics or thesis statements. [Topic Development]

One-Sentence Summary

Have students articulate in one sentence what their stories or informational texts are about (Elbow, 1973). You may have a student who proclaims, "My report is about the American Revolution." Further discussion and guidance would help the student narrow his or her topic to one facet of the Revolution. Similarly, you might have a student who decides to write about his or her week-long vacation at a theme park. Since the focus is too broad, the paper may sound like a list. Again, you could support him or her in limiting his or her paper to just one part of the vacation. The "one-sentence summary" helps students zero in on a manageable topic to develop. Think back to Tanisha and Isabella (Chapter 3), the two girls in Mr. Frank's class who were preparing a PowerPoint presentation about colonial America. If Mr. Frank had asked them to tell him in one sentence what their presentation would be about, what do you think they might have said? Perhaps it would have been: "Our presentation will describe how people in colonial times made their clothing." [Topic Development]

Somebody Wanted But So

In many narratives, writers follow a story grammar (Stein & Glenn, 1979): setting, characters, problem, and a solution. To plot out the key components of a story, have students list the words *somebody, wanted, but, so* down the left-hand side of a paper, placing one word on each line. For example:

Somebody (main character)—Caleb, a 5-year-old boy

Wanted (problem)—a puppy

But (conflict)—he knew his mother would tell him that puppies are too expensive

So (solution)—he wiggled his loose tooth until it came out, put it under his pillow, and hoped that the Tooth Fairy would leave enough money for a puppy

Students use this popular action, which is usually used for reading comprehension, to scaffold the major storyline of their pieces. Imagine what might have happened if the fifth-grade boys who were writing graphic novels (Chapter 6) had used this action to plan and/or revise their work. The stories might have been fully developed and perhaps easier to write. [Idea Generation]

Interesting or Important?

Many times when students write informational texts, their papers are filled with interesting tidbits rather than a solid body of information that addresses their inquiry question. To help students determine what's interesting versus what's a main idea that needs to be developed, have them make a two-column chart, labeling the left column *Interesting* and the right column *Important*. Next, have them reread their drafts and list ideas under the appropriate heading. Sometimes the interesting ideas are also important, so ideas might fall into both columns. Discuss the items in the *Important* column and how they can be elaborated upon to enhance the paper (Harvey, 1998). If Kristin, in Chapter 8, had used this action as she began to revise her heredity report, she might have seen that she had not yet clearly identified specific key ideas around which to develop her report. [Idea Generation]

Q and A

Pretend you have a new friend who is not at all familiar with your topic or has not shared your experiences. Predict some questions this new friend might ask you. Jot down your questions. Think about how you would answer them and what information from these answers would be important for your reader to know. Once Melissa, the novice sixth-grade writer we met in Chapter 2, was able to focus the topic of her memoir, she could use this action to add relevant, concrete, specific details to her next draft. [Detail Treatment]

Snapshots

Snapshots are used to describe physical details in writing. The writer takes a mental photograph of a person, place, thing, or action and then describes the details in the photo in words for the reader (Lane, 1992). In Chapter 6, Lucy added a snapshot to provide physical details of her dog Charly's return home after having her teeth removed: *Charly limped into the kitchen as if she had broke her legs. She collapsed on her bed. I took the blankets from the living room and toppled them on Charly.* [Detail Treatment]

Thoughtshots

Similar to snapshots, thoughtshots are used to reveal what a character is thinking or feeling (Lane, 1992). The character's inner speech and feelings can be revealed in the narrative or through dialogue. Returning again to Lucy in Chapter 6, notice the thoughtshot she used: *I wonder what they are doing to her. I imagine Charly looking at the fluid tubes and fainting.* [Detail Treatment]

Show, Don't Tell

Effective writers draw readers into texts by creating situations in which they show us (rather than tell us) what their characters are feeling and thinking. A writer, for example, might want the reader to know that the boy in the story was nervous about playing in his first high school hockey game. Rather than telling reader, the writer could show the boy's nervousness by writing, "his legs felt wobbly and his heart thumped wildly as he darted onto the ice." Provide direct instruction first, using examples from mentor texts to illustrate this action. Then, to practice show, don't tell, prepare a series of index cards. On each card, write one situation, such as *The elderly man was sore from shoveling snow, A baby was getting sleepy, A puppy was excited to play with other dogs at a park*, or *A toddler was upset when his mother wouldn't buy him candy at the store.* Have students act out the situation and then brainstorm how they could show in words, not tell, what the character was thinking or feeling.

Revision Actions for Discourse Knowledge: Genre Knowledge, Organizational Structure, Sentence Construction, Word Choice, and Conventions

Great Genre Expectations

When you read Jeff's persuasive letter in Chapter 7, you probably noticed that he identified his stand on town parking restrictions, provided evidence to support his stand, and included a counterargument and conclusion when he revised his piece. Clearly, he had learned the characteristics of a persuasive letter. After students have read mentor texts and have worked together to generate a list of typical characteristics, prepare a reference chart for them, based on the characteristics discussed in Chapters 6 and 7. As students revise their writing, have them refer to features on the chart. Are they including specific genre characteristics their readers will expect? In some cases, students might blend genres or modify a genre to meet their purposes and audiences. If so, they would need to consider characteristics from multiple genres or be able to explain why their genre characteristics differ from those on the chart. [Genre Knowledge]

Repeat a Word

This straightforward transition action can be used with almost any genre. Writers include a word in the last sentence of one paragraph and repeat the word in the first sentence of the next paragraph, thus bridging the two paragraphs as the writer gradually transitions to a new point (McMackin & Siegel, 2002). Take a look back at Kristin's heredity report in Chapter 8. See how she used the word *genes* at the end of the first paragraph and again in the first sentence of the second to provide a seamless transition between these two paragraphs. [Organization]

No Doubt About It

Writers bring closure to their pieces by stating one indisputable conclusion about the topic. Phrases such as "One thing seems certain," "Without a doubt," or "There is no question" may be used to initiate the conclusions (McMackin & Siegel, 2002). Think about the students in Ms. Smith's class who wrote persuasive letters (Chapter 7). Ms. Smith could have suggested this action for students who were uncertain about how to conclude them. [Organization]

Rearrange the Pieces

Many authors literally cut their drafts apart, move pieces around until the sequence of ideas and structure of the piece is coherent, and then tape the draft together. We often use a variation of this action by having students highlight the ideas or sentences that relate to one topic in yellow, the ideas that relate to another topic in green, and continue using different colors to distinguish different topics. We could also use software, such as Draft Builder, to help students move ideas around. Once complete, writers can easily see how related ideas should be regrouped for better organization. Although we did not see Dakarai's science report in Chapter 8, we do know that it was disorganized. If it was disorganized because he lacked discourse knowledge, he could use rearrange the pieces to group ideas into a logical order before revising his original draft. [Organization]

Sentence Sense

Have students read page 2 of *Morning Girl* by Michael Dorris (1999) and then count the number of words in each sentence of the second paragraph: 13 words, 28 words, 3 words, and 29 words, respectively. The three-word sentence—*The day wins*—catches the reader's attention. While you are on this page, look at the variety of sentence constructions: simple, complex, and compound sentences are evident. Listen, too, for the rhythm of the sentences and how smoothly they flow together as you read them aloud. Discuss with the students the impact that different sentence lengths and constructions have on what the writer is trying to communicate. Notice the variations in the construction and length of sentences in the report that students in Ms. Arnold's eighth-grade class (see Chapter 7) prepared for town officials: *On December 7, the highways were salted. As you will remember, our hypothesis was that the road salt used to melt ice was causing the high salt levels in Franklin Brook. Therefore, this was a crucial time to collect data. When we went to test the water two days later on Thursday, December 9, we found that after the salting, chloride levels had jumped to 232 mg/L. However, on December 16, the level of salt contamination dropped.* [Sentence Construction]

Sentence Combining

Writers are able to elaborate on ideas and establish relationships among ideas when they can combine thoughts into well-constructed, smooth-flowing sentences. Furthermore, students can be taught sentence combining skills that can have a positive effect on the quality of their writing (Graham & Perin, 2007; Saddler, 2007; Saddler & Graham, 2005). Try this: Place several pairs of related sentences (or sets of three sentences) on an overhead and model how you might combine each set to produce interesting sentences that sound correct and capture what you want to say. Note that there may be more than one "correct" way to combine each set of sentences. Begin with a simple example:

1. *Katie likes to play tennis.*
2. *She also likes to play basketball.*
3. *She plays these sports after school.*

These three choppy sentences can be combined into one more interesting, appealing sentence: *After school, Katie likes to play tennis and basketball.* or *Katie likes to play tennis and basketball after school.* Next, in pairs, give students similar sets of related sentences. Have them cut the sentences apart, move the words or phrases around on their desks, combining them to create as many different sentences as possible. Have students record their sentences in their writers' notebooks and share their new sentences at the end of the exercise. Gradually introduce more complex configurations: adding adjectives and adverbs, combining compound subjects or verbs, creating compound sentences with coordinating conjunctions (and, but, or), including adverbial clauses (after, because, until), and using clauses with who or which (Saddler, 2005, 2007). Check how Sue, Chapter 7, combined many ideas while describing how to set an alarm on a cell phone: *After you click the side arrow keys, located at the top of the screen, [press] until you get to the settings bar, which will most likely be in the corner of your screen and say settings right on it.* [Sentence Construction]

Eliminating Clutter

Do your sentences contain clutter—words that can be removed so that the message is clear and direct (Zinsser, 2006)? Novice and developing writers, for example, may use a series of adjectives or adverbs when one strong verb or noun would be more effective. They may also include words, such as *very*, that are not necessary and can often be replaced by a stronger adjective. For example, instead of saying "She was very pretty," we could say "She was gorgeous." In addition, writers should be encouraged to eliminate words such as *I think, I'll tell you, I believe.* Consider the following two lead sentences: "I think schools should have vending machines" versus "Schools should have vending machines." The second sentence is direct and more powerful. Have students weed their pieces, eliminating clutter or unnecessary information. Share results in a small- or large-group setting. Did you notice how many times Jeff used the word *And* to make a long run-on sentence in the draft of the persuasive letter he wrote (Figure 7.2)? For example: *And say a cop sees you in your spot and you do something else maybe pick up your kids or do library or something else and go back into town and the cop sees you again.* Wouldn't this sentence be more effective if we eliminated the *And* words to make several direct sentences? Also, wouldn't the sentences be more direct if Jeff eliminated the clutter created by the words *do something* and replaced the words with a specific example? [Sentence Construction]

Vivid Verbs

Verbs play a pivotal role in writing, enabling writers to convey precise actions; yet, writers often use weak, vague verbs to express their ideas. Try this: Use a piece of writing that you compose or one from an anonymous former student to point out how often we use weak verbs. Circle or highlight all the verbs in the piece (or in a section of the work). If you are using a narrative piece, discuss which verbs are strong, such as Tom *stormed* into the room, and which verbs do little to reveal information about the characters or events, such as Tom *went* into the room. Check to see if the verbs are passive—passive verbs always contain a form of the verb to be: *am, is, was, were,* or *are,* and the subject is being acted upon rather than initiating the action (e.g., Passive: *The teacher's request was approved by the school committee.* Active: *The school committee approved the teacher's request.*). The writing is usually stronger and less cluttered when verbs are active rather than passive. Check out some of the vivid verbs

Lucy used in her personal narrative (Chapter 6): *Mom <u>scooped</u> up Charly and walked out the door. Charly <u>limped</u> into the kitchen as if she had broke her legs. She <u>collapsed</u> on her bed. I took the blankets from the living room and <u>toppled</u> them on Charly.* [Word Choice]

Spelling and Meaning It

Many times, words that upper elementary and middle school students misspell are derived from a base word that they already know how to spell. When words are related in meaning, they are often spelled similarly, too, even when the pronunciation changes slightly (Bear, Invernizzi, Templeton, & Johnston, 2004). For example, if we know that *definitely* comes from the base word *definite*, we would know that it should not be spelled "definately," even though we might hear a short *a* in the third syllable. Kristin (Figure 8.2) did a great job spelling *combination* in her heredity report, but we can imagine that some students might be puzzled about the vowel sound in the second syllable. Knowing, however, that *combination* and *combine* are related in spelling and meaning, enabled Kristin to spell *combination* correctly. [Conventions: Spelling]

That's It, Period!

Be on the lookout for commas that are used where periods are needed! Students sometimes run two sentences together, separating them with a comma instead of a period; thus, creating a comma splice. Prepare a passage in which you have used a comma splice (or two), for example, *That's great, I'll bring the chips and dip.* Or *We're done, where do you want us to leave the dirty dishes?* Using a think-aloud, explain where the subjects and verbs are and why you need a period instead of a comma in these two examples. Have students circle all the commas in their texts to see if they can discover any comma splices. For each comma, they should check to see if a complete sentence is on each side of it; perhaps they could identify the subject and verb for each sentence. If they discover a comma splice, they need to use either a period or a coordinating conjunction (such as *for, and, nor, but, or, yet,* or *so*) and comma to separate their ideas. Original: *She was tired, she went to bed early.* Revised: *She was tired. She went to bed early.* Or, *She was tired, so she went to bed early.* Did you notice the comma splice in Kristin's heredity report (Figure 8.2): *Chromosomes are like threads, they are inside cells.* [Conventions—Punctuation]

Apostrophe Awareness

We teach the "apostrophe *s*" convention, as we do with all conventions, to help writers communicate ideas. We know that the correct use of "apostrophe *s*" can be confusing. Some writers may leave off the apostrophe when it is needed to indicate possession, or they include it when the meaning of the sentence requires a simple *s* to make a noun plural. To review the rules for possession, see the website English-zone.com (*www. english-zone.com/spelling/possessives.html*), which lists the rules in straight-forward language and includes self-correcting practice exercises. Have students use this website as a handy reference. Did you catch the place in Andy's graphic novel (Figure 6.8) where he should have used an "apostrophe *s*" but didn't: *Sadly Santas evil twin.* [Conventions—Possessives]

Revision Actions for Time and Space: Contextual Knowledge

Setting a Context with the Five W's

Writers often refer to the five W's (who, what, where, when, why) when deciding what background information to include in a piece and what to leave out. To show this strategy in action, you might read aloud *Mother to Tigers* by George Ella Lyon (2003), a nonfiction picture book that describes the work of Helen Martini, the first woman keeper at the Bronx Zoo. List on chart paper the types of information that Lyon includes in the first part of the text and how this information prepares the reader for what is to come. You could repeat this same procedure with *Bud, Not Buddy* by Christopher Paul Curtis (1999), a story that takes the reader on a journey to locate Bud's father, a person Bud has never met. After reading, you could discuss how the author provided enough informa-tion at the start of the book so the reader could easily understand the sit-uation in which Bud found himself. In Chapter 7, we included excerpts from a PowerPoint presentation eighth graders prepared to inform town officials about the salt levels in their town's drinking water. We did not include the entire text, but we know that in order for their presentation to be understood, the students incorporated the five W's early in their report. [Contextual Knowledge]

Who's That?

Often, elementary and middle school writers assume their readers have shared time and space with them. Students writing a description of a field trip, for example, might begin the summary with *We*. However, if the *we* is not first identified, a reader who did not accompany them on the field trip may not know whom the text is about. Of course, the stu-dents must determine how to define *we* by considering their relation-ship with the intended reader. If the intended reader knows who went on the field trip, students could simply use *we*, but if the reader is an adult reading the article in the local newspaper, more context would be required—"The students in Mr. Miller's fourth grade, Cummings School, Windom, MA." After modeling how authors use pronouns to refer back to other nouns or pronouns, have students look through their writing to identify places where they have used pronouns with or without providing a clear referent. Remember how Sue began the directions for setting an alarm on a cell phone (Figure 7.12): *Do you need to set an alarm on your phone but you don't know how? Well I can teach you. First make sure your phone is on. To turn it on. . . .* Sue used *phone* in the third sentence and then used the pronoun *it* to refer back to the phone in the next sentence, making a clear connection between the pronoun and its referent. [Contextual Knowledge]

Revision Actions for Sociocultural Membership: Voice

Identify Yourself

When writers draft and revise their work, they think about the words and sentences they use to identify who they are—a knowledgeable expert in an informational piece or a cranky character in a story. They also think about what they are trying to communicate and how they will communicate these ideas—will the voice be formal, casual, charming, or perhaps humorous? Students can learn a great deal about how writers reveal characters' sociocultural memberships from the information provided in texts. For example, you might share the opening page of *The Devil's Arithmetic* by Jane Yolen (1988), which begins with dialogue between a mother and her daughter. From this short exchange we learn about the religious and family communities to which the two characters belong. Have students find places in their writing where they use language to reveal the beliefs, values, or customs of their characters. Look back at the poem in two voices that the students in the fifth grade wrote (Figure 6.13). Recall how the language changed to create each voice. [Voice]

Scrutinize the Source

When we draft and perhaps more so when we revise, we adjust the voice we use to fit our topic, purpose, and audience. The use of primary sources—documents that were either created during a particular time period or created later by someone who experienced an event (*www. lib.berkeley.edu/instruct/guides/primarysources.html*)—can be studied to learn more about voice. We can analyze the purposes of those whose words and images are captured in primary source materials, ponder the sociocultural memberships of the authors, and discuss their voices. Visit *www.lib.berkeley.edu/instruct/guides/primarysourcesontheweb.html* to find a primary source document that connects to a content area you are studying and scrutinize the source for the author's voice. What can you learn? Compare and contrast the voice in the document with a voice that depicts a different perspective or to a textbook chapter, especially if it is one that lacks voice.

Hot Seat

Perhaps you are familiar with this comprehension activity, in which one student is chosen to represent a character in a book and sits on the *hot seat*. Other students ask questions that the student answers while keeping in character (e.g., What do you enjoy doing in your spare time? What do you fear? If you could be any age, what would it be and why?). Students can use this same activity to develop the characters they create. By posing questions, students help each other discover attributes of characters.

In conclusion, we have suggested a repertoire of revising and editing actions. You know that you would choose specific actions based on your students' revising and editing needs. As the year progresses, you might incorporate a number of the actions; but not all at once!

CHAPTER SUMMARY

In order to be effective, writers need to know how to evaluate and then revise and edit their drafts to account for presumed distances between themselves and anticipated readers. In Chapter 8, we discussed evaluation (the first component of reviewing). In this chapter, we discuss the last two components of reviewing: revising—making changes to the message or meaning of the text, and editing—making changes to the mechanics or conventions.

Revising and editing are cognitively demanding processes. When engaging in these processes, accomplished writers consider the whole text with purpose and audience in mind and also look at the smaller components, such as punctuation, that contribute to the reader's ability to comprehend the writer's intended message. Writers who struggle with revising and editing often cannot take the perspective of their anticipated readers when they plan, produce, and evaluate their drafts. Novice writers often confuse revision with editing, thinking they are revising when they are fixing surface features, such as spelling and capitalization.

As writers grow, they increasingly understand that revision is a recursive process that occurs throughout—as opposed to at the end of—the writing processes. To revise and edit well, writers need a repertoire of strategies or actions they can use after they have detected inaccuracies or gaps in their work.

Without a solid repertoire of revising and editing actions to call upon when needed, students often rely on one or two actions that may or may not be effective for their immediate purpose and audience. To help students acquire revising and editing options for the four dimensions of our communication model, we share 24 actions they can use to improve the quality of their texts. In the next chapter, "Preparing Students for High-Stakes Writing," we take a look at writing for high-stakes testing, knowing that the actions introduced in this chapter can play an important role in how we prepare students for standards-based testing.

APPLICATION BOX

Think about the students in your class and the type of revision and editing strategies they are currently using. Review the world knowledge section of this chapter and select a particular student in your classroom (or several students) who might benefit from one of the world knowledge actions presented. Prepare a lesson through which you can explicitly teach the target action.

Resources for Revising and Editing

Mentor Texts for World Knowledge

Topic Development

Mitton, J. (2001). *Kingdom of the sun: A book of the planets.* Washington, DC: National Geographic Society.

In this beautifully illustrated book, each planet is compared and contrasted with the God or Goddess after which it is named. This book provides wonderful examples of topics that are clearly focused and developed. Grades 3–6.

Idea Generation

DiCamillo, K. (2000). *Because of Winn-Dixie.* Cambridge, MA: Candlewick Press.

Almost any memorable text could be used as a mentor for idea generation, because every unforgettable book contains events that flow together smoothly and ideas that bring excitement to the reading. *Because of Winn-Dixie* is no exception. You might want to compare and contrast idea generation of the written text with the motion picture version of the story. Grades 5–8.

Detail Treatment

Curtis, C. P. (1995). *The Watsons go to Birmingham—1963.* New York: Yearling.

Notice a *Snapshot* in the first paragraph of this book. On page 15, the author uses a *Thoughtshot* when Kenny wonders what will become of his brother, whose lips are frozen to the outside mirror of the car. Grades 4–8.

Mentor Texts for Discourse Knowledge

Organization

Simon, S. (2003) *Earth: Our planet in space.* New York: Simon & Schuster.

Simon uses *Repeat a Word* often in this book. He concludes one paragraph about the Earth's rotation by saying, "It takes one day, or twenty-four hours, for Earth to rotate once" (unpaged) and repeats *rotate* in the first sentence of the next paragraph. Grades 5–8.

St. George, J. (2002). *So you want to be an inventor.* New York: Philomel.

St. George concludes the book using the *No Doubt About It* strategy: "One thing is certain: There will always be barriers to be broken" (p. 48). Grades 4–6.

Word Choice

Miller, D. S. (2002). *The great serum race: Blazing the Iditarod trail*. London: Walker Books.

Miller uses vocabulary such as *quarantine, diphtheria, serum, mushers, rendezvous, frostbite,* and *blubber* in this account of the 1925 race to get antitoxin serum from Anchorage to Nome, Alaska. Grades 4–6.

Steig, W. (1986). *Brave Irene*. New York: Farrar, Straus & Giroux.

Notice the strong verbs Steig uses in *Brave Irene*. In the first five pages alone, we come across the following powerful verbs: *managed, admitted, insisted, coaxed, fixed* (tea), *stumble, resented,* and *cautioned*. Grades 3–6.

Conventions

Paulsen, G. (1987). *Hatchet*. New York: Simon & Schuster.

Every text you read will have dozens of examples of conventions that you can use as mentors. Notice, for example, the following conventions on pages 52 and 53 of *Hatchet*: commas in a series of independent clauses, an ellipse, dashes, a comma with a coordinating conjunction, a colon, and several effective sentence fragments. Grades 5–8.

Mentor Texts for Time and Space

Babbitt, N. (1975). *Tuck everlasting*. New York: Farrar, Straus & Giroux.

Babbitt uses the first chapter (pp. 5–8) to describe what the narrator sees and thinks as he or she walks along the road adjacent to the Foster's woods—woods that hold an important secret. Through this description, readers begin to recognize the significance of this setting. Grades 4–6.

Yep, L. (1992). *The star fisher*. New York: Puffin Books.

Notice how Yep sets a context for this book. The first section of the book is titled "Spring 1927." In the first few pages, we learn that the family is moving from Ohio to West Virginia. Yep uses dialogue to explain how these two settings differ and how the characters feel about the move. Grades 5–8.

Mentor Texts for Sociocultural Membership

Hesse, K. (1992). *Letters from Rifka*. New York: Holt.

Based on a true story of Karen Hesse's great-aunt Lucy, this text is a series of letters Rifka wrote to her cousin Tovah. Each letter contains a date and specifies where Rifka was when she wrote it. Rifka's voice and spirit ring true in her letters. Grades 5–8.

Lowry, L. (1993). *The giver.* Boston: Houghton Mifflin.

This is an interesting book to use when discussing sociocultural member-ship because the characters live in a unique community. The values, beliefs, customs, and perspectives of the characters are clearly evident from the start of the book. Grades 6–8.

O'Brien, P. (2000). *The Hindenburg.* New York: Holt.

In this book, we hear a voice of a historian who sets a social, political, and scientific context for the Hindenburg. O'Brien also weighs conflicting perspec-tives about the cause of the Hindenburg explosion and draws conclusions about this airship. Grades 4–8.

Smith, R. K. (1987). *Mostly Michael.* New York: Dell.

Since this book is written in a diary format (first person, dated entries), readers can quickly identify the personality and traits that are represented in the voice of Michael Marder, author of the diary. Grades 4–6.

Chapter 10

Preparing Students for High-Stakes Writing

You may think high-stakes testing began with the No Child Left Behind Act of 2001, but local and federal governing bodies have been testing children for decades to evaluate teaching and learning. Standardized tests have become increasingly prevalent in education since the federal government passed the Elementary and Secondary Education Act of 1965, the first major federal law to provide local school districts with significant funding. With funding, came accountability. Local districts had to demonstrate that they evaluated the programs funded by the Elementary and Secondary Education Act. In order to abide by the requirements of the Elementary and Secondary Education Act and to counter the country's discontent with public education, a number of states legislated minimum competency tests during the 1970s (Popham, 2001).

We saw another call for testing in 1983, when the National Commission on Excellence in Education published *A Nation at Risk*, a report that claimed our educational system suffered from "mediocrity." One of the Commission's recommendations was to institutionalize standardized tests that were more rigorous than the minimum competency tests of the 1970s (Hillocks, 2002; Triplett & Barksdale, 2005). Then in the 1990s, the professional organizations, such as the International Reading Association and the National Association of Teachers of English, became involved by drafting standards-based outcomes. These national standards became the basis for many state-designed standards and assessments (Parke, Lane, & Stone, 2006).

All this brings us to the No Child Left Behind Act of 2001—an act that is being reauthorized in 2008 and that federally mandates statewide testing. These tests are designed to measure how well students have acquired the content knowledge specified in the state standards and, second, the effectiveness of instruction (Pedulla et al., 2003).

Since mandatory standardized testing plays such a prevalent role in determining curriculum, instruction, assessment, and even the "climate" of the school today (Pedulla et al., 2003), we turn our attention in this chapter to the genre of high-stakes writing. We look at high-stakes writing assessments and recommend instructional practices you can use to prepare students for this genre of writing. Specifically, we:

- Provide a rationale for defining high-stakes writing as a genre.
- Show how to use our communication model to analyze test items and then plan, produce, and review responses.
- Discuss balancing testing and teaching.

Testing has affected students and teachers but it need not dominate daily life in classrooms; learning should. Let's begin our discussion by looking at high-stakes writing as a genre.

THE GENRE OF HIGH-STAKES WRITING

Teachers throughout the country spend time preparing students for standards-based tests. Not surprisingly, as the stakes for institutions and students get higher, the influence these tests have on students, teachers, administrators, and schools increases (Pedulla et al., 2003). Preparing students for the tests can be stressful, time-consuming, and overwhelming. Yet, good writing is good writing. Our goal is to prepare students to write effectively in a wide variety of situations, including, but not limited to, mandatory testing. Therefore, we propose that writing for standardized tests should be presented as a genre of writing—a genre that should be given time and attention. We endorse a brief, focused test preparation period just before the exams are given. In our view, teachers need to prepare students for this genre, but the test preparation should not be the entire writing curriculum. Let's take a look at how writing for standards-based tests resembles other genres, including those discussed in earlier chapters of this book.

In Chapter 1, we define *genre* as communicative actions developed to serve similar purposes in response to recurring situations (Coe, 2002; Miller, 1994). With high-stakes testing, we know the recurring situation and purpose: for students to demonstrate knowledge to an unknown audience—the evaluators.

As with the genres introduced in Chapters 6 and 7, the genre of writing on standards-based tests has typical characteristics that suit the writers' and readers' purposes and needs. These characteristics include:

- Specific language usage, including the direction words used in prompts, such as *describe, compare, list,* or *persuade.*
- Prompts that require evidence, elaboration, explanation, or support for a claim.
- Formats that are found primarily in test-taking situations: filling in bubbles, writing short answers to questions, and open response.

What can be curious about this genre is that the intended audience in a prompt can be distinctly different from the actual audience. For example, a prompt might have fourth graders pretend they are writing to third graders in their school. Students need to understand, however, that the actual audience is an unknown, distant, adult evaluator. Think back to the stars we used in Chapter 1 (see Figure 1.1) to indicate distances between writers and intended readers. Students should not assume that they and their readers share the same type and amount of world knowledge and discourse knowledge, or similarities in time and space or sociocultural membership.

In the next section, we investigate ways in which we can balance quality writing and writing for standardized tests by linking our communication model to typical items on standards-based writing tests.

Teaching the High-Stakes Genre

In balancing quality writing with high-stakes writing on standardized tests, we teach different genres throughout the year, including the high-stakes writing genre. In this section we use Mr. Tucker and his class to show how we analyze a prompt using the four dimensions of our communication model. We also explain how he supports his students through planning, producing a response, and reviewing the response. In addition, because students are often asked to write responses in different disciplines on high-stakes tests, we present our analysis of a science prompt and a persuasive prompt. As in the other genre chapters, we begin the teaching section with a classroom scenario.

A Classroom Scenario: High-Stakes Genre

We step inside Mr. Tucker's classroom to illustrate how he prepares his students for writing they will do on the standards-based tests across the curriculum. The high-stakes writing tests will be given in May, so for five weeks preceding the administration of the test, Mr. Tucker's writing workshop will be devoted to how to take the state tests.

Preparing to Teach

Mr. Tucker logs onto his state's department of education website, selects three sample test types, and the rubrics used by the state to assess writing on the tests. He plans to spend about eight classes on the first test type (open response) and then reduce his instructional time for each of the other test types he introduces. He analyzes the prompts first for purpose and audience and second for the four dimensions of our communication model. Next, Mr. Tucker puts Figure 10.1 on chart paper.

Communication Model	Questions to Ask about the Prompts	Notes for Response
Purpose	• What is my purpose (reason) for writing?	
Audience	• Who will read my writing?	
World knowledge	• What topic will I be writing about? • What world knowledge do I have about this topic?	
Discourse knowledge	• What genre does the prompt ask for or, if given a choice, what genre should I pick? • What are the characteristics of the chosen genre? • Are there specific vocabulary words that I should use with this genre?	
Time and space	• What background (or contextual) information does the reader need in order to understand the content or experience?	
Sociocultural membership	• What viewpoint do I want to express? • What voice and language would be appropriate for the evaluator and would convey my message? • How long does the evaluator expect my response to be?	

FIGURE 10.1. Analyzing test prompts. From Gere, Christenbury, and Sassi (2005). Copyright 2005 by Heinemann. Adapted by permission.

Supporting Students' Exploring Ideas

Mr. Tucker begins his study of the high-stakes genre by informing his students that they will be taking the state tests in May. Amid the groans, Mr. Tucker reminds them that they have been learning about writing in different genres all year; writing on tests is just another genre. He informs them that they will use the communication model on the chart and the writing processes they have been using all year. He points out that they will have to make a few minor changes for the tests, such as having to write about an assigned topic, having a set time to write, and having to work independently.

Mr. Tucker informs students that for the next couple of days he will be modeling for them how he analyzes a prompt, plans his response by taking notes, and then writes a response to the prompt. Mr. Tucker moves to the overhead and places the following prompt on the projector:

> One day while at your grandparents' house, you notice a secret door that you have never seen before. You decided to take a peek. In several paragraphs, tell a story about what you saw.

Because this is the first lesson in Mr. Tucker's test-taking genre study, he models his thinking by explaining aloud why he underlines key words in the prompt (such as *several paragraphs*). Next, he points to the chart (Figure 10.1) and begins by reading the first question: "What's my purpose (reason) for writing?" He rereads the prompt and then writes the following phrase in the third column of the chart: *To tell an imaginary story in a few paragraphs.*

He quickly moves to the next question on the chart: "Who will read my writing?" He ponders for a second and then says, "It doesn't say." In the third column of the chart he writes: *Unknown adult evaluator.* Mr. Tucker pauses to remind students of the imaginary stories they wrote earlier in the year for the first graders. Mr. Tucker remarks, "It was fun to write for the first graders, but now I need to remember I'm writing to an adult I don't know. Because the unknown audience will evaluate my story, I need to work carefully through the dimensions of the communication model."

Mr. Tucker moves back to the chart and reads the next two questions: "What topic will I be writing about? What world knowledge do I have about this topic?" Again, he thinks aloud and records his ideas on the chart:

- Secret door
- Grandparents' house

- Imaginary world
- Like *The Lion, the Witch, and the Wardrobe* (C. S. Lewis, 1950)
- Maybe like Harry Potter's magical world

Mr. Tucker knows that he will probably continue to add to this list of world knowledge as he thinks of other ideas, but for now he has enough to get started. He turns his attention to the questions on the chart that relate to discourse knowledge.

"Hmm, Mr. Tucker begins, 'what genre does the prompt ask for or am I given a choice of genres?' The students stare at him until finally one student says, 'a story.' " "Now I need to think about the characteristics of this genre," Mr. Tucker remarks, as he points to the next question on the chart. This time, he invites the students to respond, and he records their ideas on the chart: setting, characters, a plot with a goal or problem to solve, an interesting ending. He makes connections to the story grammar they used (Chapter 6) and the *Somebody Wanted But So* revision strategy (Chapter 9). Mr. Tucker points to the last discourse question on the chart: *Are there specific vocabulary words that I should use with this genre?* He and his students have spent time this year writing fictional stories, so he asks them about the type of vocabulary words they would likely use in this genre. They respond that they should use descriptive words for the setting and character and strong, precise verbs. He applauds their answers.

Mr. Tucker stops analyzing the prompt and directs pairs of students to talk about imaginary worlds they would create and what would happen there. As they share ideas, he asks them to make brief notes (one word or short phrases) on their copies of Figure 10.1. In subsequent lessons, he will not give them time to talk or as much time to make notes. After 15 minutes, Mr. Tucker returns to the chart and focuses on time and space.

He asks pairs of students to look at each other's notes and to talk about the following questions: "What background information does the reader need in order to understand the content or experience?" "In your notes, did you include where the secret door was or when you found it?" "Do you have notes about the setting of your imaginary world?" The students review their notes and add more background information to their plans.

Moving to the sociocultural membership box on the chart, Mr. Tucker reads the three questions aloud and points out that the unknown reader is an evaluator who decides if the writer knows what a good story is. "Remember our discussions of voice? In stories, we need to show our characters' personalities. We can use narration, dialogue, and actions to reveal our characters' voices. Furthermore, the evaluator expects school language—not street language or slang." Mr. Tucker reiterates that evaluators in the testing community have beliefs and expectations about what makes an effective response. Mr. Tucker and the students discuss story lengths and how they can include additional, relevant information to elaborate on their ideas and make their stories more effective. He reminds students about revision actions, like those for details they've been practicing throughout the year (Chapter 9).

Together, Mr. Tucker and his students make notes on their charts that will remind them to pay attention to the voice, language, and length of their stories. He brings closure to the lesson, emphasizing that they need to remember the audience is unknown when they analyze prompts and make plans for high-stakes writing. In his next lesson, he'll model how he uses his plans to produce a response.

Supporting Students' Producing Texts

While one student passes out writing paper, Mr. Tucker asks the other students to look over the charts they created during their last lesson. Together, they review their notes and add any new ideas. Today, they are going to draft a response. He has students refer back to the list of lead strategies they have in their writers' notebook. Mr. Tucker taught students actions from Chapter 9 as well as strategies from professional resources (Lane, 1999; McAndrew & Reigstad, 2001; Noden, 1999). One student mentions the use of an intriguing question, as E. B. White did in *Charlotte's Web* (1952, p. 1): "Where's Papa going with that ax?" While the students try out some leads, Mr. Tucker composes his own lead.

After they share ideas for leads, Mr. Tucker asks the students to look over their plans and decide how they will develop their stories. He also reminds the students that the prompt says *several paragraphs*, so the stories should be detailed. The evaluator should be able to have the same images in his or her head while reading the stories as we have in our heads while writing them.

Mr. Tucker knows that many of his students have difficulty bringing stories to logical conclusions. Therefore, once they have thought through the story plots, he has his students return to their writers' notebooks and review some of the conclusion strategies they've practiced this year (see Chapter 9; Lane, 1999; McAndrew & Reigstad, 2001; Noden, 1999). In addition, they discuss approximately how long a story should be (not six sentences, but not seven pages either). After their discussion, he announces that they will have 30 minutes to write. If they finish early, they should reread their stories to make sure they have thoroughly addressed the entire prompt. Mr. Tucker and his students start writing, although students do exhibit varying degrees of industry.

Supporting Students' Reviewing: Evaluating, Revising, and Editing

Although Mr. Tucker knows that most students will not have time to make global revisions during the test, he hopes some students will have time to make small revisions to their work. On the next day of the high-stakes writing unit, he leads the class through an evaluation of their stories. Mr. Tucker refers back to the chart (Figure 10.1) as he asks the following questions, pausing to let pairs of students review his story and then each other's story:

1. Did I tell an imaginary story in a few paragraphs (purpose)?
2. Did I include the ideas I brainstormed about the topic (world knowledge)?
3. Does my story include characteristics of a story: setting, characters, plot events, and an ending (discourse knowledge)?
4. Does the story have vivid descriptive words and strong action verbs (discourse knowledge)?
5. Did I include the right kind and amount of information about the imaginary world so the evaluator knows when and where the story took place (time and space)?
6. Did I use language that allowed me to convey the character's voice accurately and consistently (sociocultural membership)?
7. Is the language and length of the story appropriate for what the evaluator would expect (sociocultural membership)?

Finally, Mr. Tucker asks the students to edit his paper and then their own paper by checking for misspellings, incomplete sentences, and missing punctuation.

Later that week, Mr. Tucker puts the state rubric on the overhead. Together, he and his students discuss the criteria the state uses to assess writing. Through his modeling, he has demonstrated how to use our communication model to analyze a prompt, plan, and draft a response. Now he engages in a similar process, modeling how to use the state rubric to evaluate the final products he and his students produced.

Over the next class periods, Mr. Tucker presents three additional open-response prompts that he analyzes with his students. Gradually, Mr. Tucker shortens the work time until, with the third prompt, the students have the amount of time the test allows. They use the time to independently analyze the prompt, quickly plan a response, produce a written response, make small revisions, and edit their writing. Later, they use their state rubric to evaluate their work.

Because students are often asked to respond to prompts in different content areas, we offer you two additional prompts that we have analyzed according to our communication model: a science prompt and a literary response prompt (see Figures 10.2 and 10.3) and encourage you to analyze prompts with your students.

To Inform on a Science Prompt

When writing about science on high-stakes tests, your students may be asked to respond to a prompt similar to the following:

> Describe the water cycle to a student who is unfamiliar with this topic.
> Include a diagram of the water cycle and explain each part of the cycle.

In the prompt, as in many others, the audience is confusing. The prompt says the audience is a student, but in reality the audience is an unknown evaluator who knows about the water cycle. In Figure 10.2, we list the guiding questions for purpose and audience and for the dimensions of our communication model. In the third column, we suggest language you might use in a think-aloud, just as Mr. Tucker did in our last example.

We expect that throughout the year, you and your students have written in genres that inform audiences about science and social studies topics. Reminding students about their previous experiences will help them remember to write all they know about the topic—not just the first bits of information that come to mind. We now analyze another typical type of test question—the literary response question.

To Persuade on a Literary Response Prompt

Literary response questions appear on many state exams. Often, within a limited time frame, students must read an excerpt from a novel or a poem and then write a response—often a persuasive response. The following prompt is similar to many we've seen:

> Think about a character from a book you've read who, in positive ways, has influenced how you think and act. Convince the reader that the character was a good role model for you. Provide details from the book and your life to support your answer.

Responding to literature can be challenging for students because they need to balance a great deal of information. First, they must be able to recall ample details from something they have read to take a stand and provide evidence to support their stand, framing their support within a persuasive text organization. In addition, they need to provide a context for their response because in some cases the evaluator will not be

Communication Model	Guiding Questions	Notes for Response
Purpose	• What is my purpose (reason) for writing?	• The purpose is to show all I know about the water cycle. • The purpose is to inform my audience.
Audience	• Who will read my writing?	• The prompt says that the reader is another student who is unfamiliar with the water cycle. • But, I know that the real audience is an adult who knows about the water cycle.
World knowledge	• What topic will I be writing about? • What world knowledge do I have about this topic?	• The topic is the water cycle. • Water evaporates and the vapors change into liquid water when it goes into the cold air. • Clouds form in the atmosphere, and when the water gets too heavy it eventually falls as rain, snow, or even hail. This precipitation returns to lakes, rivers, and the ocean and the cycle begins again.
Discourse knowledge	• What genre does the prompt ask for or, if given a choice, what genre should I pick? • What are the characteristics of the chosen genre? • Are there specific vocabulary words that I should use with this genre?	• I will explain information in a report. • I will use a circle sequence order to describe the water cycle and describe each step. I need to include a diagram with labels. • I'll make sure my diagram matches the sequence I've described. • I need to include and define the terms: evaporation, condensation, precipitation, and collection.
Time and space	• What background (or contextual) information does the reader need in order to understand the content or experience?	• Because the water cycle is circular, there is no real beginning or end. I need to make sure the reader knows where I start the cycle and why I begin at that point.
Sociocultural membership	• What viewpoint do I want to express? • What voice and language would be appropriate for the evaluator and would convey my message? • How long does the evaluator expect my response to be?	• I need to sound like a science teacher explaining this to a student. • The reader will expect a thorough, detailed, sequential explanation.

FIGURE 10.2. Analysis of a science prompt. From Gere, Christenbury, and Sassi (2005). Copyright 2005 by Heinemann. Adapted by permission.

Communication Model	Guiding Questions	Notes for Response
Purpose	• What is my purpose (reason) for writing?	• I need to convince the reader that a character from a book I read was a good role model for me.
Audience	• Who will read my writing?	• It doesn't state an audience, but I know it's an unknown adult evaluator.
World knowledge	• What topic will I be writing about? • What world knowledge do I have about this topic?	• I need to think back to a hero or someone admirable—someone who had a positive impact on me. • I should pick a character that I know well because I will need details from the book and my life.
Discourse knowledge	• What genre does the prompt ask for or, if given a choice, what genre should I pick? • What are the characteristics of the chosen genre? • Are there specific vocabulary words that I should use with this genre?	• It says to convince, so I will pick a persuasive genre. • I need to give reasons why a character is a role model. I may try to refute why the evaluator might not like the character. • I need to show how the character influenced my life. • I'll choose precise, compelling words.
Time and space	• What background (or contextual) information does the reader need in order to understand the content or experience?	• I can't assume that the evaluator has read the book or knows the character. The evaluator needs background information in order to understand why I chose this character.
Sociocultural membership	• What viewpoint do I want to express? • What voice and language would be appropriate for the evaluator and would convey my message? • How long does the evaluator expect my response to be?	• I need to have a clear position and use the voice of someone who feels passionately about the character. • I need to use school-appropriate words and enough factual information to help me sound convincing. • I need to write four or five paragraphs.

FIGURE 10.3. Analysis of literacy response questions. From Gere, Christenbury, and Sassi (2005). Copyright 2005 by Heinemann. Adapted by permission.

familiar with the texts students are referencing. Finally, students need to maintain a strong, consistent voice to convince the evaluators that their stand is valid. Practicing persuasive writing throughout the year will equip students for the multifaceted literary response prompts when they come across them in high-stakes testing situations.

In our experience, teachers practice writing for tests but rarely analyze prompts in a systematic manner, as Mr. Tucker did. Focusing on the key words in the prompt and the four dimensions of our communication model gives students a structure around which to plan, produce, and review their responses. Thinking about the dimensions should encourage students to access the world knowledge and discourse knowledge they need to answer the prompt. The guiding questions should also call to their attention the need to provide a context for their response and use a voice that adults in a sociocultural community of evaluators would expect for the specific prompt. In the next section, we step back and look at the big picture: how high-stakes writing as a genre can be incorporated into the writing curriculum and how *what* we teach and *how* we teach has been affected by the predominance of high-stakes testing.

BALANCING TESTING AND TEACHING

Learning the characteristics of the testing genre is definitely important—no question about it. Students need to understand the characteristics and should practice applying them in test-like situations (preferably just prior to the administration of the test), but a focused genre study should comprise only a small portion of students' test preparation. The bulk of test preparation should come from using effective instructional practices to teach students to write in diverse genres for a variety of purposes and audiences.

Researchers support this two-tiered approach to test preparation: effective year-long instruction and targeted test preparation (Parke et al., 2006; Shelton, Fu, & Smith, 2004). We'll use two specific examples to illustrate this approach. First, a teacher–researcher in a low-income Florida school (Shelton et al., 2004) used a workshop approach to teach writing for all but a few weeks preceding the state test. Because her fourth graders had never experienced writers' workshop before they entered her class, her daily mini-lessons were foreign to her students at the start of the year. Nevertheless, the teacher introduced mini-lessons that focused on writer's craft, the use of mentor texts, and the integration of reading and writing. Students in this class wrote to communicate their ideas in authentic situations, such as writing to pen pals and drafting persuasive essays to affect changes in their classroom and school. Six weeks prior to the high-stakes test, the teacher stopped workshop and worked exclusively on test taking: writing to a prompt, budgeting time for planning, producing, and reviewing texts, and working with the state rubric. The teacher's instructional practices and students' hard work were reflected in the test scores: The students scored higher on average than students across the state. In addition, the school had never witnessed as many high-scoring students as there were in this class.

Second, a teacher we know uses collaborative classroom talk and problem solving to prepare her students in the weeks leading up to the test. She begins by putting a sample prompt on the overhead and asks students to work in small groups (three or four students) to talk about the prompt. In their talk, they point out what they notice and create a plan for responding. The small groups collaboratively write up a response and share it with the larger group for feedback. Then they compare their writing to the state rubric and the sample essays the state provides. Over the next few days, the students are given a different test item. This time, each student works with a partner to prepare a plan for responding to the prompt. The pairs write a response, share it with the whole class for feedback, and evaluate it against the state rubric. Finally, the students independently plan and write a response that is shared and evaluated. Students in this class are used to collaboration and talk, which are part of their expected task environment. The teacher knows, however, she must gradually move them from their familiar environment to the high-stakes testing environment. Consequently, she systematically moves them from collaborative to independent responses. As noted in both of these examples, effective teachers prepare their students for standards-based tests by introducing them to the characteristics of this genre in short, well-designed units of study.

Although we advocate for a focused genre study for high-stakes test writing, we encourage teachers to use their daily curricula to reinforce the academic language used in prompt directions. Fleming and Trompeter (2006) used direction words from the Massachusetts' tests in the activities students completed as part of a unit on Africa:

- *Describe* the major landforms you encounter on your journey across Africa to your country.
- *Make a graph to illustrate* the annual temperature and precipitation in your country.
- *Explain* how climate influences people's activities in your country.
- *Identify* and *explain* any problems that people in your country may be facing now or in the future.

While they concentrated on learning about Africa, the students also practiced responding to test direction words. Like Fleming and Trompeter, you can include the direction words from your state's test in your directions throughout the year.

In our work with teachers, we often discuss the role that the five-paragraph essay plays in writing on high-stakes testing. Needless to say, we have had many passion-filled discussions. You may know the five-paragraph format as the "hamburger": an opening paragraph that identifies a topic and main idea (the bun); three subsequent paragraphs, each one including examples that support one aspect of the main idea or one of the main ideas (the meat, lettuce, and tomato); and a concluding paragraph that brings closure to the piece (the bun).

Educators voice strong views on both sides of the debate. Some educators defend the five-paragraph essay, noting that its format provides a structure for organizing one's ideas and that all effective expository writing adheres to this basic form (Smith, 2006). Opponents contend that we only use the five-paragraph essay in school and not in published writing (Schuster, 2003).

Although most states do not seem to openly endorse the five-paragraph essay, teachers may believe that evaluators expect to see this format and that using it will help students garner high scores. Not everyone agrees, however, that using the five-paragraph essay is the way to achieve high scores on standardized tests. Schuster (2003), a former high school and college English teacher who serves on the Writing Assessment Advisory Committee in Pennsylvania, reported that students who did well on state tests almost never organized their writing using the five-paragraph essay.

In addition, after analyzing over 1,000 eighth- and tenth-grade essays, many of which were five-paragraph essays, Albertson (2007) concluded that Delaware students who adhered to the formula did not necessarily score higher than those who did not. Most students who used the five-paragraph format earned mid-range scores, while students who used other organizations tended to score at either the higher or lower ends of the rubric. In other words, using the formula did not guarantee a high score, but it "may be a safe alternative for writers" (p. 447). You might agree with Albertson's interpretation of her data: the five-paragraph essay is "a road map for some and a road block for others" (Albertson, 2007, p. 458).

Given all the information that is available, we think that the five-paragraph essay is an acceptable format to use with inexperienced or struggling writers who might need this safe, comfortable structure to help them organize their ideas. The five-paragraph essay should not, however, be the only or even the primary form of writing for the majority of students. You probably would agree: We wouldn't want students to graduate from school thinking that a five-paragraph essay is the one-size-fits-all format to use regardless of purpose, audience, or genre, or that quality writing can be reduced to an inflexible formula. The challenge for teachers is to balance content, the characteristics of exemplary writing, and the qualities of writing that meet standardized tests' criteria (Albertson, 2007).

Across the country teachers, administrators, students, parents, and other stakeholders in our educational system have monitored the impact of high-stakes testing. Not surprisingly, what is being assessed in statewide tests has had an impact on writing instruction across the country. Our review of literature revealed the following:

- A narrowing of curriculum (e.g., teaching primarily what is likely to appear on the test) or expansion of curriculum (e.g., when content-area teachers integrate literacy skills into units of study) (Au, 2007).
- Changes in the content that is being taught—and no longer being taught (Scherff & Piazza, 2005).
- A shift away from a workshop approach to a reliance on lectures and a recitation approach to teaching writing (Hillocks, 2002).
- An increase in teacher-centered rather than student-centered pedagogy (Au, 2007).
- A decreased emphasis on process writing and less attention to revision strategies in particular, especially in states where students are not expected to revise writing samples for assessment (Hillocks, 2002).
- Disagreement across states about what constitutes quality writing (Hillocks, 2002), with some states requiring factual support for ideas, for example, and others merely encouraging the elaboration of ideas. Teachers may advise students to write longer papers, even if the papers include "irrelevancy, facetiousness, inaccuracy, and falsehood..." (Hillocks, 2002, p. 77).
- Inconsistencies in how states assess the conventions of writing: Some use multiple-choice items to assess grammar, usage, and punctuation (see, e.g., Texas Education Agency, 2002), whereas others assess conventions as a component of each student's writing sample (Baldwin, 2004).

What's clear is that standards-based testing has influenced how administrators, teachers, and students perceive both the purposes for writing as well as how one plans, produces, and reviews texts. When states endorse standards and assessments that limit the scope of possibilities for authentic writing, it can easily become formulaic, prescriptive, and artificial.

We hope that analyzing prompts and treating test writing as a genre will help students feel comfortable with high-stakes writing. We clearly recognize the consequences for students, teachers, and schools, but having students practice test-taking skills alone or teaching to the test will not help your students become better writers. Teaching students to recognize the variety of situations and the appropriate communication response to each situation will build awareness of writing in the testing situation. What you teach them about writing throughout the rest of the year will prepare them to do well in all writing situations, including high-stakes testing.

As we write this chapter, Congress is in the process of reauthorizing the No Child Left Behind Act of 2001. Those who champion the Act and those who oppose it are trying to have their voices heard. Although there are bound to be at least some changes, one thing seems certain: Standards-based testing will live on. High-stakes tests existed well before the No Child Left Behind Act of 2001, and stakeholders in public education will undoubtedly continue to turn to them to measure student achievement. We give students every advantage to demonstrate their writing accomplishments when we prepare them well to write for a multitude of purposes, a variety of audiences, and a range of genres—including, but not limited to, the genre of high-stakes writing.

CHAPTER SUMMARY

Although accountability tests have been administered for decades, today's teachers and schools are experiencing pressure to produce high scores. Therefore, we propose that high-stakes writing be taught as a genre unit in the weeks just prior to the administration of the state tests. We consider writing on high-stakes tests to be a genre—writing that occurs in recurring situations and containing particular characteristics that audiences, in this case evaluators, expect.

In the classroom scenario, we illustrate how a teacher prepares instruction for an open-response prompt common to many tests. The teacher and students analyze the prompt, paying particular attention to purpose, audience (evaluators), and the four dimensions of our communication model. Asking specific questions for each dimension, the teacher guides students through the analysis and then through planning, drafting, and reviewing of their responses. Concluding the scenario, we show how the guiding questions can be used to analyze and plan for a science prompt and a literacy response prompt.

State tests have had an impact on decisions about curriculum and instruction in schools across the country and will probably continue to do so for the foreseeable future. We contend that spending the year writing for a variety of purposes and audiences, writing in many genres including the high-stakes writing genre, and applying the elements of effective writing will prepare students to write in test situations.

In the next chapter, the final chapter of this book, we turn our attention away from students and focus on you, the teacher. We celebrate you, the teacher of writers and writing, and explore ways in which all of us can continue to grow and develop as writers.

APPLICATION BOX

As we've emphasized throughout this chapter, we believe that writing for high-stakes testing should be approached as a genre that is taught for a limited amount of time just prior to the administration of your state's test. Although you may not teach this genre until later, you will probably want to prepare for this instructional unit earlier in the year.

If you haven't done so already, you might begin preparing for high-stakes tests by visiting your state's department of education website to download and print a copy of the rubric(s) evaluators will use to score student responses. You might also gather sample test items ahead of time to analyze with your students as you model the writer's cognitive processes: planning, producing, and reviewing responses. Before you begin to teach this unit, analyze the prompts for purpose and audience as well as the four dimensions of our communication model. As Mr. Tucker did in this chapter, you might even want to enlarge Figure 10.1 and make it into a chart so students have ready access to it as they prepare for their high-stakes writing tests. Finally, you may want to seek out samples of student responses on similar test items so that you and your students have exemplars to refer back to during test preparation. Remember to reassure your students that high-stakes writing is just another genre that they will meet again and can conquer.

Chapter 11

Teachers as Writers

Throughout this book we have written about students as writers and the various purposes and audiences for student writing. In this final chapter, we shift our focus to you, the teacher, as a writer. We write this chapter knowing that our audience will have different responses to this chapter. Some of you will nod at the title and feel perfectly comfortable with the image of yourselves as writers. You may be one of the 141,000 teachers who annually take part in the National Writing Projects summer workshops or activities, in which teachers help teachers become better writers at almost 200 local sites around the country (Freeman, 2007). Others will begin reading this chapter by questioning the title: "Me—a writer?" Recognizing that each of you has a different comfort level, we invite you to give yourself permission to experiment with writing for different purposes and audiences. We celebrate those of you who are writers and encourage those who haven't yet taken this step. Our goal in this chapter is to reinforce what you do as a competent writer by highlighting the role writing plays in your classroom and extending the invitation to write in your personal and professional life.

In the sections that follow, we describe teachers as they engage in writing for purposes and audiences that span the audiences of our communication model—oneself, familiar audiences, and unknown audiences. As you read this chapter, consider the situations in which you already write and then consider new situations—purposes, audiences, and genres—for your writing.

In this chapter, we:

- Encourage teachers to write with their students in order to share their own writing processes.
- Identify how teachers write to explore ideas in order to inform classroom instruction and assessment.

- Suggest local situations for teachers' writing.
- Encourage teachers to write for unknown audiences, as professionals sharing their knowledge, as citizens advocating for social change, and as published authors informing and entertaining readers.

We begin this chapter with a discussion of teachers writing with their students—a comfortable audience with whom to begin a writing journey.

WRITING WITH STUDENTS

If you are timid about writing for different audiences, writing with your students provides a forgiving audience, usually. Your students are more likely to take risks in their writing when they see you, their teacher, risk writing for new purposes and real audiences in genres not often found in school. Most importantly, writing with your students exhibits how one writer works at writing. Working through the processes of crafting a piece, you can discuss your decisions and even ask your students for help. When you experiment with writing in genres that are new to you, your students will come to understand that adults (even teachers) do not produce perfect writing in their initial attempts.

Let's take a look into Ms. Chu's fifth-grade classroom. Ms. Chu is the proud owner of a rambunctious young chocolate Labrador retriever named Max. Max is perpetually getting into mischief and Ms. Chu regularly shares stories about his antics with her students. Sometimes she incorporates these stories into her morning meeting; like today, she threw her hands up in the air exclaiming, "Max met a skunk last night!" Through the cries of "eeyuw," her students ask if Max was sprayed. As the students ask questions, Ms. Chu records her answers in her writer's notebook. Rereading the information generated by their questions, Ms. Chu asks her students where to start the draft: when she let Max out or when Max saw the skunk. She's pleased students remembered they could start the story where the action begins (Gilmore, 2007). Writing on the overhead projector, she begins a draft with Max encountering the skunk and then dismisses the class to work on their own pieces. She will finish the draft at night and bring it in for her students to review. Ms. Chu wants the students to evaluate her word choice when she describes Max's and the skunk's actions and the smell of the skunk's spray. She has been reading *Marley and Me: Life and Love with the World's Worst Dog* by John Grogan (2005) to the class and will refer to it as a mentor text for her Max stories. After reading tips for submitting stories for children's magazines on *Writing-World.com* (*www.writing-world.com/foster/foster10.*

shtml), Ms. Chu has decided eventually to submit the story about Max's escapade to a children's magazine.

In the above scenario, you can easily find the cognitive processes and text elements that Ms. Chu demonstrates for her students. When producing text in front of her students, Ms. Chu explains the decisions she makes both in her writer's notebook and in the beginning of her draft. Although she has a real purpose for the draft (a magazine story), she uses her initial draft to teach her students to evaluate and revise text. Her decision to focus on word choice for details was based upon a need she observed in her students' drafts. Like most fifth graders, they do not easily evaluate their own texts or view revision suggestions as helpful.

When writing with students, teachers often fashion their drafts to demonstrate and discuss writing needs they have assessed in their students' writing processes or texts, like Ms. Chu. You recall Ms. Alverez in Chapter 6. While writing a memoir about her recess experience in second grade, she modeled and explained how to choose a focused topic and how to cut irrelevant information that was not about the recess event. Also recall the classroom scenario in Chapter 7 in which Ms. Smith evaluated her first attempt at teaching persuasive writing. Looking back on the unit, Ms. Smith stated that next year she would write with her students because the students encountered two major stumbling blocks: a lack of factual information and inexperience with refuting counter positions to their positions. When writing with her students next year, Ms. Smith will discuss her process, explain the decisions she makes, and solicit suggestions from her students.

When we informally poll teachers in our graduate courses, we find that few write to entertain or to inform, except writing they do for their course work or as part of their job responsibilities. In our writing courses, we regularly write with our graduate students and explore our processes across several genres as we write for real purposes and a variety of audiences. We usually begin with personal narratives and memoirs. By sharing our childhood memories while teachers are sharing their memories, we help to build a classroom community of writers. As we explore other genres throughout the semester, we continue to model and explain our writing processes. Here are just a few of the topics that we have discussed when writing with the teachers in our courses:

- Changing an entertaining story from third person to first person.
- Critiquing the voice of a letter written in response to a *New Yorker* article.
- Evaluating word choice in a complaint letter to a phone company.

- Demonstrating how to show-not-tell in character sketches of assisted living residents.
- Brainstorming ideas for a poem contrasting how 20 year olds versus 60 year olds use cell phones.
- Beginning a story where the action starts.

These topics emanate from both our writing and from the teachers' writing. All of us learn that we do not initially produce perfect drafts, but we do produce drafts that can be revised. We post our drafts online using a secure web-based discussion board and seek each other's evaluation and revision suggestions. After several drafts, we eventually produce effective pieces that accomplish our purposes and meet the needs of our audiences.

We encourage you to experiment with new purposes, audiences, and genres. In our experience, students of all ages are appreciative of teachers' struggling efforts! Plus, by struggling to write, you are legitimizing your students' struggles. If you show a willingness to experiment and a dedication to improve your writing, your students will most likely follow your lead.

As you and your students write for new purposes, you will explore the challenges of writing to audiences who differ from you in world knowledge, discourse knowledge, time and space, and sociocultural membership. Using our communication model, you and your students will learn to write more effectively for a variety of audiences. We recommend actually sending both the students' and your pieces to the intended readers. While you are exploring writing with your students, you know you are also exploring ideas about your teaching—the next section.

WRITING TO EXPLORE

When students write to explore ideas in journals, they show their understanding of the concepts they are learning and reflect on how they are learning. We presume that you write to explore your teaching and your students even if you do not formally keep a journal.

- When attending conferences, you jot down "take away" ideas on the handouts.
- At a faculty meeting, you record notes about upcoming parents' meeting.
- During class or after school, you make notes about students' progress for upcoming conferences.
- When planning a lesson, you post it on a Wiki so other teachers in your school or district can make changes, suggest alternatives, and discuss the plans.

- After a lesson, you note how you will customize the activity for a particular group of students for when you will use the lesson again in the future.
- After school, you plan what to explicitly teach based on your students' needs: vivid verbs or rearranging pieces.

If you have notes in your head, notes in your plan book, and notes in your grade book, you might want to consider keeping a teaching journal. Some teachers prefer keeping a journal because all their explorations into their teaching are in one place. Plus, they can reread entries, reflect on what happened last month, and find patterns in their teaching practices or in their students' learning.

A teaching journal can also be a place to conduct informal research into our teaching and our classrooms. Perhaps you have designed a teacher-as-researcher project as part of a course or as professional development for yourself. In our graduate programs, we ask teachers to explore inquiry questions they have about their teaching, their students, or their curriculum. In the beginning, they write freely about their teaching and their students, searching for an inquiry topic that intrigues them. They may choose to investigate a small group of students, a particular teaching practice, or a change in the curriculum. When they have settled on an inquiry question, the teachers keep a double-entry journal or a field notebook. On one page or one column, they record their observations, data from student work, and descriptions of the lesson or situation. On the opposite page or second column, they reflect, analyze, search for patterns, question, and wonder about their observations, data, and descriptions. Over the semester, they conduct classroom inquiry (Hubbard & Power, 2003) by posing a question, collecting data over time, and then analyzing and sharing the results.

For example, one teacher investigated how students incorporated their understanding of math concepts into a creative writing piece (Boisvert, 2007). The students wrote "Polygon High School Reunion" stories in which they imagined meeting all the other polygons and seeing who had changed. Students were encouraged to use dialogue and give their characters personality traits. The teacher evaluated how well they incorporated their understanding of plane geometry and how well they personified the polygons. Analyzing the students' products, the teacher found a range:

1. Stories containing no explanation of polygons: "surprised to see how friends had changed."
2. Stories containing meager mention of polygons: "The jocks were all triangles."
3. Stories containing personification: "Only one of my angles has to stay over 90 degrees and under 180 degrees. Also two of my

angles are acute, But I make sure every day that I add up to 180 degrees exactly, says Obtuse. How do you *do* all that? Asks Equilateral."

The teacher concluded that creative writing in math benefited both the students and her. Many students thought more thoroughly about polygons and found the assignment interesting. She found the creative writing pieces provided an alternative assessment instrument—a twist to the typical "What have I learned?" end of chapter reflection prompt or essay.

We recommend pursuing an inquiry question that fascinates you. Now that you have reached the end of our book, brainstorm various inquiry questions you could ask:

- How does writing for real situations or purposes motivate students to write?
- How does student writing change when students write for real audiences beyond the school?
- How does the writing of three students' change when they write different genres?
- Which revision strategies produce more effective student writing?
- How can students include more of their world knowledge into their informational writing?

While the teaching journal is generally a private forum, writing can also be used as a more public reflection tool. You might decide that you want to participate in an online discussion forum sponsored by a professional teaching organization. In these forums, teachers have the opportunity to share successful practices, pose questions to the online community, and share teaching resources. If you Google "blogs for elementary teachers" or "blogs for middle school teachers," you will find an array of sites where you can read and share thoughts about educational topics and ideas. You might find that participation in forums and communities inspires you to think about the decisions you make as a teacher. If you are the type of person who prefers face-to-face discussion, you might consider forming or joining a teacher study group that includes written reflection. Generally, teacher study groups agree on a topic for discussion and prepare for discussion meetings by recording thoughts, observations, and notes from readings to share with the group.

Whether you use your teaching journal as a place to plan lessons and to assess students or as place to reflect on and to investigate your teaching practices, writing allows you to slow down the hectic pace of teaching and to re-see yourself and your students. Use your teaching journal to brainstorm wonderings or questions, to record data, and to reflect on your observations and your students' work. Don't forget to reread previous entries; your thinking may have changed or a pattern may emerge. In the next sections of this chapter, we move to audiences beyond you and your classroom to discuss writing for the local community and writing for unknown audiences.

WRITING FOR THE LOCAL COMMUNITY

To enhance communication between schools and the community, teachers write about their classrooms and schools to inform parents and citizens. Although teachers have traditionally written letters to parents requesting field trip permission, classroom supplies, or a conference, today teachers are writing:

- *Classroom newsletters.* Teachers periodically produce a newsletter for parents. Usually, teachers inform parents about units of study that have been completed. Students may contribute work they have produced during the units or compose original pieces for the newsletter.
- *School or classroom websites.* Many schools now have websites that provide information about schedules, personnel, and upcoming events. Teachers create a classroom web page as a link from the school's website or as their own site. Classroom web pages can be used to post written descriptions of important classroom information such as daily schedules, classroom rules and procedures, homework and grading policies, and curriculum overviews. Tech-savvy teachers regularly update their sites by incorporating images and descriptions of student work or announcements.
- *Blogs.* Serving as an ongoing diary or journal of classroom activity, blogs chronicle life in the classroom. Students and parents can check the blog frequently to read the teacher's descriptions of the learning and post responses to the entries.
- *Articles for the local paper.* Although few teachers write for the local town paper, we think citizens not directly connected to the school need to be informed about the learning events in classrooms. Writing an article is similar to writing a newsletter except that you need to pay careful attention to the time and space dimension of our communication model because citizens have less contextual knowledge about your classroom than parents do. You could build a rationale for the unit you are teaching, chronicle the events in the unit, highlight learning outcomes, and reproduce selected student work. Recall the salt investigation in Chapter 7. We learned about the project because a newspaper reporter wrote an article that emphasized the results of the students' investigation. If Ms. Arnold had written the article, she could have emphasized the learning students acquired—not just the results.

As you can see, teachers often report the learning events in their classroom (world knowledge), give details about the context of the learning since readers were not there (time and space), and use the voice of a friendly and knowledgeable educator (sociocultural membership). We are sure other forums could be added to the list above and we encourage you to explore your options. Writing about your classroom to local audiences—some who are familiar (neighbors and parents of students) and some who are unknown (senior citizens)—is an excellent way to get your feet wet. Then, maybe you will venture into writing for more distant unknown audiences—our next section.

WRITING FOR UNKNOWN AUDIENCES

When we write for unknown audiences, we accept a greater challenge than writing for known audiences because we estimate, rather than know, what our unknown audiences need. In writing this book, for example, we think of teachers we have known and base our estimates about you on them. We work to build common world knowledge about teaching writing and the classroom context in which writing would occur (time and space) since you can't go with us to classrooms. Although we write in the professional book genre, we choose not to write in the stuffy academic voice. Instead we strive to use our teacher voice to communicate what we know about classrooms and teaching (sociocultural membership) even though we no longer spend all day with young students. Writing for unknown audiences forces all writers to consciously address the dimensions of our communication model. We encourage you to accept the challenges unknown audiences bring to your writing when you write as a professional sharing your knowledge, as a citizen advocating for social change, and as a published author informing and entertaining readers.

Like many teachers who are producers of knowledge, not just consumers, we encourage you to share your practices and experiences with audiences in the profession by presenting at conferences and writing articles for professional journals. By reading professional journals, you can become familiar with the journal's style of writing and find their guidelines and themes for upcoming issues. Since regional journals have fewer submissions than national journals, you may succeed in having an article published sooner in one of them than if you submit to a more competitive national journal.

Or when attending conferences, you can obtain proposals for next year's sessions and attend sessions that offer help to new presenters. For example, at the 2006 Massachusetts Reading Conference, Renae Stockton presented, "Feature Articles: Promoting Nonfiction Reading and Writing," a unit she taught her fourth graders. In 2005, Stockton taught the unit, collected students' writing samples, and submitted a written proposal to the conference organizers. As the conference date approached, she referred back to her proposal to compose her Power-Point presentation and made notes to elaborate on for each slide. For example, Stockton (and her students) compared the characteristics of feature articles to encyclopedia articles. On the PowerPoint, Stockton showed the students' Venn diagram of the comparison as she stressed that the key point was the narrow focus of the feature article. Stockton took the audience of teachers through the unit from the rationale for teaching nonfiction feature writing to the final products—the students' nonfiction feature articles. Her teaching rationale, samples of students' work, as well as hints and pitfalls were well received by the teachers in attendance. They recognized Stockton's expertise exhibited in the reality of the classroom.

Although Stockton presented by herself, we recommend finding another teacher with whom to collaborate. Together you can outline the learning events, collect student work, and evaluate the learning outcomes. We recommend not just telling what happened in the classrooms but also documenting and evaluating how students learned.

While we suggest collaborating with a partner in your school, you may know a college or university person who wants to collaborate with a classroom teacher. Across the country, teachers and university teachers collaborate to inform the profession. You probably know that now-familiar classroom activities, such as author's chair (Hansen & Graves, 1983) and book club (Raphael & McMahon, 1994), began as collaborations between schools and universities. We like collaborating with teachers also and did collaborate with teachers when writing this book.

Think about what you are doing in your classroom that other teachers would like to know about. What twist are you putting on a familiar writing genre? How are your students using their math journals? What progress have you noticed in your students' revision strategies? How do you incorporate high-stakes writing into your classroom? Busy classrooms have a million topics that could turn into conference presentations or journal articles.

As professional educators, we have knowledge and views not only about our classroom and our students, but we have knowledge and views about issues that affect education in our district, our state, and our nation. For example, in September 2007, Education and Labor Committee Chair George Miller (Democratic Representative from California) held hearings in the House of Representatives regarding the draft revisions to the reauthorization of the No Child Left Behind Act. During the summer of 2007, professional organizations, such as the National Council of Teachers of English, informed their members of the revisions and encouraged members to write their representatives. Writing was a powerful instrument through which teachers could express their opinions and try to affect change.

Undoubtedly, you have professional experience and local knowledge about the effects of No Child Left Behind, bilingual education, or school funding. Perhaps you've read some of the articles on the International Reading Association's *Reading TODAY* website and have provided your own comments in response to the article(s) (*blog.reading.org*). You can contribute to your professional organizations' efforts to inform and persuade local, state, and federal politicians to enact laws and policies favorable to children and schools. In addition, you can write your representatives to inform and persuade them to support educational acts.

Not only are we educators, but we are ordinary citizens concerned about the issues in society. As private citizens, we give voice to our views on current issues, such as presidential candidates, the near extinction of the albatross, or global warming. We may join advocacy groups, participate with volunteers at food banks, or run for cancer research. We may speak at public forums, ask questions of local officials, write elected representatives, and create posters for advocacy groups. When we write as citizens, we take a political stand and recognize that not everyone will agree with us. In fact, at times we take the stand to inform and change our audience's views.

Finally, we encourage you to become a published author, a published journalist, or a published poet writing for children, adolescents, or adults. In her writing classes, published author Anne Lamott often finds an adult seeking to write the great American novel. Instead, Lamott recommends writing small first—a story rather than a novel (Lamott, 1994). Based on her advice, we recommend writing stories, articles, essays, poems, or columns for newspapers and magazines. Writers have also been advised to write about what they know. What are you passionate about? What topic do you have an abundance of knowledge about? What really interests you so much you want to learn more about it? What are mentor texts you could read for writer's craft?

Do you know that some published authors were or are teachers? One example is children's author Mem Fox, who taught teachers for 24 years, although she did not begin "small." She wrote her first book because she was assigned to write a book in a children's literature course. Because the instructor suggested she have it published, Fox sent it to nine publishers, all of whom rejected it. The tenth accepted it with changes. They asked Fox to switch the mice to possums, cut the manuscript by two-thirds, make it more Australian, and write more lyrically. *Possum Magic* was published in 1983 and is still in publication. Retiring from her first love, teaching, in 1996, Mem Fox continues to write books and presents to teachers and parents around the world. You may want to listen to the story behind her books, such as *Possum Magic* and several others, at her website (*www.memfox.net*).

CHAPTER SUMMARY

Many teachers find the time and purposes to write for themselves and others, as evidenced through the work of organizations such as the National Writing Project, which helps over 141,000 teachers improve their writing skills each year (Freeman, 2007). Yet, not all teachers view themselves as writers.

Teachers who write with and for their students recognize the benefits of sharing their work: They reveal their writing processes and their writing decisions; they show their struggles to communicate messages to an intended audience so that students know struggles are okay; and perhaps most important, they convey the message that most writing is not "done" after the first draft.

Very often, teachers engage in writing to explore ideas when they record observations for anecdotal records, keep notes from a workshop or conference, and revise lesson plans. We encourage you to keep a teacher's journal—a safe place where you can record your thoughts, as well as plan, collect, and analyze data from teacher inquiry projects.

Teachers who keep journals may have no intention or need to share the writing with others, but occasions occur when teachers write for audiences other than themselves. For example, they correspond with students and parents. Less often, but equally as important, they share their ideas with people they have never met. They write proposals for conference presentations, write to a member of Congress to take a stand on a civic issue, and may write the next Newbery medal winner.

No matter the audience, writers consider how an understanding of their anticipated readers' world knowledge and discourse knowledge, temporal and geographic differences, and recognition of sociocultural memberships impact what they write and how they write. These considerations are even more crucial when writers compose for people they have not met. Potential distances along the four dimensions of our communication model need to be accounted for in order for the writer's message to be conveyed accurately and completely.

We hope that opportunities you and your students find to write throughout the school day and outside of school will enable you to become purposeful and effective communicators in a variety of genres that fit different situations and audiences.

References

Albertson, B. R. (2007). Organization and development features of grade 8 and grade 10 writers: A descriptive study of Delaware student testing program (DSTP) essays. *Research in the Teaching of English, 41*(4), 435–458.

Anderson, C. (2000). *How's it going?: A practical guide to conferring with student writers.* Portsmouth, NH: Heinemann.

Anderson, J. (2006). Zooming in and zooming out: Putting grammar in context into context. *English Journal, 95*(5), 28–34.

Anderson, M. (2003). Reading violence in boys' writing. *Language Arts, 80*(3), 223–230.

Angelillo, J. (1999). Using the writer's notebook across the day and beyond the writing workshop. *Primary Voices K–6, 8*(1), 30–36.

Angelillo, J. (2002). *Making revision matter: Strategies for guiding students to focus, organize, and strengthen their writing independently.* New York: Scholastic.

Applebee, A. N. (2000). Alternative models of writing development. In R. Indrisano & J. R. Squire (Eds.), *Perspectives on writing: Research, theory, and practice* (pp. 90–110). Newark, DE: International Reading Association.

Atwell, N. (1998). *In the middle: New understandings about writing, reading and learning.* Portsmouth, NH: Boyton/Cook/Heinemann.

Au, W. (2007). High-stakes testing and curricular control: A qualitative meta-synthesis. *Educational Researcher, 36*(5), 258–267.

Auster, P. (Ed.). (2001). *I thought my father was God and other true tales from NPR's National Story Project.* New York: Henry Holt.

Baldwin, D. (2004). A guide to standardized writing assessment. *Educational Leadership, 62*(2), 72–75.

Ball, A. F. (1992). Cultural preference and expository writing. *Written Communication, 9*(2), 501–532.

Bangert-Drowns, R. L., Hurley, M. M., & Wilkinson, B. (2004). The effects of school-based writing-to-learn interventions on academic achievement: A meta-analysis. *Review of Educational Research, 74,* 29–58.

Beal, C. R. (1990). The development of text evaluation and revision skills. *Child Development, 61,* 247–258.

Bear, D. R., Invernizzi, M., Templeton, S., & Johnston, F. (2004). *Words their way: Word study for phonics, vocabulary, and spelling instruction* (3rd ed.). Upper Saddle River, NJ: Pearson.

Bearse, C. (1992). The fairy tale connection in children's stories: Cinderella meets Sleeping Beauty. *The Reading Teacher, 45*(9), 688–695.

Beaufort, A. (2006). Writing in the professions. In P. Smagorinsky (Ed.), *Research on composition* (pp. 217–242). New York: Teachers College Press.

Bereiter, C., & Scardamalia, M. (1987). *The psychology of written composition*. Hillsdale, NJ: Erlbaum.

Berger, L. R. (1996). Reader response journals: You make the meaning...and how. *Journal of Adolescent and Adult Literacy, 39*(5), 380–385.

Black, R. W. (2005). Access and affiliation: The literacy and compositon practices of English-language learners in an online fanfiction community. *Journal of Adolescent and Adult Literacy, 49*(2), 118–129.

Black, R. W. (2008). Just don't call them cartoons: The new literacy spaces of anime, manga, and fanfiction. In J. Coiro, M. Knobel, C. Lankshear, & D. Leu (Eds.), *Handbook of research on new literacies* (pp. 583–610). New York: Erlbaum.

Boisvert, K. T. (2007). *Exploring creative writing in the middle school math classroom.* Unpublished inquiry report for Lesley University, Cambridge, MA.

Boraks, N., Hoffman, A., & Bauer, D. (1997). Children's book preferences: Patterns, particulars, and possible implications. *Reading Psychology, 18*(4), 309–341.

Brannon, L., Griffin, S., Haag, K., Iannone, T., Urbanski, C., & Woodward, S. (2008). *Thinking out loud on paper: The student daybook as a tool to foster learning.* Portsmouth, NH: Heinemann.

Bratcher, S. (1994). *Evaluating children's writing: A handbook of communication choices for classroom teachers.* New York: St. Martin's Press.

Brenner, R. (2006). Graphic novels 101: FAQ. Retrieved September 6, 2006, from *www.hbook.com/publications/magazine/articles.mar06_brenner.asp.*

Britton, J., Burgess, T., Martin, N., McLeod, A., & Rosen, H. (1975). *The development of writing abilities* (11–18). London: Macmillan Education.

Brown, D. (2003). *The Da Vinci code: A novel.* New York: Doubleday.

Buckner, A. D. (2005). *Notebook know-how: Strategies for the writer's notebook.* Portland, ME: Stenhouse.

Bulla, C. (1985). *A grain of wheat: A writer begins.* Boston: Godine.

Cairney, T. (1990). Intertextuality: Infectious echoes from the past. *The Reading Teacher, 43,* 478–484.

Cairney, T. H. (2000). The construction of literacy and literacy learners. *Language Arts, 77*(6), 496–505.

Calkins, L. M. (1983). *Lessons from a child.* Portsmouth, NH: Heinemann.

Calkins, L. M. (1991). *Living between the lines.* Portsmouth, NH: Heinemann.

Calkins, L. M. (1994). *The art of teaching writing* (2nd ed.). Portsmouth, NH: Heinemann.

Carvalho, J. B. (2002). Developing audience awareness in writing. *Journal of Research in Reading, 25*(3), 271–282.

Cervetti, G. N., Pearson, P. D., Bravo, M. A., & Barber, J. (2005). Reading and writing in the service of inquiry-based science. In *Seeds of science / roots of reading.* Retrieved December 10, 2007, from *seedsofscience.org/PDFs/ Science&Literacy.pdf.*

Chambliss, M. J., Christenson, L. A., & Parker, C. (2003). Fourth graders composing scientific explanations about the effects of pollutants. *Written Communication, 20*(4), 426–454.

Chapman, M. (2006). Preschool through elementary writing. In P. Smagorinsky (Ed.), *Research on composition: Multiple perspectives on two decades of change.* (pp. 15–47). New York: Teachers College Press.

Chapman, M. L. (1995). The sociocognitive construction of written genres in first grade. *Research in the Teaching of English, 29*(2), 184–192.

Clark, R. A., & Delia, J. G. (1976). The development of functional persuasive skills in childhood and early adolescence. *Child Development, 47,* 1008–1014.

Coe, R. M. (2002). The new rhetoric of genre: Writing political briefs. In A. M. Johns (Ed.), *Genre in the classroom: Multiple perspectives* (pp. 197–207). Mahwah, NJ: Erlbaum.

Coiro, J. (2003). Rethinking comprehension strategies to better prepare students for critically evaluating content on the Internet. *NERA Journal, 39,* 29–34.

Coiro, J., & Dobler, E. (2007). Exploring the online reading comprehension strategies used by sixth-grade skilled readers to search for and locate information on the Internet. *Reading Research Quarterly, 42*(2), 214–257.

Coles, M., & Hall, C. (2002). Gendered readings: Learning from children's choices. *Journal of Research in Reading, 25*(1), 96–108.

Countryman, J. (1992). *Writing to learn mathematics.* Portsmouth, NH: Heinemann.

Crowhurst, M. (1990). The development of persuasive/argumentative writing. In R. Beach & S. Hynds (Eds.), *Developing discourse practices in adolescence and adulthood* (pp. 200–223). Norwood, NJ: Ablex.

Curtis, C. P. (1999). *Bud, not Buddy.* New York: Random House.

Dahl, K. (1988). Peer conferences as social contexts for learning about revision. In J. Readance & S. Baldwin (Eds.), *Dialogues in literacy research: Thirty-seventh yearbook of the National Reading Conference* (pp. 307–315). Chicago: National Reading Conference.

Dahl, K., & Farnan, N. (1998). *Children's writing: Perspectives from research.* Newark, DE/Chicago: International Reading Association/National Reading Conference.

Dahl, R. (1986). *Boy: Tales of childhood.* New York: Putnam.

Daiute, C. (2000). Narrative sites for youths' construction of social consciousness. In L. Weis & M. Fine (Eds.), *Construction sites: Excavating race, class, and gender among urban youth* (pp. 211–234). New York: Teachers College Press.

De La Paz, S. (2005). Effects of historical reasoning instruction and writing strategy mastery in culturally and academically diverse middle school classrooms. *Journal of Educational Psychology, 97*(2), 139–156.

De La Paz, S, & Graham, S. (1997). Effects of dictation and advanced planning instruction on the composing of students with writing and learning problems. *Jouranl of Educational Psychology, 89*(2), 203–222.

Delpit, L. D. (1995). *Other people's children: Cultural conflict in the classroom.* New York: New Press.

de Paola, T. (1999). *26 Fairmont Avenue.* New York: Putnam's.

Dix, S. (2006). I'll do it my way: Three writers and their revision practices. *The Reading Teacher, 59*(6), 566–573.

Donovan, C. A. (2001). Children's development and control of written story and informational genres: Insights from one elementary school. *Research in the Teaching of English, 35*(3), 394–447.

Donovan, C. A., & Smolkin, L. B. (2002). Children's genre knowledge: An examination of K–5 students' performance on multiple tasks providing differing levels of scaffolding. *Reading Research Quarterly, 37*(4), 428–465.

Dorfman, L. R., & Cappelli, R. (2007). *Mentor texts: Teaching writing through children's literature, K–6.* Portland, ME: Stenhouse.

Dorris, M. (1999). *Morning girl.* New York: Hyperion.

Duke, N. (2000). Print environments and experiences offered to first-grade students in very low- and very high-SES school districts. *Reading Research Quarterly, 35*(4), 456.

Duke, N. K., & Pearson, P. D. (2002). Effective practices for developing reading comprehension. In A. E. Farstrup & S. J. Samuels (Eds.), *What research has to say about reading instruction* (3rd ed., pp. 205–242). Newark, DE: International Reading Association.

Duke, N. K., Purcell-Gates, V., Hall, L. A., & Tower, C. (2006). Authentic literacy activities for developing comprehension and writing. *The Reading Teacher, 60*(4), 344–355.

Dworin, J. E. (2006). The family stories project: Using funds of knowledge for writing. *The Reading Teacher, 59*(6), 510–520.

Ebbers, M. (2002). Science text sets: Using various genres to promote literacy and inquiry. *Language Arts, 80* (1), 40–50.

Elbow, P. (1973). *Writing without teachers.* New York: Oxford University Press.

Elementary and Secondary Education Act, Public Law 89-10, 79 Stat. 77, 20 U.S.C. Ch 70 (1965).

Emig, J. (1971). *The composing processes of twelfth graders.* Urbana, IL: National Council of Teachers of English.

Englert, C., Raphael, T., Anderson, L., Anthony, H., & Stevens, D. (1991). Making strategies and self-talk visible: Writing instruction in regular and special education classrooms. *American Educational Research Journal, 28,* 337–372.

Englert, C. S., Mariage, T. V., & Dunsmore, K. (2006). Tenets of sociocultural theory in writing instruction research. In C. A. MacArthur, S. Graham, & J. Fitzgerald (Eds.), *Handbook of writing research* (pp. 208–221). New York: Guilford Press.

Faigley, L., & Witte, S. (1981). Analyzing revision. *College Composition and Communication, 32*(4), 400–414.

Felton, M., & Kuhn, D. (2001). The development of argumentative discourse skill. *Discourse Processes, 32,* 135–153.

Ferretti, R. P., MacArthur, C. A., & Dowdy, N. S. (2000). The effects of an elaborated goal on the persuasive writing of students with learning disabilities and their normally achieving peers. *Journal of Educational Psychology, 92*(4), 694–702.

Fitzgerald, J. (1988). Helping young writers to revise: A brief review for teachers. *The Reading Teacher, 42*(2), 124–129.

Fitzgerald, J., & Markham, L. R. (1987). Teaching children about revision in writing. *Cognition and Instruction, 4*(1), 3–24.

Fleischman, P. (1988). *A joyful noise: Poems for two voices*. New York: Harper & Row.

Fleming, D., & Trompeter, A. (2006). *Letters to literacy: Improving student learning through research and writing*. Presentation at the annual conference of the Massachusetts Reading Association, Sturbridge, MA.

Fleming, S. (1995). Whose stories are validated? *Language Arts, 72*, 599–596.

Fletcher, R. (2001). The writer's notebook. *School Talk, 6*(4), 1–2.

Flower, L., & Hayes, J. R. (1981). A cognitive process theory of writing. *College Composition and Communication, 32*, 365–387.

Fox, M. (1983). *Possum magic*. San Diego, CA: Harcourt.

Freedman, A., & Medway, P. (1994). Locating genre studies: Antecedents and prospects. In A. Freedman & P. Medway (Eds.), *Genre and the new rhetoric* (pp. 1–20). Bristol, PA: Taylor & Francis.

Freeman, M. (2007). National Writing Project's time-tested approach evolves and adapts to a new millennium. *Reading Today, 24*(6), 41.

Frey, J. (2003). *A million little pieces*. New York: Talese/Doubleday.

Fritz, J. (2004). *The lost colony of Roanoke*. New York: Putnam.

Fulwiler, B. R. (2007). *Writing in science: How to scaffold instruction to support learning*. Portsmouth, NH: Heinemann.

Fulwiler, T. (Ed.). (1987). *The journal book*. Portsmouth, NH: Boynton/Cook.

Gantos, J. (1998). *Joey Pigza swallowed the key*. New York: Farrar, Straus & Giroux.

Gardiner, J. R. (1980). *Stone fox*. New York: HarperTrophy.

Gee, J. P. (1996). *Social linguistics and literacies: Ideology in discourses* (2nd ed.). London: Taylor & Francis.

Gee, J. P. (2001). Reading as situated language: A sociocognitive perspective. *Journal of Adolescent and Adult Literacy, 44*(8), 714–725.

Gee, J. P. (2004). Language in the science classroom: Academic social languages as the heart of school-based literacy. In E.W. Saul (Ed.), *Crossing borders in literacy and science instruction: Perspectives on theory and practice* (pp.13–36). Newark, DE: International Reading Association.

Gere, A. R., Christenbury, L., & Sassi, K. (2005). *Writing on demand: Best practices and strategies for success*. Portsmouth, NH: Heinemann.

Gilmore, B. (2007). *"Is it done yet?" Teaching adolescents the art of revision*. Portsmouth, NH: Heinemann.

Grabe, W. (2002). Narrative and expository macro-genres. In A. M. Johns (Ed.), *Genre in the classroom: Multiple perspectives* (pp. 249–267). Mahwah, NJ: Erlbaum.

Graham, S., & Harris, K. R. (2005). *Writing better: Effective strategies for teaching students with learning difficulties*. Baltimore: Brookes.

Graham, S., Harris, K. R., & MacArthur, C. (2006). Explicitly teaching struggling writers: Strategies for mastering the writing process. *Intervention in School and Clinic, 41*(5), 290–294.

Graham, S., MacArthur, C., & Schwartz, S. (1995). The effects of goal setting and procedural facilitation on the revising behavior and writing performance of students with writing and learning problems. *Journal of Educational Psychology, 87*, 230–240.

Graham, S., & Perin, D. (2007). *Writing next: Effective strategies to improve writing of adolescents in middle and high school.* A Report to the Carnegie Corporation of New York. Washington, DC: Alliance for Excellent Education.

Graves, D. H. (1975). An examination of the writing processes of seven-year-old children. *Research in the Teaching of English, 9,* 227–241.

Graves, D. H. (1983). *Writing: Teachers and children at work.* Portsmouth, NH: Heinemann.

Green, S., & Sutton, P. (2003). What do children think as they plan their writing? *Reading: Literacy and Language, 37*(1), 32–39.

Grogan, J. (2005). *Marley and me: Life and love with the world's worst dog.* New York: Morrow/HarperCollins.

Hamilton, V. (1988). *In the beginning: Creation stories from around the world.* San Diego, CA: Harcourt Brace Jovanovich.

Hansen, J., & Graves, D. (1983). The author's chair. *Language Arts, 60,* 176–183.

Harper, L. (1997). The writer's toolbox: Five tools for active revision instruction. *Language Arts, 74*(3), 193–200.

Harvey, S. (1998). *Nonfiction matters: Reading, writing, and research in grades 3–8.* Portland, ME: Stenhouse.

Hayes, J. R. (2000). A new framework for understanding cognition and affect in writing. In R. Indrisano & J. R. Squire (Eds.), *Perspectives on writing: Research, theory, and practice* (pp. 6–44). Newark, DE: International Reading Association.

Hayes, J. R. (2004). A new framework for understanding cognition and affect in writing. In R. B. Ruddell & N. U. Unrau (Eds.), *Theoretical models and processes of reading* (pp. 1399–1431). Newark, DE: International Reading Association.

Heard, G. (2002). *The revision toolbox: Teaching techniques that work.* Portsmouth, NH: Heinemann.

Heath, S. B. (1983). *Ways with words: Language, life, and work in communities and classrooms.* New York: Cambridge University Press.

Heath, S. B., & Mangiola, L. (1991). *Children of promise: Literate activity in linguistically and culturally diverse classrooms.* Washington, DC: National Education Association.

Hiebert, E. (1994). Becoming literate through authentic tasks: Evidence and adaptations. In R. Ruddell, M. Rudell, & H. Singer (Eds.), *Theoretical models and processes of reading* (pp. 391–413). Newark, DE: International Reading Association.

Hillocks, G. (1982). Inquiry and the composing process: Theory and research. *College English, 44,* 659–673.

Hillocks, G. (1995). *Teaching writing as reflective practice.* New York: Teachers College Press.

Hillocks, G. (2002). *The testing trap: How state writing assessments control learning.* New York: Teachers College Press.

Hillocks, G. (2007). *Narrative writing: Learning a new model for teaching.* Portsmouth, NH: Heinemann.

Holliway, D. R. (2004). Through the eyes of my reader: A strategy for improving audience perspective in children's descriptive writing. *Journal of Research in Childhood Education, 18*(4), 334–349.

Hubbard, R. S. & Power, B. M. (2003). *The art of classroom inquiry: A handbook for teacher–researchers.* Portsmouth, NH: Heinemann.

International Reading Association. (n.d.). *Reading Today.* Available at *www.reading.org/publications/reading_today.*

Jablon, P. (2006, April/May). Writing through inquiry. *Science Scope,* pp. 2–4.

Jacobson, S., & Colón, E. (2006). *The 9/11 report: A graphic adaptation.* New York: Farrar, Straus & Giroux.

Jarmer, D., Kozol, M., Nelson, S., & Salsberry, T. (2000). Six-trait writing model improves scores at Jennie Wilson Elementary. *Journal of School Improvement, 1*(2), 29–32.

Johns, A. M. (2002). Destabilizing and enriching novice students' genre theories: In A. M. Johns (Ed.), *Genre in the classroom: Multiple perspectives* (pp. 237–246). Mahwah, NJ: Erlbaum.

Johnston, J. (2006). Connecting middle schoolers with the community through writing. *NERA Journal, 42*(1), 45–50.

Johnston, P., Woodside-Jiron, H., & Day, J. (2001). Teaching and learning literate epistemologies. *Journal of Educational Psychology, 93*(1), 223–233.

Kamberlis, G. (1999). Genre development and learning: Children writing stories, science reports, and poems. *Research in the Teaching of English, 33*(4), 403–460.

Kaufer, D. S., & Carley, K. (1994). Some concepts and axioms about communication: Proximate and at a distance. *Written Communication, 11*(1), 8–42.

Kiefer, B. Z. (2007). *Charlotte Huck's children's literature.* Boston: McGraw-Hill.

Koch, K. (1970/2000). *Wishes, lies, and dreams: Teaching children to write poetry.* New York: HarperPerennial.

Koch, K. (1973/1990). *Rose, where did you get that red?* New York: Vintage.

Kohn, A. (2006). The trouble with rubrics. *English Journal, 95*(4). Retrieved June 23, 2008, from ProQuest database.

Kos, R., & Maslowski, C. (2001). Second graders' perceptions of what is important in writing. *Elementary School Journal, 101,* 567–584.

Lamott, A. (1994). *Bird by bird: Some instructions on writing and life.* New York: Random House.

Lane, B. (1992). *After THE END: Teaching and learning creative revision.* Portsmouth, NH: Heinemann.

Lane, B. (1999). *Reviser's toolbox.* Shoreham, VT: Discover Writing Press.

Langer, J. (1986). *Children reading and writing: Structures and strategies.* Norwood, NJ: Ablex.

Langer, J. A. (1995). *Envisioning literature: Literary understanding and literature instruction.* New York: Teachers College.

Langer, J. A., & Applebee, A. (1987). *How writing shapes thinking.* Urbana, IL: National Council of Teachers of English.

Langer, J. A., & Flihan, S. (2000). Writing and reading relationships: Constructive tasks. In R. Indrisano & J. R. Squire (Eds.), *Perspectives on writing* (pp. 112–139). Newark, DE: International Reading Association.

Lauber, P. (2006). *What you never knew about beds, bedrooms, and pajamas.* New York: Simon & Schuster.

Lawson, R. (1939). *Ben and me: A new and astonishing life of Benjamin Franklin as written by his good mouse Amos.* Boston: Little, Brown.

Lea, M. R., & Street, B. V. (2006). The "academic literacies" model: Theory and applications. *Theory Into Practice, 45*(4), 368–377.

Lemke, J. (1990). *Talking science: Language, learning, and values.* Norwoord, NJ: Ablex.

Lemke, J. L. (2004). The literacies of science. In E. W. Saul (Ed.), *Crossing borders in literacy and science instruction: Perspectives on theory and practice* (pp. 33–47). Newark, DE: International Reading Association.

Lewis, C. S. (1950). *The lion, the witch, and the wardrobe.* New York: Macmillan.

Lipson, M., Mosenthal, J., Daniels, P., & Woodside-Jiron, H. (2000). Process writing in the classroom of eleven fifth-grade teachers with different orientations to teaching and learning. *Elementary School Journal, 101*(2), 209–231.

Louie, A. L. (1982). *Yeh-Shen, a Cinderella tale from China.* New York: Philomel.

Lowther, D. L., Ross, S. M., & Morrison, G. M. (2003). When each one has one: The influences on teaching strategies and student achievement of using laptops in the classroom. *Educational Technology, Research, and Development, 51*(3), 23–44.

Lyon, G. E. (2003). *Mother to tigers.* New York: Atheneum.

MacArthur, C. A. (2007). Best practices in teaching evaluation and revision. In S. Graham, C. A. MacArthur, & J. Fitzgerald (Eds.), *Best practices in writing instruction* (pp. 141–162). New York: Guilford Press.

MacArthur, C. A., Schwartz, S., & Graham, S. (1991). Effects of a reciprocal peer revision strategy in special education classrooms. *Learning Disability Research and Practice, 6*, 201–210.

Manning, P. L. (2007). *Dinomummy: The life, death, and discovery of Dakota, a dinosaur from Hell Creek.* Boston: Kingfisher.

Many, J. E., Fyfe, R., Lewis, G., & Mitchel, E. (1996). Traversing the topical landscape: Exploring students' self-directed reading–writing research processes. *Reading Research Quarterly, 31*(1), 12–35.

Martlew, M. (1983). *The psychology of written language: Developmental and educational perspectives.* New York: Wiley.

Mayher, J. S., Lester, N., & Pradl, G. M. (1983). *Learning to write: Writing to learn.* Upper Monclair, NJ: Boynton/Cook.

McAndrew, D. A., & Reigstad, T. J. (2001). *Tutoring writing: A practical guide for conferences.* Portsmouth, NH: Heinemann.

McCutchen, D. (1994). The magical number 3, plus or minus 2: Working memory in writing. In E. Butterfield (Ed.), *Children's writing: Toward a process theory of the development of skilled writing. Advances in cognition and educational practice* (Vol. 2, pp. 1–30). Greenwich, CT: JAI Press.

McCutchen, D. (2000). Knowledge, processing, and working memory: Implications for a theory of writing. *Educational Psychologist, 35*(1), 13–23.

McCutchen, D. (2006). Cognitive factors in the development of children's writing. In C. A. MacArthur, S. Graham, & J. Fitzgerald (Eds.), *Handbook of writing research* (pp. 115–130). New York: Guilford Press.

McCutchen, D., Francis, M., & Kerr, S. (1997). Revising for meaning: Effects of knowledge and strategy. *Journal of Educational Psychology, 89*(4), 667–676.

McIntosh, M. E., & Draper, R. J. (2001). Using learning logs in mathematics: Writing to learn. *Mathematics Teacher, 94*(7), 554.

McMackin, M., Allan, K. K., & Topham, V. (in progress). To rhyme or not to rhyme: Students' criteria for poems.

McMackin, M. C., & Siegel, B. S. (2002). *Knowing how: Researching and writing nonfiction 3–8.* Portland, ME: Stenhouse.

Miller, C. R. (1994). Genre as social action. In A. Freedman & P. Medway (Eds.), *Genre and the new rhetoric* (pp. 23–42). Bristol, PA: Taylor & Francis.

Moffett, J. (1981). *Active voice: A writing program across the curriculum.* Upper Montclair, NJ: Boynton/Cook.

Mueller, L., & Reynolds, J. D. (1990). *Creative writing: Forms and techniques.* Lincolnwood, IL: National Textbook.

Murphy, P. (2003). Discovering the ending in the beginning. *Language Arts, 80*(6), 461–469.

National Commission on Excellence in Education. (1983). *A nation at risk.* Washington, DC: U.S. Government Printing Office.

National Council for the Social Studies. (1994). *The curriculum standards for social studies: Expectations of excellence.* Retrieved February 17, 2008, from *www.social studies.org/standards/introduction.*

National Council of Teachers of English/International Reading Association. (1996). *Standards for the English language arts.* Urbana, IL: National Council of Teachers of English.

National Council of Teachers of Mathematics. (2000). *Principles and standards for school mathematics.* Reston, VA: National Council of Teachers of Mathematics.

Newkirk, T. (1987). The non-narrative writing of young children. *Research in the Teaching of English, 21*(2), 121–144.

Newkirk, T. (1989). *More than stories: The range of children's writing.* Portsmouth, NH: Heinemann.

Newkirk, T. (2002). *Misreading masculinity: Boys, literacy, and popular culture.* Portsmouth, NH: Heinemann.

Newkirk, T. (2004). Misreading masculinity: Speculations on the great gender gap in writing. *Language Arts, 77*(4), 294–300.

Nippold, M. A., Ward-Lonergan, J. M., & Fanning, J. L. (2005). Persuasive writing in children, adolescents, and adults: A study of syntactic, semantic, and pragmatic development. *Language, Speech, and Hearing Services in Schools, 36*, 125–138.

No Child Left Behind, Public Law 107-10 (2001).

Noden, H. R. (1999). *Image grammar: Using grammatical structures to teach writing.* Portsmouth, NH: Heinemann.

Nystrand, M. (1986). *The structure of written communication: Studies in reciprocity between writers and readers.* New York: Academic Press.

Nystrand, M., & Graff, N. (2001). Report in argument's clothing: An ecological perspective on writing instruction in a seventh-grade classroom. *Elementary School Journal, 101*(4), 470–494.

Ochsner, R., & Fowler, J. (2004). Playing devil's advocate: Evaluating the literature of the WAC/WID movement. *Review of Educational Research, 74*(2), 117—141.

Olson, M. W., & Raffeld, R. (1987). The effects of written comments on the quality of student compositions and the learning of content. *Reading Psychology, 8*(4), 273–293.

Olson, V. (1990). The revising processes of sixth-grade writers with and without peer feedback. *Journal of Educational Research, 84*, 84–106.

Osborne, M. P., & Christensen, B. (2006). *Pompeii lost and found.* New York: Knopf.

Pantaleo, S. (2007). Exploring the metafictive in elementary students' writing. *Changing English, 14*(1), 61–76.

Parke, C. S., Lane, S., & Stone, C. A. (2006). Impact of a state performance assessment program in reading and writing. *Educational Research and Evaluation, 12*(3), 239–269.

Paterson, K. (1991). *Lyddie.* New York: Puffin.

Patthey-Chavez, G., Matsummura, L. C., & Valdés, R. (2004). Investigating the process approach to writing instruction in urban middle schools. *Journal of Adolescent and Adult Literacy, 47*(6), 462–479.

Pearson, P. D., & Gallagher, M. C. (1983). The instruction of reading comprehension. *Contemporary Educational Psychology, 8*, 317–344.

Pedulla, J. J., Abrams, L. M., Madaus, G. F., Russell, M. K., Ramos, M. A., & Miao, J. (2003). *Perceived effects of state-mandated testing programs on teaching and learning: Findings from a national survey of teachers* (Executive Summary). Chestnut Hill, MA: National Board on Educational Testing and Public Policy.

Pennypacker, S. (2006). *Clementine.* New York: Hyperion.

Perkins, L. R. (2005). *Criss cross.* New York: Greenwillow.

Peterson, S. (2000). Fourth-, sixth-, and eighth-graders' preferred writing topics and identification gender markers in stories. *Elementary School Journal, 101*(1), 79–100.

Peterson, S. (2006). Influence of gender on writing development. In C. A. MacArthur, S. Graham, & J. Fitzgerald (Eds.), *Handbook of writing research* (pp. 311–323). New York: Guilford Press.

Pinsky, R., & Dietz, M. (Eds.). (1999). *Americans' favorite poems: The Favorite Poem Project anthology.* New York: Norton.

Pinsky, R., & Dietz, M. (Eds.). (2004). *An Invitation to poetry: A new Favorite Poem Project anthology.* New York: Norton.

Popham, W. J. (2001). *The truth about testing: An educator's call to action.* Alexandria, VA: Association of Supervision and Curriculum Development.

Publisher's Weekly. (2007, March 5). Graphic novels by the numbers. *Publishers Weekly, 254*(10), 9.

Purcell-Gates, V., Duke, N., & Martineau, J. A. (2007). Learning to read and write genre-specific text: Roles of authentic experience and explicit teaching. *Reading Research Quarterly, 42*(1), 8–45.

Ranker, J. (2006). "There's fire magic, electric magic, ice magic, or poison magic": The world of video games and Adrian's compositions about Gauntlet Legends. *Language Arts, 84*(1), 21–33.

Raphael, T. E., & McMahon, S. I. (1994). Book club: An alternate framework for reading instruction. *The Reading Teacher, 48*(2), 102–117.

Rief, L. (1992). *Seeking diversity: Language arts with adolescents*. Portsmouth, NH: Heinemann.

Rentel, V., & King, M. (1983). Present at the beginning. In P. Mosenthal, L. Tamor, & S. Walmsley (Eds.), *Research on writing: Principles and methods* (pp. 139–176). New York: Longman.

Roe, B. D., & Ross, E. P. (2006). *Integrating language arts through literature and thematic units*. Needham, MA: Allyn & Bacon.

Romano, T. (2004). The power of voice. *Educational Leadership, 62*(2), 20–23.

Rosenblatt, L. (1995). *Literature as exploration*. New York: Modern Language Association. (Original work published 1938)

Rubenstein, S. (1998). *Go public! Encouraging student writers to publish*. Urbana, IL: National Council of Teachers of English.

Saddler, B. (2005). Sentence combining: A sentence-level writing intervention. *Reading Teacher, 58*(5), 468–471.

Saddler, B. (2007). Improving sentence construction skills through sentence-combining practice. In S. Graham, C. A. MacArthur, & J. Fitzgerald (Eds.), *Best practices in writing instruction* (pp. 163–178). New York: Guildford Press.

Saddler, B., & Graham, S. (2005). The effects of peer-assisted sentence-combining instruction on the writing performance of more and less skilled young writers. *Journal of Educational Psychology, 97*(1), 43–54.

Scherff, L., & Piazza, C. (2005). The more things change, the more they stay the same: A survey of high school students' writing experiences. *Research in the Teaching of English, 39*(3), 271–304.

Schirmer, B. R., & Bailey, J. (2000). Writing assessment rubric. *Teaching Exceptional Children, 33*(1). Retrieved July 23, 2008, from ProQuest database.

Schuster, E. H. (2003). *Breaking the rules: Liberating writers through innovative grammar instruction*. Portsmouth, NH: Heinemann.

Schwartz, A., & Rubinstein-Avila, E. (2006). Understanding the manga hype: Uncovering the multimodality of comic-book literacies. *Journal of Adolescent and Adult Literacy, 50*(1), 40–49.

Scieszka, J. (1989). *The true story of the 3 little pigs as told by A. Wolf*. New York: Viking.

Shanahan, T. (1990). Reading and writing together: What does it really mean? In T. Shanahan (Ed.), *Reading and writing together: New perspectives for the classroom* (pp. 1–18). Norwood, MA: Christopher-Gordon.

Shanahan, T. (2004). Overcoming the dominance of communication: Writing to think and to learn. In T. L. Jetton & J. A. Dole (Eds.), *Adolescent literacy research and practice* (pp. 59–73). New York: Guilford Press.

Sheehy, M. (2003). The social life of an essay: Standardizing forces in writing. *Written Communication, 20*(3), 333–385.

Shelton, N. R., Fu, D., & Smith, K. (2004). Creating space for teaching writing and for test preparation. *Language Arts, 82*(2), 120–128.

Shepardson, D. P., & Britsch, S. J. (1997). Children's science journals: Tools for teaching, learning, and assessing. *Science and Children, 34*(5), 12–17, 46–47.

Shermis, M. D., Burstein, J., & Leacock, C. (2006). Applications of computers in assessment and analysis of writing. In C. A. MacArthur, S. Graham, & J. Fitzgerald (Eds.), *Handbook of writing research* (pp. 403–416). New York: Guilford Press.

Short, K., Harste, J., & Burke, C. (1995). *Creating classrooms for authors and inquirers.* Portsmouth, NH: Heinemann.

Smith, K. (2006). In defense of the five-paragraph essay. *English Journal, 95*(4), 16–17.

Smith, M. W., & Wilhelm, J. D. (2002). *"Reading don't fix no Chevy's": Literacy in the lives of young men.* Portsmouth, NH: Heinemann.

Smolkin, L. B., & Donovan, C. A. (2004). Developing a conscious understanding of genre: The relationship between implicit and explicit knowledge during the 5-to-7 shift. In J. Worthy, B. Maloch, J. V. Hoffman, S. L. Schallert, & C. M. Fairbanks (Eds.), *53rd Yearbook of National Reading Conference* (pp. 385–399). Oak Creek, WI: National Reading Conference.

Spandel, V. (2004). *Creating writers through 6-trait writing assessment and instruction* (4th ed.). New York: Addison Wesley Longman.

Spandel, V. (2006). In defense of rubrics. *English Journal, 96*(1). Retrieved June 23, 2008, from ProQuest database.

Spiegel, D. L. (1998). Reader response approaches and the growth of readers. *Language Arts, 76* (1), 41–48.

Spiegelman, A. (1997). *Maus: A survivor's tale.* New York: Pantheon.

Spivey, N. N., & King, J. R. (1989). Readers as writers composing from sources. *Reading Research Quarterly, 24*(1), 7–26.

Stein, N. L., & Glenn, C. G. (1979). An analysis of story comprehension in elementary school children. In R. O. Freedle (Ed.), *Advances in discourse processing: Vol. 2. New directions in discourse processing* (pp. 53–120). Norwood, NJ: Ablex.

Steptoe, J. (1987). *Mufaro's beautiful daughters: An African tale.* New York: Lothrop, Lee, & Shepard.

Stockton, R. (2006). *Feature articles: Promoting nonfiction reading and writing.* Presentation at the annual conference of the Massachusetts Reading Council, Sturbridge, MA.

Stone, J. C. (2005). Textual borderlands: Students' recontextualizations in writing children's books. *Language Arts, 83*(1), 42–51.

Strum, B. W. (2003). The information and reading preferences of North Carolina children. *School Library Media Research, 6.*

Swinburne, S. R. (1999). *Once a wolf: How wildlife biologists fought to bring back the gray wolf.* Boston: Houghton Mifflin.

Texas Education Agency. (2002, September). *Texas assessment of knowledge and skills: Blueprint for grades 4 and 7 writing.* Retrieved February 22, 2008, from *www.tea.state.tx.us/student.assessment/taks/blueprints/writ4-7.pdf.*

Tiedt, I. M. (1969). A new poetry from: The diamante. *Elementary English, 4*(5), 588–589.

Tomlinson, C. A. (2004). *The differentiated classroom: Responding to the needs of all learners.* Alexandria, VA: Association for Supervision and Curriculum Development.

Triplett, C. F., & Barksdale, M. A. (2005). Third- through sixth-graders' perceptions of high-stakes testing. *Journal of Literacy Research, 37*(2), 237–260.

Troia, G. A. (2006). Writing instruction for students with learning disabilities. In C. A. MacArthur, S. Graham, & J. Fitzgerald (Eds.), *Handbook of writing research* (pp. 324–336). New York: Guilford Press.

Turner, J., & Paris, S. (1995). How literacy tasks influence children's motivation for literacy. *Reading Teacher, 48,* 662–673.

Umland, K., & Hersh, R. (2006). Mathematical discourse: The link from pre-mathematical to fully mathematical thinking. *Philosophy of Mathematics Education Journal, 19.* Retrieved December 10, 2007, from *www.people.ex.ac.uk/PErnest/pome19/Hersh%20&%20Umland%20-%20Mathematical%20Discourse.doc.*

Vacca, R. T., & Vacca, J. L. (2000). Writing across the curriculum. In R. Indrisano and J. R. Squire (Eds.), *Perspectives on writing* (pp. 214–276). Newark, DE: International Reading Association.

VanSledright, B. A. (2000). Can ten-year-olds learn to investigate history as historians do? *Organization of Historians Newsletter.* Retrieved December 10, 2007, from *www.oah.org/pubs/nl/2000aug/vansledright.html.*

Viorst, J. (1984). *If I were in charge of the world and other worries: Poems for children and their parents.* New York: Aladdin.

Walshaw, M., & Anthony, G. (2007). The role of pedagogy in classroom discourse. In J. Watson & K. Beswick (Eds.), *Mathematics: Essential research, essential practice* (pp. 765–774). Proceedings of the 30th annual conference of the Mathematics Education Research Group of Australasia, Wahroonga, Australia. Retrieved December 10, 2007, from *www.merga.net.au/documents/RP722007.pdf.*

Weih, T. G. (2005). The genre of traditional literature influences student writing. *Reading Horizons, 46*(2), 77–91.

Wells, G., & Arauz, R. M. (2006). Dialogue in the classroom. *Journal of the Learning Sciences, 15*(3), 379–428.

Wells, G., & Chang-Wells, G. L. (1992). *Constructing knowledge together: Classrooms as centers of inquiry and literacy.* Portsmouth, NH: Heinemann.

White, E. B. (1952). *Charlotte's web.* New York: Harper/Collins.

Willems, M. (2006). *Don't let the pigeon stay up late.* New York: Hyperion.

Willis, M. S. (1993). *Deep revision: A guide for teachers, students, and other writers.* New York: Teachers and Writers Collaborative.

Worthy, J. (1998). "On every page someone gets killed": Book conversations you don't hear in school. *Journal of Adolescent and Adult Literacy, 41*(7), 508–518.

Yeh, S. S. (1998). Empowering education: Teaching argumentative writing to cultural minority middle school students. *Research in the Teaching of English, 33*(1), 49–83.

Yolen, J. (1988). *The devil's arithmetic.* New York: Puffin.

Yolen, J. (1992). *Encounter.* New York: Harcourt Brace.

Yoshina, J. M., & Harada, V. H. (2007). Involving students in learning through rubrics. *Library Media Connection, 25*(5), 10–14.

Zinsser, W. (2006). *On writing well: The classic guide to writing nonfiction* (30th Anniversary Edition). New York: Harper & Row.

Index